Praise for *Seal the Deal*

"*Seal the Deal* is an excellent source for anyone in business. Suzi's powerful insights and practical tools will enable business people in organizations of all sizes. Whether you are inside a large organization and want to increase your visibility, a retiring executive about to launch your own consulting effort, or a sales executive wanting to unlock your best performance, you will find valuable ideas, tools, and methods in this book. For those newer to solopreneurship, Pomerantz' book is an integrated system that functions as a personal sales coach throughout a 10-week course. I'm hooked! I kept intending to just skim but I couldn't seem to skip any of it. Of the 14 books 'in progress' on my reading table, none has captured my attention like *Seal the Deal!* This is a 'must have' for anyone who wants to increase the effectiveness of his or her networking, marketing, and sales efforts."

—Angela Wagner, CPCC, executive coach and
top-performing executive, Accenture.

"This book is structured brilliantly—you have a chance to 'eavesdrop' on an actual telecourse, on the *Seal the Deal* approach, where actual participants voice their questions, anxieties, and insights. It puts the reader right in the learning experience. *Seal the Deal* is very readable with a professional yet conversational tone. And you're never in doubt that Suzi knows what she's talking about!"

—Mary Beth O'Neill, author of *Executive Coaching with
Backbone and Heart*

"I've experienced the system personally and can say that the 'Seal The Deal Formula' belongs in any professional's chemistry kit."

—Mike Jay, CEO of B-Coach Systems and
author of *CPR for the Soul*

"With *Seal the Deal,* Suzi Pomerantz masterfully guides new and experienced professionals alike to grow their business to the next level. Suzi reminds us that selling is not about being inauthentic, it's about clear, honest communication and cultivating win-win relationships."

—Karlin Sloan, author of *Smarter, Faster, Better: Strategies for
Effective, Enduring, and Fulfilled Leadership*

"*Seal the Deal* is packed with worksheets, templates, personal action plans and homework action steps—just what anyone who sells services or ideas needs to build or transform a successful business."

—Agnes Mura, MA, MCC, founder of PCMA and author
of *Ten Themes and Variations for Postmodern Leaders and
Their Coaches*

"Have you ever wanted to 'eavesdrop' on a highly successful coach who is sharing words of wisdom? Well, in *Seal the Deal,* you get to do just that when you follow the conversations between Suzi Pomerantz and several of her coaching colleagues. I've known Suzi for many years and she has never failed to amaze me with her intelligence and skills as a coach. This time she graciously shares her knowledge, experience and best practices as she helps professional services providers to sidestep the pitfalls and mistakes most beginners (and even seasoned practitioners) make in networking, marketing and selling their services. There's a wealth of information with strategies, tips, tools, powerful questions, checklists, and even a 10 step plan to follow. It's all just waiting for you to implement. Am I a Raving Fan of Suzi and *Seal the Deal?* Absolutely!"

—Syl Leduc, M.Ed., MPEC, Certified Executive
Coach and Leadership Development Strategist,
www.TurningPointLeaders.com

"If there ever were an Oscar given for 'Super Coach,' Suzi Pomerantz would be my nominee. Her book, *Seal the Deal,* is a masterful production and destined to become a classic for any executive or personal coach. Not only is the networking, marketing and sales content of the book superb, but also watching her coaching technique throughout the book adds incredible value to any coach practitioner. Two thumbs up on this one."

—Steve Gladis, Ph.D., former professor and associate
dean/director at the University of Virginia, author
of 11 books including *Survival Writing for Business* and
The Manager's Pocket Guide to Public Presentations

"Over the years I've discovered that you can have the best products and services in the world, but if you don't have a plan and tools for building your business with your key clients and referral systems, you will remain an unknown commodity. *Seal the Deal* demystifies networking, marketing, and sales—and most of all will boost your confidence to go after the clients you really want to work with. *Seal the Deal* is destined to be a classic— it's what everyone needs to build a successful business."

—Judith E. Glaser, CEO Benchmark Communications, Inc.
and author of two best selling business books—*Creating We*
and *The DNA of Leadership*

"In reading Suzi Pomerantz' book I feel like I am participating in a Master Mind group or in one of her teleclasses—and I'm the center of attention. Everything that Suzi has to say about networking, marketing, and sales relates directly to me and my life as a coach and consultant. I also learned quite a bit about how to get out of my own way—I wish I had her book 40 years ago when I first began consulting and coaching!"

—William H. Bergquist, Ph.D., president of the Professional
School of Psychology and author of 42 books, including
Executive Coaching: An Appreciative Approach

"Entrepreneurs looking for a way to differentiate themselves in an overcrowded marketplace have a new handbook, and it's needed by the many service professionals who soon realize that substantial industry expertise and impressive talent are simply not enough. In *Seal the Deal,* Suzi Pomerantz takes talented entrepreneurs behind the business-building curtain and gives them a six-figure formula for success. By teaching the reader how to use marketing, sales, and networking in strategic concert, and how to weave individual success strategies into a comprehensive, proven success formula, *Seal the Deal* empowers entrepreneurs with a logical and manageable system for substantial growth."

—Jennifer Kalita, entrepreneurial consultant to the
National Association of Baby Boomer Women and
author of *In Business & In Balance*™

"I started my consulting/coaching company three years ago, after 20 years of quota-breaking sales and management for Fortune 100 companies like GE and McGraw-Hill. I have been in almost any sales situation that is possible and find myself awed by *Seal the Deal.* This book offers incredible real-life situations and the solutions we all need when we are selling our own services. Professionals of all kinds will greatly benefit by reading this book and applying the selling solutions. *Seal the Deal* will greatly increase your revenue through improved confidence. After reading it, I signed my first six-figure client!"

—Nancy McCarthy, president of DC Rainmakers

"If you are a professional services provider, here is an offer you can't refuse. In her ten-step model for growing your business, Suzi Pomerantz shows you how to network, market and sell as a natural act—a game that you can play and win and have fun while you're doing it. Reading this book is like having Suzi as your personal sales coach, while you follow her roadmap and dramatically expand your business in a systematic and sustainable way. *Seal the Deal* is the real deal!

—Don Arnoudse, executive coach and
founder of The 2nd Half

"*Seal the Deal* is a great resource for new and experienced coaches, consultants and others! I found the straightforward approach that Pomerantz used to share her considerable wisdom and experience to be very effective. It can reduce the learning curve for anyone that wants to make a difference and make money. I highly recommend that others read her book and buy one for someone else that would benefit from it as well."

—Beverley Alridge Wright, president of Wright Choice Group

"In *Seal the Deal,* Suzi Pomerantz takes the intimidating world of networking, marketing, and sales and teaches simple, real-world, road-tested steps for how to integrate these key elements of business development into an actionable, sure-fire business development plan. Networking made fun, marketing made simple, and sales demystified . . . *Seal the Deal* is a winner! If you're looking to build a prosperous coaching practice while also making a difference in people's lives, you have to get this book!"

—Felice Wagner, Esq., CEO, Sugarcrest Development Group

Seal the Deal

The Essential Mindsets for Growing Your Professional Services Business

The book that demystifies how successful coaches and consultants make money while making a difference

Suzi Pomerantz

HRD Press, Inc. • Amherst • Massachusetts

Published by: HRD Press, Inc.
            22 Amherst Road
            Amherst, Massachusetts 01002
            1-800-822-2801 (U.S. and Canada)
            1-413-253-3488
            1-413-253-3490 (fax)
            http://www.hrdpress.com

ISBN 10: 0-87425-934-7
ISBN 13: 978-0-87425-934-6

First Edition

This publication is designed to provide accurate and authoritative infor-mation with regard to the subject matter covered. It is sold with the understanding that neither the author nor the publisher is engaged in rendering legal, accounting, or other professional service. If legal advice or other expert assistance is required, the services of a competent professional person should be sought.

—From a *Declaration of Principles* jointly adopted by a Committee of the American Bar Association and a Committee of Publishers and Associations

Editorial services by Sally Farnham and Leslie Stephen
Production services by Anctil Virtual Office
Cover design by Eileen Klockars
Back cover photo by Ellen Cohan, www.ellencohan.com
Makeup by Karen Allyn

Available through HRD Press and Amazon.com

Dedication

To the loves of my life:
- To Sir Bryan the Brave, for making sure no dragons got in my way
- To Princess Samantha Ladybug, for being the CEO of everything
- To Bruceasaurus, for infinite love
- To Tadpole, for believing in me
- To Jack-O, for unwavering support

To my grandparents, who were my best teachers:
- Samuel J. Benoff taught me humor and patience
- Helen Benoff taught me to view life as simply happy
- Leon Shmukler taught me to swim with the sharks
- Tania Shmukler taught me to temper life's tragedies with sweetness

Table of Contents

Dear Reader,

In order for you to be able to better use the templates in this book, I'd like to send you the worksheets from the chapter titled Integrating it All. Just send me your e-mail address with the words REQUEST TEMPLATES in the subject line and I will send you (for free) a PDF file of the Personal Action Plan (page 310), Personal Strategic Business Development Action Plan (page 311), and My Individual Selling System (page 318). Send your request to templates@sealthedealbook.com.

Also, we update the website frequently, so please be sure to visit www.sealthedealbook.com often for free reports and other resources.

Thanks for reading and recommending the book!

Suzi

Acknowledgments

It truly takes a village to raise a child, and birthing a book is no different. I am so grateful to the people of my virtual village, who have supported my crazy ideas and helped to make this book possible. If it weren't for Jeremy Robinson, I wouldn't have done a telecourse about *Sealing the Deal* in the first place, and his generosity, encouragement, and support in many ways contributed to the launch of this endeavor. If Felice Wagner hadn't partnered with me to provide sales training to our joint clients I wouldn't have had nearly as much to say in this book, since she taught me how to shift my own mindset about sales and selling. Many friends and colleagues supported the development of the book directly: Thanks to Mark Cappellino, Darryl Salerno, and Kat Kadin for selflessly providing feedback as my content readers in the early stages of the book. Thank you to my terrific telecourse participants over the years, and all my clients (you know who you are) who have taught me so much and who live in my heart long after our coaching engagements have ended. Thanks to Tom Finn, Steve Gladis, Bill Bergquist, Judith Glaser, Sue Bethanis, Rebecca Merrill, Ginny O'Brien, Len Merson, Bud Bilanich, and Linda Finkle for sharing resources and many conversations about book writing, editing, publishing, and promoting. Thanks to Suzanne Levy and Lisa Nabors for coaching me to design an expanded strategy around my telecourse content. To my fabulous and very vital brothers of the law, Todd Benoff and Stewart Pomerantz, who kept asking me the tough questions and supported me with both legal counsel and brotherly advice. To Popster Bob Silberfarb, who helped with my sub-title and computer issues. Many thanks to Leslie Stephen, my editor extraordinaire, who tightened up and organized my thoughts so well. To Bob Carkhuff, my miraculous publisher, who showed up at the right time and took a chance on this unknown author. To Kyle King and the Amazons, Nancy Wunderlich, Dani Pardo, Sarah Sneed, Kim Komrad, Sandor Kovacs, Wendy Capland, Shawn and Cynthia Adler, Eric and Lori Marshall,

Jackie Eiting, Roberta Greenberg, Padma Ayyagari, Kim Cox, Suzy Pereira, Patricia Bowens, Linda Lang, and my brother, Jack Benoff who provided sanity, enthusiastic interest, willing ears, emotional fuel, and strong shoulders to lean on while I rode the crests and dips of the entire book process. I'm so thankful for my wonderful family: my soul mate and husband-partner Bruce, and my delicious and magical children Samantha and Bryan who make every day worth living joyfully and who make the concept of legacy important. My most enthusiastic cheerleader and biggest support is my amazing mom, Bethany Portner Silberfarb, who is always there for me in life, business, and the pursuit of all things meaningful. You can't write a book without wonderful people in your corner, and I am truly blessed with an abundance of wonderful people. My corner runneth over!

Preface

It is no longer good enough to be good at what you do. You must demonstrate a baseline of excellence just to survive. The thing that will really make you stand out in your market is how effectively you can communicate about what it is that you do and how happy your clients are to have had you do it. You have to demonstrate results. You have to be able to sing your own praises, toot your own horn, and stand up and shout to the world, in a variety of different formats, why anyone should buy your services. Specifically, what you have to tell the world is why they should buy your services from YOU. It is not how good you are at what you do that matters; it is how effective you are at marketing and selling what you do. The good news is that you already have the skills to do this. You know who your audience is and what your message is. Now you just need to figure out how you can communicate your message in multiple different ways to reach all the varied styles out there in your intended customer base.

Not unlike the frustrated artist who lines the walls of his home with his own paintings and wonders why he hasn't been discovered, those of us who are just good service providers and not good networkers, marketers, and salespeople will be sitting home alone. Example: Many attorneys have told me that they create great work product or are fabulous litigators and they assume clients should just know that and somehow find them. It would be nice if it worked that way, but it doesn't.

That's why I wrote this book. **Tons of coaches, trainers, and consultants are great at their craft, but don't know how to sell their services to corporations and organizations.** Whether you are selling to companies or to individuals, if you are a self-employed professional, you will find in this book the essential mental perspectives that will open the floodgates to new business and repeat business. You will also find the all-access pass to expanding new business with your current clients. There are many books saturating the market about sales and selling. You can also find a fair number of books on networking. There are quite a few materials about marketing. However, **it is the intersection of networking, marketing, and sales that is the sweet spot where you can seal the deal. There's no class that you took in school that taught you how to integrate the critical trinity of networking, marketing, and sales.** This book shows you how.

Seal the Deal will save you time. Attorney clients have told me that as associates, they were actually taught to expect it to take them seven years to get business from their marketing and rainmaking activities. SEVEN YEARS?! With integrated activity in the three domains (networking, marketing, and sales) mapped out in this book, you can reduce that cycle time by 85 percent or more. Some people believe that if you are good at networking, sales will happen. Others believe that if you are good at marketing, sales will happen. Many will tell you that if you are good at sales, there's a pretty good chance sales will happen. *Seal the Deal* will show you that if you are good at all three (networking, marketing, and sales), then sales are guaranteed to happen and you will build a six-figure business in a relatively short time.

> **THE SWEET SPOT is not only where networking, marketing, and sales intersect; it is where you SEAL THE DEAL!**

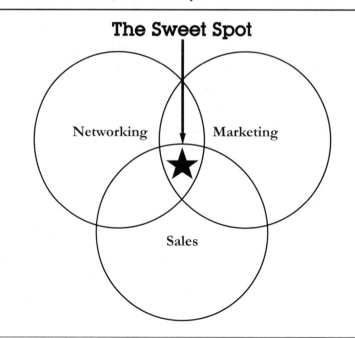

The Sweet Spot

About the Format and How You Might Choose to Approach This Book

Seal the Deal is written from a coaching perspective, so it gently guides you through specific action steps to be taken to get your ideal clients. Each step of the book is set up as if you were taking a 10-week course on this material. Thus, if you approach this book as a self-study course, you'll be serious about trying out the suggested actions and you will see evidence of results in as little as 10 weeks.

Each chapter at the heart of the book is a step of the 10-step proven process. The first part of each chapter is a condensed actual transcript of a telecourse session on that subject, followed by additional explanation and worksheets to bring each step to life. The telecourse scripts offer several benefits, for those of you who choose to read them. You will get to know the participants, their fears, their successes, and their experiences as they learn the same 10-step process you will be learning. You will see their humanity and be able to form an emotional connection to the material through their experiences. The telecourse scripts are full of anecdotes that demonstrate the real-world relevance and examples of each of the 10 steps in the process. You will be able to be a "fly on the wall," observing a group of highly educated, highly degreed professionals engaged in a powerful, real-life learning dialogue. You will find that you are being coached right along with these participants.

If you opt to approach *Seal the Deal* as a 10-week self-study course, I recommend that you put the book down between each chapter: Read one each week for 10 weeks and do the homework, try the actions, and use a journal to capture your observations and progress as you move through the steps. There is a good amount of worksheet space so that you can also write in the book and use it as a workbook.

Another option is the quick-study approach, for those of you who don't have time to complete the steps thoroughly. You can still get powerful results if you want to just get the highlights and skip the telecourse material in each chapter. Just read the second part of each chapter, do the worksheets, and take the action steps. Be sure not to miss the summary points and worksheets in the last two chapters of the book.

You're too busy for that much? Then I recommend taking the Self-Assessment Quiz on the next page, and then going through the table of contents to hit just the specific highlights that were illuminated by your quiz results. For the impatient, I definitely recommend skipping the telecourse transcripts.

And maybe some folks will approach this book in the random inspiration method—meaning you could just pop it open on any given day and read whatever paragraphs jump out at you. That would be a great way to dive in if you are already a seasoned, successful sales practitioner seeking a quick review to fire yourself up and motivate targeted action.

However you choose to approach it, I appreciate your commitment to try something new, and I applaud your efforts at all levels. You are on your way to *Seal the Deal.*

Self-Assessment Quiz:
How ready are you?
Test your "seal the deal-ability."

TRUE or FALSE?

1. _____ I am confident and comfortable in the process of selling professional services.

2. _____ I no longer feel like I am just winging it or hoping for the best.

3. _____ I have a model, a process, and a roadmap in place for sales.

4. _____ I know the distinctions between networking, marketing, and sales, and I know how and when to use each one and all three together in my business development strategy.

5. _____ I know the nine mindsets of networking and how to leverage my networking skills in alignment with my business development goals.

6. _____ I know how to play the numbers game, manage my time inside the sales process, and easily set up meetings with prospects.

7. _____ I know the specific goal for each step of the sales process.

8. _____ I know how to handle gatekeepers and objections.

9. _____ I have a genuine and natural style for leading sales conversations with clients and I do not use any techniques, gimmicks, or tricks.

10. _____ I quickly build trust and rapport and I demonstrate my credibility right off the bat.

11. _____ I am adept at quickly grasping the client's situation and I know how to integrate my success stories into the conversation to demonstrate how my services can help them with what the client's business is going through.

12. _____ I provide value and support in the first conversation and create collaborative partnerships with my clients.

13. _____ I know how to subtly and masterfully seal the deal and seamlessly manage the transition from sales to service.

14. _____ I have sustainable systems in place for tracking my progress and managing follow-up.

15. _____ I have fabulous resources for proposals, pricing, and contracting.

16. _____ I know how to leverage excellent customer service into new business; I consistently expand the sale while serving the client.

17. _____ I know how to build business while billing time through referrals and lessons-learned meetings.

18. _____ I am skilled at letting go of my attachment to any particular outcome. I focus my energy on following the ten steps of the sales process and trust that the results will come.

If you answered true to all of the above statements, then put this book down and walk away! There's nothing in here for you. If you answered false to fewer than five of the above statements, then you are well on your way to sales success, and the notions in this book will help you fine-tune your business development efforts for ultimate success. If you answered false to more than five of the above statements, this book is just what you've been looking for to help you get on the path to sealing deals and succeeding in your business, so read on.

Introduction

This is a book about relationships. More specifically, it is about managing relationships as assets. I know, I know—you thought it was about sales. It is. I once heard a speaker named Lou Heckler say, "Business moves at the speed of relationships." He's right. You may have heard the term *relationship asset management*.[1] If you constantly manage your relationship assets, your business will move at a constant speed. If you shift your focus or divert your attention, even for a moment, from relationship asset management, you will find that your business will slow down proportionately. If you think of sales as the vehicle that propels business, relationships are the engine and you are the driver. This book is your road map. How fast and how far you want to go is up to you. There are no limits. As Yogi Berra once said, "If you don't know where you're going, you'll wind up somewhere else." Selling professional services does not have to be one of those happenstance, if-you're-lucky kind of things. You can have a plan, you can have systematic steps to get there, and you can have a road map to follow.

What's in It for You

You are great at what you do. You are so good at it, you've entered the world of self-employment and you have your own business as a consultant, a coach, a therapist, an attorney, a facilitator, an accountant, a chiropractor, a project manager, a trainer, an advisor, a whatever! Do you have a selling system that integrates networking, marketing, and sales? Where will your next clients come from? Where will your leads come from? Do you think of yourself as a consultant, a coach, a counselor, an advisor, a chiropractor, a project manager, a whatever, and not as a salesperson? As a sole proprietor or small business owner, chances are you are not only the president/CEO, but you are also the janitor, receptionist, CFO, and COO! And, you are, whether reluctantly or not, the *sales executive* for your business. As Sam Horn of TongueFu has said, "a sole proprietor is a *sale* proprietor." Likewise, if you are a solo practitioner, you must also be a *sale* practitioner.

You may be an experienced solopreneur looking for a structured format for sealing the deal and supercharging your sales to take your business to the next level. (A system is defined as a set of connected things or parts forming a complex whole, and as a set of principles or procedures according to which something is done; an organized scheme or method.[2]) The system set forth in this book applies equally well to seasoned practitioners as well as "the newbies."

Or maybe you're a retiring baby boomer looking for your next avocation. You may be an employee, tired of slaving away for someone else's gain, ready to break out on your own to join the global, networked economy of free agents. Either way, you've probably considered some form of consulting as an option for what you can do to leverage and apply your corporate experience as a free agent. This book can help you make it a reality. In fact, I was already doing a six-figure business when I started applying the 10 steps I've laid out for you, and in the first year of using the system, I saw a 95.6 percent increase in revenues.

Your success is hinged on your sales ability. *Sales* is not a dirty word! Selling executive coaching, consulting, or any professional services to corporations can be challenging, particularly given the abstract, intangible nature of those services. Complicating that is our sometimes-negative perception about sales and selling. For many of us, the concept of sales conjures up images of sleazy used car salesmen, pushy telemarketing calls during dinner, the onslaught of catalogs that clog our mailboxes, or a sales pitch from a door-to-door solicitor or vendor. Worse yet, we think of spam, phishing, and other e-mail evils. For others of us, the activity required to generate sales causes us anxiety or feels intrusive or uncomfortable. We don't want to force ourselves on others—we want to help them! Particularly for the coaching industry—which in spite of itself is a $1 billion industry and second in growth only to information technology—generating business is a major stumbling block. The only way to impact this reality is to recognize that we can't afford to be naïve about what it takes to create business opportunities. We have to get good at it so that it will take us less time to get the clients and we can spend more time doing what we love, which is working with the clients. Most of the helping professions are a lot like coaching—they don't want to sell. They love the client work, but hate the work of getting clients. Yet we know that no clients equals no business. The most important part of running a business is keeping existing clients and acquiring new ones.

Developing New Business, Your Way

Seal the Deal will guide you to take new actions and alter your mindsets about business development in a way that will open the door for you to grow your coaching/professional services business in the way *you* want. Once you understand and can use this book's systematic process, concrete approach, and focused format for selling professional services into organizations, you can easily *Seal the Deal* using your own natural style and personality. The steps are easily customizable and user friendly. If you picked up this book looking for tips, tricks, gimmicks, magic, secret formulas, or other marketing wizardry, you won't find them here. There will be no manipulative or pressure techniques, fear tactics, or slick shadiness of any kind. The system in this book is about honor and integrity, genuineness, authenticity, and honesty. It is a straightforward, no-nonsense approach, which is why it works for everyone who applies it in a way that is true to his or her natural self. There are no shortcuts. If you are willing to do the work, take the risks, and shift your perceptual framework, you will see results.

Many of the points in this book are discussed in terms of coaching and consulting, but these steps apply equally well to any professional service. Also, the discussion is primarily organized around the idea of a sole practitioner or small partnership selling into organizations at the executive level or to Human Resources; but with only slight shifts in mindset, it can also apply to business-to-business selling or to selling large-scale multi-coach interventions, large-scale change initiatives, or large-scale strategic implementation projects. None of the concepts presented here is rocket science or truly new information—but you might not have thought of them in the context of business development before.

A notable feature of this book is that you will learn an action-oriented selling system through an edited transcript of our *Seal the Deal* telecourse. The telecourse is a mastermind group of coaches and consultants who are taking their networking, marketing, and sales to the next level (the participants' names have been changed to protect the innocent). There are 10 sessions of live group coaching conversation, and while we've edited out the small talk and personally identifying information, we've left the course content essentially intact. I have also included some of our most popular worksheets, templates, samples, and tip sheets for you to use as you create and fulfill your own Personal Strategic Business Development Action Plan in three distinct domains: networking, marketing, and sales. If you wish to listen in, audio of our telecourses is available for purchase. You can contact Innovative Leadership International for one-on-one sales coaching as well.

Endnotes

1. Richardson, T., & Vidauretta, A., (2002). *Business is a contact sport.* Indianapolis, IN: Alpha Books.

2. *Oxford American Dictionaries.* New York: Oxford University Press USA, Oxford University Press, Inc.

Overview of
Seal the Deal

Each step begins with the dialogue from the corresponding telecourse session for that topic, and it is followed by additional guidance, strategies, worksheets, and guidelines. I recommend going through the sessions in order, as they build on one another, but each chapter is also usable on its own, so if you prefer to skip around, you will still benefit. At the end of the book, you will find additional resources and your own Strategic Business Development Action Plan for Networking, Marketing, and Sales template. If you approach this book as a self-study course, you will alter your mindsets about sales and walk away with actionable steps for building your business your way.

Why do I know this stuff works? Here's a bit of my story. When I left my career as a schoolteacher, I learned how to network by spending six months engaged in informational interviews—meeting everyone I could possibly meet to figure out what I would do next. How would my teaching skills transfer to the corporate workplace? The pattern that emerged from that experience was that people kept saying I should get into consulting and coaching. In fact, a few of the folks I met during that six months of interviewing wanted to hire me as the coach for their employees and clients! Thus, I started my business because I had clients. After two years, the initial engagements came to their natural conclusion, and I had to quickly learn how to generate new business. Applying what I knew about networking, and integrating a few marketing activities, I was able to go from $10K in debt at year two, to generating sustainable six-figure revenues by year three of my business. Then I learned how to integrate sales activities into the game. The first year that I used the whole system in an integrated way in my own business, I was already six years into self-employment. I formatted the selling system by combining my networking and marketing experiences with the core concepts from sales training that I had been co-facilitating for lawyers and legal service providers—and I began to apply it to my own business. The system works for experienced consultants as well as those just starting out. How do I know it works? Because I've sealed the deal in more than 110 companies and firms worldwide, and I started as a schoolteacher!

In my first year of applying the selling system you are about to learn, I saw a 95.6 percent increase in annual revenues. Does that sound like something that would interest you? If so, I encourage you to systematically do the homework actions and answer the questions in this book, and treat this book as if it were your personal sales coach. Here are some of the basics we'll be exploring more fully:

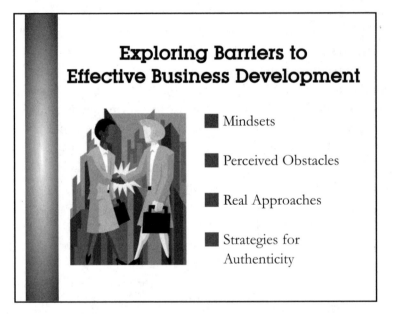

Exploring Barriers to Effective Business Development

■ Mindsets

■ Perceived Obstacles

■ Real Approaches

■ Strategies for Authenticity

Barriers to Effective Business Development

- What are your current mindsets about sales and marketing? About business development in general? About networking?
- What gets in your way? What are the obstacles that prevent you from making lots of sales?
- Where do you get in your own way?
- Where are you repressing your real and authentic self in an effort to fit in, impress partners or clients, or manage others' perceptions about you?

- What strategies can you employ that will allow you to bring forth your full and authentic self toward a meaningful purpose?

- Who are your allies?

- Where can you deepen relationships or create partnerships that will expand your sphere of influence and forward your business development goals?

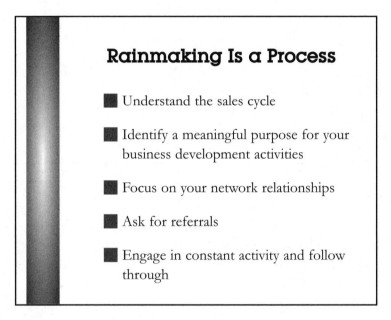

The Power of Rainmaking

Successful rainmaking begins with developing your own concept of what result you want from your business development efforts—you can't get there if you don't have a clear idea of where *there* is. Know where you want to go with your business and design steps to take it in that direction. The first step for many of us is to perfect a deep understanding of the sales cycle— and when and how to bring our best targets into it. Key strategies are to zero in on prospective clients you have identified in or through your network and to never, ever fail to ask for referrals. In other words, rainmaking means you are in perpetual business development mode—continually networking, marketing, and selling.

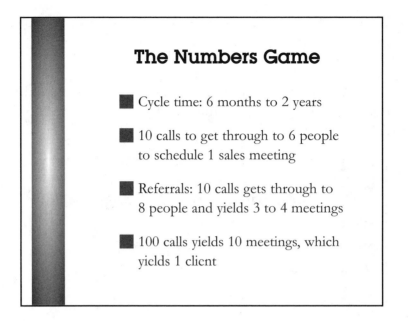

Playing by the Numbers

Allow me to explain. The numbers I quote throughout *Seal the Deal* are based on general research and, of course, vary greatly depending on the individual, but you can use these numbers as a baseline for understanding the numbers game involved.

- It takes 10 calls to get through to six to seven people to set up one meeting.
- It takes 10 meetings to get 5 second meetings to get one client.
- Therefore, it takes 100 calls to get 10 meetings to get one client!
- The figures for referrals are much better: 10 calls will get through to eight or nine people and yield three to four meetings or more.
- The entire process, from meeting a prospective user of your services to getting business from them, could take anywhere from six months to two years. That means that if you stop making calls to set up meetings to get new clients, in roughly six months, you will find yourself with a paucity of work.

This is why you need to engage in constant activity and follow through! Much of the sales process is about momentum.

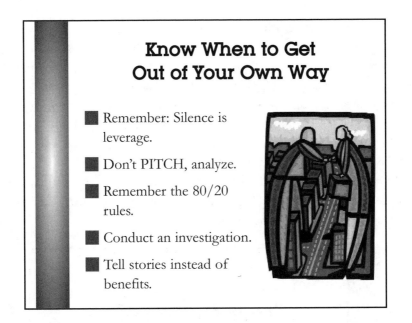

Know When to Get Out of Your Own Way

- Remember: Silence is leverage.
- Don't PITCH, analyze.
- Remember the 80/20 rules.
- Conduct an investigation.
- Tell stories instead of benefits.

Getting Out of Your Own Way

An ongoing theme throughout *Seal the Deal* is avoiding self-sabotage—learning ways to get out of your own way. For example, know when to stop talking. Listening is the key to getting golden nuggets of information from your prospects as well as to eventually getting the business. Use silence to put the ball in their court.

No one likes to be pitched. It is better to use the time to determine with the prospect if it makes sense to do business together. Analyze their needs, their situation, what they are committed to doing/accomplishing, and where you might help. Approach the conversation with the assumption that you may not be the best match for their needs—and a willingness to walk away.

In the long run, 80 percent of your business comes from 20 percent of your clients, so focus on providing excellent customer care and seeking repeat business from current clients. Ask them for referrals frequently throughout the engagement life cycle. Do not just ask for referrals at the end of a project, but plant seeds at the beginning and make referral requests throughout your service cycle with a client.

In any sales meeting, the listening/talking rule is 80/20—you should do 80 percent listening and only talk 20 percent of the time; the client should do 80 percent of the talking. Thus, to prepare for client meetings, you will be well served to prepare questions that will open up the client responses.

Apply the investigative, inquiry skills you already have to the sales meeting. Don't assume they can use your services; investigate the possibility with the prospect of where it makes sense to work together in a way that best serves their commitments/goals/objectives.

Tell stories that illustrate your results, wins, and successes with other clients so that your prospects can see themselves in your story and assume your services are the solutions to their needs.

Create Space, Be Real

■ Trust yourself.

■ Listen.

■ Create space to breathe.

■ Align with your authenticity and commitments.

People Buy from You for a Finite Set of Reasons

Once you understand that there is a set number of possible reasons someone might buy your services, you can step aside from the personal attachment to the outcome of getting clients. Once you know the finite list, you can have more control over your reactions to the process. Your list might be like what the Sandler Institute teaches: People buy from you either because of their pain and the belief that your products or services can eliminate that pain for them, or because they believe that your products and services will increase their pleasure or joy in some way.[1]

While the Sandler training is very powerful and useful, my list is a little bit different. Inquire within yourself to determine what your list looks like. People buy from you because:

- They like you.
- They trust you.
- They value the service you provide.
- They want your products or think your services will help them.
- They have some problem that you can help them solve.
- They trust the person in their life who told them about you.

If you keep your list in mind during your sales process, you'll know that once one or more of those things are sufficiently present in the other person (organization, etc.), then you can close the deal. The list above provides your litmus test for readiness to approach the close. Likewise, if none of the above is present in sufficient quantities to score the sale, it would be foolish to ask for business at that time.

No One Is on the Bench

Networking and business development are not spectator sports. Not only do you have to be in the game, on the court, out in the field, or whatever metaphor speaks to you, you must think of everyone else in the world as also being in the game with you. There are no benchwarmers, which means that none of your interactions with any other human being is ever wasted. Every moment is an opportunity for building relationships—for speaking your vision to everyone all the time. Another critical piece of this mindset is to operate from the assumption that everyone wants to help you. This assumption will allow you to make big, bold, outrageous requests that will encourage and invite people to contribute to your growing business and blossoming self.

How do you actively stay competitive in this rapidly expanding market? If you are not networking all the time, what is in the way of that? Even if you spend most of your time with fellow coaching or consulting colleagues, they can be great networking and business development resources for you. Staying competitive in the market may not actually be about competition.

Competition

Think about competition for a minute. In a personal services business such as consulting or coaching in organizations, even though you and all your would-be competitors offer similar or even the same services (assessments, 360-degree assessments, Myers-Briggs Type Indicator, individual coaching, team coaching, situational leadership, presentation skills, etc.), so much of what you do is unique to you as an individual. When you think about it that way, do you truly have competitors in your market?

Here's a mindset that better serves coaches to expand their offering into organizations and be able to provide larger-scale interventions than individual coaches: I've heard it referred to as *coopetition,* an amalgam of *cooperation* and *competition.* The idea is one of collaboration with competitors, or turning competitors into partners, by building alliances and joint ventures as a business development strategy. If you struggle with staying competitive in the market, identify those you perceive to be your biggest competitors and approach them to create coopetition arrangements that serve everyone and the greater good of the client organization. It is the old win-win concept that we facilitate our clients to attain, now applied to your own business growth strategy.

There is a psychology of selling, and it is equally important to manage your own psychology as well as understand the game from the prospective buyer's perspective. Selling coaching and other professional services is very different from selling products or programs. These services are abstract and intangible—it's not like you're selling Fuller brushes or Girl Scout cookies! You're selling concepts, competence, confidence—a host of outcomes that often are years in the making.

Navigating the System

The *Seal the Deal* process uses clear navigation points and basic foundational elements. There's an assumed baseline of credibility: You have the training, experience, education, and credentials to deliver the service (whatever it may be) and get results. You have a track record of proven value (results/worth). You understand and can facilitate a sophisticated interview. You recognize when your prospective client is an educated and savvy consumer/user of your services. You are aware of and can manage your mindsets and attitudes during the process. You understand and can keep all your activities clear and consistent within a specific sales cycle. You constantly fill and track your pipeline of leads. You know your numbers and what it takes to play the numbers game to move people through your sales process. You build your business routinely using the technology of referrals, and you are always networking.

These are the basics. Of course, there's much, much more to each one of these elements, hence this book. Read on and have fun!

Endnote

1. See their website at www.sandler.com/.

Step 1

Demystifying Selling and Distinguishing Networking, Marketing, and Sales

"We are all continually faced with a series of
great opportunities brilliantly disguised as insoluble problems."
—John Gardner

In this chapter, you will find the first telecourse dialogue, which covers the initial context setting for the course, and the theory and practice of the 30-second commercial. You will learn how to create, refine, and practice your own 30-second commercial to use when introducing yourself on the phone or in person, and when networking in order to have a response to that question everyone asks when they first meet you: "So, what do you do?" This first live script includes more dialogue than the others so that you can get a feel for the participants and their baseline of comfort or discomfort with the notion of business development. Hopefully, you will recognize elements of yourself among them and feel confident that this system will work for you.

After the dialogue piece, selling is further demystified with a few suggestions for how to reframe your thinking and understand your current mental barriers so that you can get your head in the game. There are a few worksheets for you to use to explore mindsets and mental positioning with respect to sales as well as a chart depicting the distinctions between the three critical domains of networking, marketing, and sales. From there we'll explore time management, both as a mental barrier to selling and as an organizational process.

Telecourse Session #1:
Your 30-Second Commercial

The Difference between Marketing and Sales

[Suzi] Before we get into the specifics of a 30-second commercial, I want to talk a little bit about the difference between marketing and sales activities. To start, let's have each of you say what you see to be the distinction between marketing and sales. If you don't know, that's okay too. I just want to get a sense of your thinking.

[Len] I think marketing is partly studying the market, and shopping around in the market, and sales is giving the pitch, and getting the contract.

[Suzi] What does that mean to you, making the pitch?

[Len] Telling people exactly what you do, and also connecting with what people need.

[John] I think of marketing as a kind of a strategy, planning and strategy, and that includes research. And I think of sales as the implementation, where you actually get out there and pound the pavement, press the flesh, make the human connection, and do the follow-up. But one of them seems more strategic, and conceptual, than the other.

[Bill] To me the marketing is stuff that I can do by myself, alone in my office, and the sales is stuff I have to do with another person.

[Jeremy] I've heard you speak on this topic before, Suzi, so I'm going to be giving some of your answers. Marketing to me is positioning yourself, deciding your strategy, and providing information. And sales is developing the relationship with a customer and getting them to sign contracts.

[Suzi] Yes, marketing and sales go hand-in-hand. Marketing activities are the things that you can do by yourself, in front of your computer, creating text, writing letters, doing research, all of those things that you said—that's right on target. Also marketing includes building a website, fine-tuning your website, writing articles, getting articles or books published, and creating your letterhead, your logo, and your business card. Those things, image and collateral kinds of things, are the marketing activities. It's very easy to spend lots and lots of time on marketing activities. The bad news is, those things alone don't get you the contracts. They help, but in and of themselves, they don't get you the contracts.

So the time you're spending working on marketing is time that you're not spending on sales activities, and the trick with sales is that it's all about the numbers. (More on that later). It's all about how many sales activities you're undergoing in a day, how many prospective clients you have in your pipeline, how many times you're following up with folks in your pipeline. Because sales is a process, it takes time to move through that process. So all that time you're spending on marketing activities, while they're important and necessary, they're not moving you toward getting the contract. So I just want to make that distinction up front, because there's nothing wrong with doing marketing activities, but if you're like I was, maybe you're kind of afraid of sales because you're afraid of rejection, or you feel like you're bugging people, or you're just resisting it for whatever reason. It's much easier to focus on marketing and pat yourself on the back and say, "You know what? I'm doing what I need to be doing. I'm spending hours each day writing these letters, I've got it all fine-tuned and I'm ready to go, I've got all my materials in place, I've got my brochure ready." Well that's great, but it's not sales. I just want to make sure that we're not tricking ourselves into thinking that all the time we're spending on marketing is forwarding our sales.

[Len] I think that's a very important distinction because I have fallen into that trap. I am a sinner and I confess. And then you can really get discouraged—"How come I'm not getting the clients? What's going on here?"

[Suzi] Right, and it feels like, "Oh I'm working so hard. I've spent hours writing these articles. I've really got the words the way I want them. I've got all my materials ready. My letterhead looks great." You feel like you're working a lot, and you are, but it doesn't get you the clients directly. So I'm not discouraging those activities, but it's important to be very clear with yourself that on any given day, whatever amount of time you spend on marketing, developing marketing materials, or on marketing activity, you want to spend at least that time plus 50 percent more on sales activities so that you're getting a good balance. We all slip into wanting to do the marketing stuff, "cause it's much easier." And we can see the accomplishment much more quickly. You write a document, you end up with a document. It's not like the sales process, where you can be in it for two years before you see results. Any thoughts on that?

[Len] I have a humorous take on it: Companies create marketing departments to keep their salespeople from wasting time. Get people who won't sell to stay home and do marketing.

[Suzi] Yes, getting out there and selling is hard at first. I've heard people refer to it as pounding the pavement, pressing the flesh, making the pitch, while it's really just about getting out there and creating relationships and talking to people.

What would you say is your gut reaction to the concept of sales and sales activities? Is it something that feels good to you, or is it something that you're resisting? Is it something that feels positive or effortless, or bad or uncomfortable—how does it feel to you?

[John] Maybe the word would be threatening.

[Jeremy] I guess my humorous response, if I could summarize in 10 words or less would be, "Isn't there something else I have to do?"

[Len] Sales makes me uncomfortable, especially if I don't really understand it. If I think that I have some sort of understanding about what I'm doing, I feel better, but sales is foreign to me, basically.

[Bill] Before Christmas I went into a cycle of going to meetings and all kinds of Christmas parties, the local business association, this association, that association. I was nervous and uptight, but I pretty quickly became used to it. It's just a lot of people like me showing up at these places, we're having the same feelings, but it's quickly dispelled. It's not so bad when you get in it. It's kind of like swimming in cold ocean water; you get used to it and later on it seems you're fine. You just have to be in it for a while.

[Suzi] You're talking about networking types of events?

[Bill] Yeah, Christmas parties plus a presentation at a Chamber of Commerce meeting where I met a lot of people, collected a lot of cards, and another presentation at a financial services company. It was all very exhilarating actually. It created kind of a high—because I was walking and quacking like a duck, and I seemed to be seen as one. And that seemed to be a good first step. And it's also good for me to be able to transfer, to feel like my skills are generic and portable, and to know that this is a viable thing I'm trying to do—at least it seems like it from the response. It's encouraging when you get past worrying about if you'll pass for whatever you want to be passing for. And it's confidence building, and that's how you become what you say you are, in my mind.

[Suzi] Well, in one of our later classes, we're going to get into networking, and how to make the most of those networking situations, but right now I want to get back to basics. Just as there is a distinction between marketing and sales, there's also a distinction between networking and sales. So it's wonderful to go to networking activities, go to these meetings, meet people, give out your card, develop the beginnings of relationships. But again, that's not direct sales activity.

[Bill] Well, there's two things about what you're saying that explain my own psychological process. After the first week of January, I went into a crash. After spending a lot of time creating a flyer for a different type of business, and then going through all this networking, nothing emerged except people calling me up wanting to have lunch. But I don't have time for lunch. I wasn't selling anything.

[Suzi] Right—you weren't selling. You were networking, you were marketing, but you weren't selling.

[Bill] And it seemed discouraging. I was doing some right things, but I wasn't selling.

[Suzi] Right, all of these activities are right things, and I'm not going to say "Stop marketing, stop networking." You've got to keep doing all of that. But let's not delude ourselves into thinking we're selling, and let's not be surprised when that doesn't yield contracts, clients, business dollars, etc.

[Bill] In other words, I hadn't taken a shot at the eight ball yet . . . I think I need to do that.

30-Second Commercial Basics

[Suzi] Ready? Let's start with the 30-second commercial. We're going to get into what is sales, and the sales process, in later classes, and I hope that you can be patient with postponing that, because I want to give you something to use right away: the 30-second commercial. This is not your typical elevator-speech or an infomercial to memorize and deliver with robot-like precision. It is an introduction you can actually start working with right away.

As we build skills in this telecourse over the next nine sessions, you'll start to get an understanding that there is a sustainable, repeatable process behind sales; there are specific steps and activities that you can embark upon. You'll know how to do it, and one of the first steps is nailing down your 30-second commercial. Because that's the thing that's going to open doors for you, get phone calls through for you, and help you fine-tune some of your networking activities.

So we'll start with the basics of your 30-second commercial so that you can take a modular approach. The first thing you want to have in it is, of course, your name. And then you want to have something in there right off the bat that gives the sense of what you do in a very concise way.

Key Pieces in Crafting a 30-Second Commercial

- Your name, and how to remember it
- Credibility points about you or your work
- Whom do you help?
- What do you help them do?
- What energizes and excites you about what you do?
- Other impressive factoids

Why don't we go around the group and each tell a little bit about our coaching experience and what we hope to get out of this first class, and then we'll get into fine-tuning your 30-second commercial. You want to kick it off, Jeremy?

[Jeremy] Why don't I kick it off with my 30-second commercial? I provide Leadership-Development and Coaching to Executives. I partner with businesspeople to solve the kinds of dilemmas that wake them up at 3:00 in the morning. I'm known for being both a trusted advisor and an intuitive person. I love what I do, and I'm relentless in my determination to help organizations and individuals develop. I've been doing coaching for about 15 years, and I've decided that that's all I'm going to say—it's always going to be 15 years from now on.

[Suzi] Why is that?

[Jeremy] Something about getting older, you want to stop the clock on things you can stop the clock on. Some recent initiatives: I'm going to be giving a talk at a large psychological conference on executive coaching, I've been asked to be on some panels at the International Coach Federation (ICF), I'm nominating people to the Board of Directors, and something to do with grandfathering Master Certified Coaches (MCC).

[Bill] I'm a full-time psychologist and psychotherapist in Manhattan and Westchester, and I've been doing little bits of coaching in my office here for a couple of years, getting referrals from a friend of mine who has a full-time business. I do it to get out of the office more, and just take on a new challenge—because I'm pretty comfortable with what I do, I've been licensed since 1977. Around Christmastime, I thought I was all but signed off to coach two senior executives from a major financial services company with the promise of more to come. That got quashed by January 7, and I've been in the doldrums since. Still, I want to gear up, because I think the business cycle will reverse, and I'll have some big opportunities down the line to be coaching higher-up. That's the only place I'm really interested in coaching, because I make a decent living as a clinical psychologist, and I'm not interested in personal coaching. I really want to do corporate stuff. So I want to develop my sales approach so that when the pieces begin to fall back into place, I'm there and I'm ready.

[John] I'll go next. I'm John. I have a Ph.D. in Organizational Behavior, and I was on the Business School faculty of University of Florida for 20 years, and 6 years ago it came time for the mid-career change. So I created my own small consulting firm, and we specialize in dissolving resistance to change. I've had a lot of Organizational Development consulting in my past, and wanted to add the executive coaching to my bag of tricks. So I just did an Executive Coach Academy class, and I've written a book that will be out soon hopefully, on how to dissolve resistance to change in the workplace. Also, I'm giving a paper, if I ever get the damn thing written, at a conference in D.C. on how to dissolve resistance to e-learning. So resistance to change is kind of my niche, or my specialty. My dilemma is I'm very, very good at the technical part, but not so good at the marketing and sales piece. So I'm hoping this class will imbue the skills—and probably more important some confidence—to take on that sales part of the buy.

[Suzi] John, what is your evidence that you are not good at the sales and marketing part?

[John] When given the chance, I don't do it.

[Suzi] But does that mean that you're not good at it, or that you would prefer not to do it?

[John] It probably means I'm scared of rejection. If someone holds my hand and does the introductory paragraph to someone, then I'm wonderful. But getting the ball rolling in the first place, and doing the self-presentation from ground zero, that's the part that seems to be the hang-up.

[Suzi] Thanks, John. That leaves Len.

[Len] I'm a clinical psychologist, just about as long as Bill has been. I've gotten into coaching and consulting because the idea really appealed to me, beginning a couple of years ago, and I've been refining my skills since then. At first I was practicing on a non-commercial model. I was working with families with a developmentally-disabled or a Downs Syndrome child, and coaching them in terms of managing their everyday kinds of issues. After a while, I moved my focus into commercial areas, and now I want to work more as a consultant and coach for upper-level executives in financial institutions. So I've been drafting and re-drafting a letter of introduction to one particular bank that I'm thinking of approaching, and I also wrote a newsletter, and I'm going to be writing more. Also, just yesterday I contacted a local Chamber of Commerce; I was scouting around to find information about the CEO of the particular bank that I'm interested in working with, and I contacted the Chamber of Commerce where he is a member. And they were so very welcoming of my call, I have an appointment with them and will introduce myself to them at the next meeting.

[Suzi] And Len, what has drawn you to the financial services world as your clients?

[Len] Well, the kind of consultation I want to do is with executives. For two reasons: One, there are a lot of very good banks in the area where I live. And the one that I'm focusing on is a growing bank. I've done a lot of investigation and basically I'm experimenting. I've talked with different businesspeople about my new endeavor in consulting. And while talking with a particular stockbroker about the bank that I'm interested in, I learned that he knew the philosophy of the bank CEO. Basically the CEO wants everybody to be very people-oriented in his banks, and very service-with-a-smile kind of thing. His service model is McDonald's, so I did my research: for example, McDonald's posts statements about its service approach on its website. So I felt great about that, plus I know this bank is a growing bank and I found a *Harvard Business Review* article that's really relevant. So I put together the ideas from McDonald's and the article and cast them in a way that I think would be quite appealing to the CEO; when he reads my newsletter he'll see I'm right on target for his concerns.

[Suzi] So you've tailored your marketing materials to what you have learned to be his philosophies and beliefs.

[Len] Right. Very specific that way. And so this has been a practice run. I wish it will turn out to be something, but it's really practice in refining my skills. And so I've also just begun to develop various kinds of inserts for a folder, so when I meet with people in banks, I'll have appropriate materials to show them. Besides referring them to my website, I'll have a little brochure that I can show them.

[Suzi] Keep in mind that marketing actions are not the same as sales actions. I'd like you to think about a strategy for making direct contact with the CEO or other decision makers in these banks, and asking for a meeting.

[Jeremy] Okay, Suzi, over to you.

[Suzi] My name is Suzi Pomerantz, and I lead leaders from chaos to clarity. I'm an executive coach, and I'm the owner of Innovative Leadership International, LLC, which is a leadership-development firm that specializes in executive coaching and training. And I have my master's degree in teaching, and I'm internationally certified as a master-certified coach. My coaching business began in 1993, and mostly I coach executives from corporate law departments, such as DuPont, Sears, Welch's, Tyco, and also across the country. I have coached and trained executives at Lockheed Martin, at American Express, at the U.S. Postal Service and other government agencies, and primarily what we do in my company is help leaders exceed prior levels of performance and improve their leadership skills. So that's me, and what you just heard is my 30-second commercial. So part of what we're going to work on is . . .

[Len] Do you have that spiel posted on every wall in your residence?

[Suzi] No, I don't. I've just done it so many times I kind of have a bullet list in my head. It doesn't sound exactly the same every time. Jeremy can attest to that, because he's now heard it three, four times?

[Jeremy] Yeah, three times.

[Suzi] So it doesn't sound exactly the same every time, but I have the bullet list in my head for what I want to cover each time. I have a longer version for when I'm standing up in front of a room introducing myself. I have shorter versions of it for when I'm at cocktail parties, or for example, Len, when you go to your Chamber of Commerce meeting—that would be a good opportunity to have a finely-tuned **30-second** commercial when you walk around the room meeting people.

[Bill] What would your 10-second commercial be?

[Suzi] That I'm an executive coach and I focus on leaders to help them find clarity within chaos and I've coached and trained in over 110 organizations worldwide. That's basically the short version. Sometimes, when I have a little more time than that, I might throw in that I primarily work with attorneys and managers of corporate law departments, and I might list a few of the organizations I've worked with—particularly if I know my audience. When I'm talking to attorneys and executives, they want to know where I've worked before. They want to know if I'm capable of handling executives of their caliber. So I find that that's important for my target audience, but it may not be for yours. So part of delivering your 30-second commercial is to know whom you're targeting. You don't need to know that right off the bat to design your 30-second commercial, but it is helpful for fine-tuning it later on.

So Jeremy said, "I coach executives." That's very clear. Mine is "helping leaders find clarity" or "helping leaders exceed prior performance." To start putting your 30-second commercial together, think first about who you want to help, and what you want to help them do. You also want to include something that gives you a credibility boost right up front. Jeremy's credibility boost was "I've been an executive coach for 15 years." Bill, your credibility boost is "I'm a psychologist and psychotherapist." You might want to throw in the number of years you've been doing that.

[Bill] I'm concerned that it wouldn't sound very impressive.

[Suzi] Well, it is when you talk about executive coaching. First of all, if you're talking to executives, you're a doctor, and that's impressive. You know what you're doing. With a psychology background, you know a lot about emotional intelligence that you can transfer to the workplace. Now, you also have to know your audience. I know that when I work with attorneys, many don't want to deal with psychologists, because then they feel like they're getting into something like psychotherapy, rather than executive coaching.

It depends on knowing to whom you're talking. If there's anything negative going on about therapy, you might not want to take that route. You might want to say what you've been doing as a therapist over X number of years, and how that's helped certain people. I'll give you an example: My husband is a clinical psychologist. Over the past couple of years, he has been branching into executive coaching. And when he talks to prospects, he doesn't necessarily have to mention that he has a private practice in psychology. He might say he's been working with high-powered executives on issues such as X, Y, or Z, and he might talk about the issues they've been working on in therapy, but he can talk about it in the context of business.

You can take your experience in your practice and turn it into language that's going to be relevant to the audience that you're speaking to. But that takes knowing something about them, too. So when you're designing your 30-second commercial, you want to design it to be generic enough that you can use it in most cases. You want something that you practice over and over and over again—something that you know so well that if I woke you up in the middle of the night and asked you to introduce yourself, you would be able to rattle it off.

So in crafting your 30-second commercial, the key points are your name, some credibility points about you, what it is that you do, and for whom you do it—whom you help and what you help them do. And anything else that you think might be impressive in the first **30 seconds.** I'd definitely recommend writing out your 30-second commercial.

But for now, let's just practice by thinking out loud: Knowing those key points, let's see what comes off the top of your head. Who wants to go first?

[Len] I'm Len, I've been a clinical psychologist for the past 25, 26 years, and I do consultation assessments, data-based feedback, and executive coaching for corporations and upper-level executives.

[Suzi] Great. Now one question I have for you is did you say "data-based feedback"?

[Len] Meaning based on data. If you do an assessment of some sort, like a 360-degree assessment, it's like an evaluation of skills within that office environment, and you do an assessment and then you get back together with the person that the assessment was about or focused on, and you go over the data with that person.

[Suzi] Okay. So you might want to find a more generic way of saying that. Because not everyone you're talking to is going to ask you, like I just asked, if they don't know what that means. A lot of folks are going to assume that they know, or they're not going to want to look stupid. Because here you've been a doctor for 26 years, so they're not going to want to show you, especially if they're a high-level person, that they have ignorance in any area. So you might want to find a very straight-forward, elementary way of expressing that so that it's not a jargon term that might cloud over for somebody the real effectiveness of what you do. That was an excellent first shot. Next?

[John] I help leaders build support for and lead controversial change projects. I've just written a book describing a new way to dissolve resistance to change in the workplace. You know how employees and managers treat change with skepticism, even outright hostility? I turn that resistance into commitment and support. I specialize in coaching executives who are leading a difficult change project, and I'm particularly effective at helping leaders deal with the people problems of change.

[Suzi] All of that is great, but it sounded like you were reading rather than talking. Can you do that without reading it?

[John] Not today, but yes I can. By the way, a tool I often use for memorizing lines in situations like this is just writing it down. A lot of times, that helps me a lot. So if I wrote something down a hundred times, I would remember it.

[Suzi] Well, it also depends on your learning style, too. I'm the kind of person who'd feel trapped by having to have the same words every time, which is why I opt for the bullet list in my head of the points I want to cover. That way I have the flexibility to have it sound slightly different every time, but still have the same points. I get bored easily, so the modular approach allows me to mix it up a bit.

[Jeremy] My style is to have a trigger word for each thought, so there are four or five trigger words that I can use to remember five things.

[Suzi] Excellent. So that's something to take into consideration as you're writing and practicing your 30-second commercial. What's your learning style? Are you like John where you need to write it down 100 times? Are you like me where you just want to write a bullet list? Do you want trigger words like Jeremy? Part of having an effective 30-second commercial is knowing how you work best, and imagining yourself in different situations. The best one is the elevator test. Nine times out of 10, you'll be in an elevator, riding up with somebody to a different office in the building, and you and that person are the only people in the elevator. Well, you could stare at the floor, you could stare at the numbers, or you could talk to the person. And in an elevator, you have **30 seconds** or less to actually make your point.

Think about that scenario, or think about being at networking meetings and how quickly you meet people there. Think about being at conferences when you have a break in between sessions and you're meeting people, or think about being at social parties or weddings or brunches or lunches with family and friends and meeting people there. Strategize various contexts in which you'd want to introduce yourself. As you think through different scenarios where you might say your commercial, determine what your method will be for practicing it.

[John] I have a question on credibility. The only credibility piece I've mentioned is books that I've written. Should I throw in something about my Organizational Development consulting past?

[Suzi] I would definitely say you have a Ph.D. in organizational behavior. That's definitely credible when you're talking about executive coaching. Other credibility points include the number of years you have worked in a particular field, any books you have written, any degrees (master's, doctorate) that you have earned, and any impressive clients you have worked with. For example, I don't have a doctorate, but I have the credibility of having worked with some of the big Fortune 500 companies. So that's what I use. Okay, who haven't we heard from?

[Bill] Me. I'm Bill, I'm a psychologist with 25 years of experience. I coach senior executives and high-potential employees in the banking and financial markets to achieve performance—wait a second, I'm reading this, hold on.

[Suzi] That's okay.

[Bill] My name is Bill. I am a psychologist with 25 years of experience coaching high-potential employees and senior executives to achieve superior performance and results in leadership through a high-impact coaching relationship.

[Suzi] That's great! Now, another thing to think about is that you never know whom you're going to be meeting at any stage of your life, no matter where you are. So your 30-second commercial has to be simple enough that you could communicate to someone who's not an executive, because they might be married to an executive, they might be the son or daughter of an executive, or they might have a client who's an executive to whom they might want to refer you.

I think all of you did a really good job of having your 30-second commercials be clear and simple enough that they don't just speak to the executive-level person. That was great. So I would say in terms of fine-tuning them, practice them on people in your family or with people you see on a regular, daily basis. And if you're isolated and you don't see anybody, call somebody up and practice on them. Your homework assignment is going to be to practice this at least 15 times between now and next week's call.

[Jeremy] I have an image of sitting down at a table with a two year old, and they look at you and they don't blink. You're sitting at the table and you're giving them dinner, and then you're telling them, "Hi, my name is Jeremy," and doing the commercial.

[Suzi] Yeah, why not?

[Jeremy] Oh, it was just a funny idea to me.

[Suzi] Well, what's going to happen is, depending on the people you practice it on, you're going to get different reactions. And if you're open to coaching from the people you practice it on, you'll find different ways of fine-tuning it. You don't have to take everybody's feedback to heart, but I would think a three year old would have a lot of valuable points for you, if you're open to it.

So back to the homework assignment: Practice your 30-second commercial 15 times—you have to find 15 different ways to practice it. So that means 15 different people, and include yourself as one of those people, meaning practice it in front of a mirror. I would try to do it face-to-face. If you can't, do it over the phone. As you find different ways of practicing it, allow it to evolve and be fine-tuned, but keep in mind the key points: that you want to have credibility, you want to say what you would do, whom you help, and what you help them do. And then you want to make sure it's within 30 seconds.

The shorter and more succinct you can get it, the better. But practice it until it starts to feel natural, and see what happens. Observe as you practice it 15 times over the next week. Observe how it evolves, and observe how you feel about it, and observe how natural or fluid it starts to feel. We'll kick off next week by talking about that. Any questions? Comments? Thoughts? Observations that anybody wants to share at this point?

[Jeremy] Well, this is backing up a little bit at this point, but one of the advantages of this class being small is that Suzi's really going to have a chance to coach us in depth, and maybe we'll have a chance to coach each other, getting to the nitty gritty. And I guess that's a disadvantage, too—there'll be no hiding here.

[Suzi] I want you to feel free to be as vulnerable and open as you can on these calls, because that's how you're going to make real progress and find out where your personal stumbling blocks and barriers are so that we can move through them.

[Jeremy] Before we all hang up the phone, I'd like to say that your process, Suzi, reminds me of what's called stroke production in tennis, which is as you get more efficient with your strokes, you can produce them better and play the game faster and harder. So one of my goals is not only to be out selling, but to get two more company clients, which could be either large or small companies, by the end of the 10 weeks. That's a personal goal I'm going to set for this.

[Suzi] Okay. I want to tell you that's a stretch goal.

[Jeremy] Yeah, I like stretch goals.

[Suzi] Good, because 10 weeks is a very short time in the sales cycle, and we're going to talk about the sales cycle next time.

[Jeremy] I know, but I have a couple irons in the fire, so I'm cheating a little bit.

[Suzi] Oh good, because if you were aiming for two new clients from start to finish within 10 weeks, I'd say that's very aggressive, I just wanted to be clear about that. Yeah, absolutely nothing wrong with aggressive goals.

[Jeremy] Suzi, do you want to comment?

[Suzi] First of all, I want to completely acknowledge that Jeremy gave me my first experience as a teleclass instructor a few months back. He said, "Why don't you just come and do one and see how it goes?" That made this teleclass possible, and I have to tell you that I really enjoy this format, much to my surprise. My formal training is as a teacher, and I do a lot of teaching in front of the room, plus I'm a visual learner. So I had a lot of preconceived notions that teleclass learning might not be the best format—and I'm happily proved wrong. So I'm really looking forward to working with you all for the next 10 weeks and having all of you accomplishing what you want to accomplish in terms of sales.

So, Len, we'll look forward to hearing how your 30-second commercial went at your Chamber group.

Homework

Practice your 30-second commercial 15 times. Practice it in front of a mirror, practice it over the phone, and practice it as many times as possible face-to-face with different people.

Fine-tune it as it evolves and observe how you feel about it, and how natural or fluid it starts to feel. As you experiment with different ways of saying it, keep in mind the key points: that you want to have credibility, you want to say what you would do, who you help, and what you help them do. And then you want to make sure it's within 30 seconds.

Losing Negative Baggage

In his book *Let's Get Real or Let's Not Play,* Mahan Khalsa shows us the problem: "With due respect to true sales professionals, the notion of sales and selling carries a lot of negative baggage. It is the second oldest profession, often confused with the first. No matter what you put in front of or in back of the word 'selling' (consultative, solution, visionary, creative, integrity, value-based, beyond), it still ends up with the sense of doing something 'to' somebody rather than 'for' or 'with' somebody."[1] Often, even the best-intentioned sales and marketing books out there teach us tips, techniques, gimmicks, tricks, or other manipulations. Until you are clear about who you are, who you help, and what you help them to do, you are ill-equipped to make any kind of offer to your prospective buyers. The whole goal is to make them an offer they can't refuse. Mark Joyner calls it "the irresistible offer" and in fact wrote a fabulous book[2] by that title. Joyner says that in their busy lives, prospective buyers are being bombarded by thousands of marketing messages daily, which means we have less than three seconds to get their attention and make an offer so attractive that they simply must buy our services.

Once we take the time to understand our mindsets and the societal/cultural mindsets pertaining to sales, then we can begin to reframe these important activities in a way that supports us and sustains us, rather than depletes us or stresses us. It is possible to transcend dysfunctional sales practices and simply help people in ways that they will appreciate. Sales feels uncomfortable when it is not aligned with core values. My Grandma Helen always said, "Life can be beautiful." Well, I'll borrow her attitude here and assert, "Sales can be beautiful." You get to break out of the mental chains, change the game, and create a new dynamic around selling—one that is meaningful to you. When it is integrity-based, it gives you energy because it is linked to your core values.

Helping Professions and the Conflict with Sales

Coaches and consultants are not unlike the other helping professions. Self-employed doctors, lawyers, accountants, artists, and mental health professionals often sabotage their own efforts to make a healthy living or amass personal wealth by not engaging in prosperity-generating mindsets. They are rarely taught or trained in a systemic sales process, and often are not aware that one even exists, so they find themselves truly committed to helping others and hoping that that will be sufficient to attract clients. They have a helping mindset and are hoping for sales. Often they have a negative view of sales and perceive it to be about forcing oneself on others, or pushing people to do something they don't want to do. Reframing their current sales mindset to one of helping and meaningfulness would allow them to integrate their commitment with sales activity.

The other thing I see a lot is people who may be excellent practitioners, but often are not businesspeople or salespeople. To truly succeed in business, we must be coaches who think like businesspeople and we must consider ourselves to be the sales executive in our own businesses. If we think of sales as helping others determine if our services and products would be useful to them or not, we can begin to integrate our commitment to helping with our need to sell. I approach every sales conversation seeking ways in which I might help. There are no pitches, no agendas, no attachments to closing. In this way, I can feel good about selling—I have reframed it from being something that people do to move used cars off a lot to being about making a difference with people, which is one of my core values. Identify your current mindsets about sales and see how you can reframe it for yourself to be something that aligns with what's true for you.

Use the Understanding Your Mindsets Worksheet to explore your mindsets and identify the changes you want to make to set off on your new adventure.

Worksheet:
Understanding Your Mindsets

1. How do you perceive sales? What is your definition of sales?

   _____

   _____

2. How would you describe your job? _____

   _____

3. How do you view your job in the context of the sales process/cycle?

   _____

   _____

4. What are your core values? _____

   _____

5. How do you define success at prospecting? _____

   _____

6. How do you organize the prospecting portion of your day? _____

   _____

7. How do you measure your results? What do you measure? _____

   _____

8. What obstacles or barriers exist in your work? _____

   _____

9. What changes would you put in place if it was up to you to re-design
   your job description and work responsibilities? _____

   _____

(continued)

Worksheet:
Understanding Your Mindsets *(continued)*

10. How do you prepare to call prospects? _____

_____

11. How do you identify targets and prospects?_____

_____

12. How do you qualify leads? _____

_____

13. What are the preconceived assessments you already have of the person you'll be talking to on the other end of the phone line? How do you view the person you are calling? How do you think they perceive you?

_____

_____

14. What is your intention on every call? Do you set goals for each call?

_____

_____

15. How much importance do you place on creating relationships with the targets you call? _____

_____

16. What structures for accountability have you developed and are they effective? _____

_____

(continued)

Worksheet:
Understanding Your Mindsets (concluded)

17. What motivates you? How can you motivate yourself:

    A. To generate more calls? _____

    _____

    B. To generate more appointments? _____

    _____

    C. To generate more qualified leads? _____

    _____

18. What will it take to align your thoughts about selling with a key core value? _____

    _____

Notes: _____

_____

_____

_____

_____

_____

_____

_____

Partnership and Service: Mental Positioning

If you approach sales activities with a reframed belief system, it might look like partnership and service rather than bugging people or needing to sell stuff. In the Mental Positioning Worksheet, write an example of what each mindset means to you or what it could mean to your business development and delivery efforts. Try these mental shifts as you go about your sales actions each day and see what opens up for you.

Worksheet:
Mental Positioning

Write an example of what each mindset means to you or what it could mean to your business development and delivery efforts.

Authenticity _____

_____

Being useful _____

_____

Abundance _____

_____

Listening _____

_____

Imagination _____

_____

Creating team or partnership _____

_____

Enrollment _____

_____

Loving your work _____

_____

Distinguishing Between Networking, Marketing, and Sales

People often misuse the term *marketing* to be an all-encompassing concept to mean everything from press, exposure, pricing, referrals, networking, and branding to sales, business development, rainmaking, and getting new clients. Marketing is often broadly used to refer to the act of getting your message/product/service to market as well as to define the materials and design of your image. I'd like to try to un-co-mingle the three main concepts of networking, marketing, and sales for you. Once you have a clear understanding of the distinctions between these terms, you will be able to manage your time so that you are leveraging each piece of this critical trinity to get to the sweet spot where deals are sealed.

In a nutshell, networking is about relation, marketing is about preparation, and sales is about implementation. What does that mean? Figure 1.1 will give you specifics about each one, but basically, networking is the relational aspect of your business. It is connecting with others for the purpose of sharing resources, information, leads, referrals, ideas, etc. Cultivating a working network of relationships is crucial to your business development system, but in and of itself will not be the way you build or expand your client base. Marketing is how you will prepare yourself to take your unique identity package, your irresistible offer, and your message to market. This involves a lot of strategy, design work, writing, and outreach, but those things alone will not get you the clients you want. Sales activities are about implementing your business development strategies. Simply put, sales involves making appointments, seeking to be of service, making fabulous and bold offers, and asking for the business. Your goal is to master the integration of where preparation and relation meet implementation.

Relation + Preparation + Implementation = CLIENTS

Or, stated another way,

Networking + Marketing + Sales = $$$$

Many savvy and successful businessfolk will tell you that it is not a 1-to-1 ratio, and that it is most important to spend the bulk of your time in networking or relational activities. If you think of systems, you have to put a lot into the system up front to yield the desired output. Networking and marketing activities are the precursors to sales activities, all of which are necessary input. It isn't magic. Your networking and marketing activities do not always just naturally lead to a hot prospect and then you turn on the sales juice or begin the sales process. Although that will happen on occasion, wouldn't you rather be in the driver's seat than waiting for your networking and marketing efforts to pay off? There's no need to wait for someone to ask you to dance; you get to take the lead and thereby control your time, your efforts, your results, your business. Taking action in your sales process from the start will dramatically reduce the time to close even while you are building your network and creating your marketing materials and strategies.

Figure 1.1 provides more detail about the distinctions between the three keys to success. If you take only one thing away from this book, my core message is that you need to be taking action in *all three domains* simultaneously to grow your business.

Figure 1.1:
Distinguishing Networking, Marketing, and Sales

Networking	Marketing	Sales
Relation	Preparation	Implementation
Pipeline building	Positioning yourself	Contracting
Connection-seeking with genuine interest in others	Market research—studying the market, knowing what the market will yield, understanding market trends and influences, shopping the market for your competitors	Understanding sales cycle and process
Meeting people	Strategy, conceptual approaches	Knowing your hit rates and numbers
Talking to people and getting to know them better	Planning activities for acquisition, retention, or reacquisition of buyers	Tracking progress

(continued)

Figure 1.1:
Distinguishing Networking, Marketing, and Sales
(continued)

Networking	Marketing	Sales
Relation	Preparation	Implementation
Getting out there and creating relationships of all kinds	Alone in your office, in front of your computer	Making calls
Asking to meet other people—asking for introductions or at least contact information and permission to use you as a contact reference	Providing information about who you are and what you do: shameless self-promotion!	Setting up appointments with the express agenda of finding out about the current issues a prospect is facing
Follow-up	Showing people what you do, perhaps including pro bono work	Client meetings to tell people what you do
Manners, etiquette, social graces	Creating text, writing letters, researching clients and prospects	Proposals
Introducing people to each other with an eye to expanding others' networks	Writing and publishing articles, columns, books	Follow-up
Activities that yield human connection and interaction, not necessarily related to business	Speaking engagements, teaching opportunities	Moving people through your pipeline

(continued)

Figure 1.1:
Distinguishing Networking, Marketing, and Sales
(concluded)

Networking	Marketing	Sales
Relation	Preparation	Implementation
Nine mindsets of networking	Public relations and media, advertising	Activities that directly yield clients, contracts, business dollars
Finding out what people do, where they do it, why they do it, and what they want to do	Website or brochure building, fine-tuning, management	Action selling system
	Image and collateral things: logo, letterhead, business cards, etc.	
	Activities that yield informative materials (documents, speeches, advertising, promotional materials, stuff to hand out or direct people to)	
	Branding (sustainable, consistent, recognizable, uniqueness)	

Practice Tips:
Networking, Marketing, and Sales

- It is easy to spend lots of time on marketing activities, but those alone don't get you contracts.

- Time spent on networking and marketing activities is time not spent on sales activities. The ideal would be a 3-to-1 ratio: three units of time spent on networking for every one unit of time spent on marketing and three units of time spent on sales for every one unit of time spent on networking.

- The trick with networking is to keep active about following up with folks, even if they are not prospective clients and are not in your sales pipeline. Just keep looking for ways to help people you interact with and keep looking for more people to meet.

- The trick with sales is it's all about the numbers and tracking those numbers: How many sales activities are you doing each day? How many prospective clients are in your pipeline at any given moment? How many times are you following up with folks in your pipeline?

- Sales is a process, and it takes time to move through that process.

- If you are resisting sales (afraid of rejection, not wanting to bug people, feeling uncomfortable), the tendency is to focus on marketing activities and congratulate yourself for getting all your ducks in a row . . . that's not sales. Don't trick yourself into thinking time spent on marketing activities is directly forwarding your sales. Spend more time instead on networking so that you can collect people without feeling like you are asking for anything. Then look to see how you can link sales to your core values.

- Marketing activities are easier for most people in that you can see accomplishment more quickly. You write a document, you end up with a document. Sales activities can be ongoing for weeks, months, even years before you see a tangible result.

Time Management: The Accordion Effect

"We have far more control over our energy than we ordinarily realize.
The number of hours in a day is fixed, but the quantity and quality
of energy available to us is not. It is our most precious resource.
The more we take responsibility for the energy we bring to the
world, the more empowered and productive we become."[3]
—Jim Loehr and Tony Schwartz

The biggest complaint I hear from coaches, consultants, and self-employed professionals is that you simply don't have time to add sales or networking or marketing activities into your busy life. You know you should, but you are overwhelmed as it is. It's like exercise. You know you should do it, but for some reason that extra hour of sleep seems more important, or you just don't see how you could possibly fit one more thing into your already packed day.

Before we get into the subject of time and how to manage it, I have to tell you about a dynamic law called the Accordion Effect. The Accordion Effect applies to money as well as time, and both are important to any discussion of sales. The bellows of an accordion expand and contract in order to push the air through to make music. Time and money work the same way. Both expand and contract, come and go. Just as we know with certainty that the ocean tide will go out and it will come back in, both money and time follow the same energetic laws. They ebb and flow. Knowing this will give us access to a sense of continuity or even security.

If we apply this dynamic law to money, it means that money comes and money goes, and the good news is that it will always do this. Why is this good news? Because when applied to sales, it means that you can trust that money will always, eventually, come to you—and this concept allows you to give up the desperation and fear and attachment to "making the sale" or to seal the deal. It gives you the freedom to approach sales as a game. Like chess, once you know each piece and how it moves, you can begin to learn various strategies for success in the game.

With sales, once you know the 10 steps outlined in this book and the mindsets that support them, you can customize the game so that you will use your knowledge of how the numbers work to freeing yourself up to play. With money, once you know the dynamic laws of how it operates, you can let go of the belief systems that keep you stuck in a scarcity mentality. Likewise, with time, if you know that time can expand and contract like the accordion, then you can free yourself from the restraints of not having time to take the 10 steps delineated in this book (among other things). You have already had personal experiences of time expanding and contracting. For example, have you ever been waiting for something you eagerly want and felt that one hour seemed like an eternity? Similarly, when having fun or focused on something intently, you can find yourself in a zone where time (that same one hour) will seem like just a few minutes. Yet we can all agree that one hour is always 60 minutes and each minute is always 60 seconds, and that remains constant.

The application of this Accordion Effect is that it gives you some access to control or freedom, whichever motivates you. If time expands and contracts, that means you have the ability to cause it to do so, because the expansion and contraction of time exists primarily in your perception of it. You can control your perception, particularly in a busy, fast-paced world, by not giving in to the temptation of thinking you don't have time. You can impact your very real sense of not having time. You can practice intentionally causing time to expand. Try it next time you find yourself saying, "I'm too busy" or "I don't have time for that." If you have a commitment to any particular goal or result, you can overcome your timelessness by creating time. In other words, one way to manufacture time for yourself is to practice the mental shifts described above—to reframe time for yourself not as an immutable constant in life, but as something that can move and breathe, expand and contract, and be manipulated to create space for the music of life. When you experience time as compressed, breathe air into it by slowing down, practicing yoga or meditation, taking a walk, recharging your soul in whatever way you choose, and then returning to the tasks at hand.

It seems counterintuitive, but the act of taking your time when you seem to have none is exactly what allows time to expand. "Time management is not an end in itself," say Jim Loehr and Tony Schwartz. "Rather it serves the higher goal of effective energy management. Because we have a limited number of hours in a day, we must not only make intelligent choices about how to use them but must also insure that we have the energy available to invest in our highest priorities. Too often, we devote our time to activities that don't advance our mission, depleting our energy reserves in the process."[4]

Understanding the Accordion Effect frees you from all sorts of limitations, ultimately providing the doorway to accessing power. The ability to focus on following recommended practices, step by step, while letting go of the results, letting go of expectations, letting go of judgments and assessments of yourself and your performance, and letting go of the outcomes, while at the same time having a clear focus on what is beyond the desired outcomes: This is the formula to get what you want in sales and in life. It is never just about the money. There is a purpose behind what you want money for. Holding a clear vision of what you want as the ultimate end result of what money can provide for you is the goal to strive for unflappably. There is an opposing push and pull, just like in the accordion, that will help you achieve your goals. Focusing on doing the practices, without attachment to any particular result, trusting that the process works, and relaxing into the game will guarantee a different operational space for you—one that is absent of fear and anxiety, and one that is playful and productive. Part of grounding your mindset in abundance involves expanding your inner capacity to accept and attract what you want. There are numerous practices in every spiritual and religious doctrine in the world that you can employ to open to joy and tap into trust. Figure out what practices will give you access to that place of effortless flow, and then go apply your 10 steps in the sales process.

Worksheet:
Time Management

As you explore how you currently go about organizing your time as it pertains to business development, don't concern yourself with recommended percentages or the right way of doing it. Simply observe and record how you are actually already organizing your time and see what shows up for you.

1. What percentage of your time is dedicated to sales activities as distinct from networking and marketing activities? _____

   _____

2. Of that percentage, what percentage of your time do you spend in each of the following:

   _____ Identifying targets

   _____ Setting appointments

   _____ Client meetings

   _____ Follow-up

   _____ Professional development

   _____ Other: _____

   (Total should be 100%)

3. How would you prioritize and rank the activities in item 2 above? List in order of importance below:

   _____

   _____

   _____

   _____

   _____

Practice Tips:
Planning Your Week

1. Decide what in your life is most important to you and make certain to allocate time to those items first.

2. Allocate time to make calls to set appointments. (How many calls does it take you to set up one appointment? How many appointments do you want to set up for each week? How many calls does that mean you have to make each day? How long will it take you to make those calls?)

3. Schedule any sales appointments you have set for yourself. (Include travel time and plan to arrive 5 to 10 minutes early. Include any preparation time you may need to prepare for the meeting.)

4. Allocate time for target research, proposal development, letter writing, card sending, and other marketing correspondence.

5. Allocate time for follow-up calls or account-servicing activities.

6. Allocate time for special projects and tasks that are non-sales or service related activities (i.e., networking meetings, marketing activities, expense reports, administrative duties, paperwork, other projects, and billable work).

Endnotes

1. Khalsa, M., (1999). *Let's get real or let's not play: The demise of dysfunctional selling and the advent of helping clients succeed.* Salt Lake City, UT: Franklin Covey, p. 3

2. Joyner, M., (2005). *The irresistible offer: How to sell your product or service in 3 seconds or less.* Hoboken, NJ: Wiley.

3. Loehr, J., & Schwartz, T., (2003). *The power of full engagement.* New York: The Free Press, p. 5.

4. Loehr, J., & Schwartz, T., (2003). *The power of full engagement.* New York: The Free Press, p. 106.

Step 2
The Sales Process, Targeting Prospects, and Branding

"Leap, and the net will appear."

—Julia Cameron

"All life is an experiment.
The more experiments you make, the better."

—Ralph Waldo Emerson

We'll begin with the telecourse in which you will have a chance to see the participants fine-tune and get coaching about their 30-second commercials in more depth. During this session, I introduce an integrated model of the sales cycle and the service cycle. This model is named the Bowtie Model because the shape of the figure illustrating the model looks like a bowtie. After introducing the sales process, I briefly introduce the concept of targeting.

You'll have a chance to think through how you define your services. Then you will address "moments of truth" in your service cycle and ways to build your brand. The chapter includes a couple of worksheets for you to use in creating your brand and developing your own strategic target list.

Telecourse Session #2: The Sales Process and Introduction to Targeting

Fine-Tuning Your 30-Second Commercial

[Suzi] Your homework was to practice your 30-second commercial 15 times, so I want to give everybody a chance to give us your 30-second commercial, without reading it—because if you've practiced it 15 times, it should be able to roll right off your tongue and off your mind! Then we'll talk about the sales process, and look at targeting: how to do some strategic targeting to figure out who your clients are, where they are, and how to get at them. As we do the 30-second commercial, I also thought this would be an opportunity for you to coach each other so that we can start to create a community that supports each other in our growth. So who wants to go first with your commercial?

[Len] Let me just try. Hi, I'm Len. I'm a psychologist and organizational development specialist, and I help corporate executives repeatedly achieve objectives for advancement, and get back on track and take constructive action for many of the changes that are occurring within the corporate environment.

[Suzi] Okay, so repeatedly achieve what?

[Len] Repeatedly achieve objectives for advancement.

[Suzi] What does that mean?

[Len] So that they can get promoted.

[Suzi] Oh, get promoted! My first recommendation would be that you say that. "Get promoted" resonates much more quickly than "repeatedly achieve objectives for advancement."

[Len] Okay.

[Suzi] Just simplify it. Part of what happens in a 30-second commercial is people listening don't have the words in front of them. When we read the words, we can visually target their meaning in different ways. But when we're listening to someone talk, especially when you're meeting them for the first time and giving them your 30-second commercial,

they're going to be looking at a lot of other things. So you want your words to be very simple so that they get the concept quickly, while they're busy trying to memorize your face or noticing things about your nonverbal communications, etc. Particularly with that first phrase, I think that's where I started to get lost. And then you had a couple of phrases after that.

[Len] Getting back on track.

[Suzi] Okay, "getting back on track," that's clear.

[Len] And taking constructive action.

[Suzi] Okay, "taking constructive action," I'm just writing these down so that I can look at them. Let's get some other feedback from around the room.

[Jeremy] Speak faster.

[Len] Oh really? Okay, I'll try it.

[Len] Okay. Hi, I'm Len, I'm an Organizational Development specialist. I help executives get promoted, get back on track, take constructive action, and deal with corporate change.

[Suzi] Good. I like that much better than the first one.

[Len] Okay. It's easier to understand?

[Suzi] It's more like cocktail party language. If you're hanging out at a cocktail party and you're telling somebody what you do, that sounds much more natural than the first way you said it. Which is really the point—to sound natural. The first way you said it you used great words, and if I were reading that on a document, I would have thought "Yeah, this guy really knows what he's doing. This is a great introduction." But when you're doing it orally, you're meeting somebody face-to-face, there's so many other things going on that you want your concepts to be as simple and as full of imagery as possible. So you want things that people can get their brains around quickly, even as they're focusing on your face or your nonverbals.

[Deb] What are some words to paint pictures with, Suz?

[Suzi] Well he said "corporate executives," and I think that paints a picture in a lot of people's minds about who he's looking for—who he works with. I think that Len, you did a great job with your credibility—

establishing your credibility up front about being a psychologist in Organizational Development. I think that "helping executives get promoted" paints a picture in people's minds because, depending on how visual the listener is, some people might picture a corporate ladder, or they might picture someone they know who wants to get promoted. They might think of themselves and whether they want to get promoted. I think "getting back on track," "taking constructive action," and "dealing with change" will all speak to different people differently, so I think you've done a good job covering the spectrum that they might be coming to you to deal with.

[Len] Exactly. That's what I was hoping to do.

[Suzi] Yeah. That's great. I might want to tweak the phrase about getting back on track. The reason being that it may be perceived as somewhat negative, and an executive might not want to admit that he or she has gotten off track and needs to get back on.

[Len] Well then, I can simply eliminate it and "taking constructive action" can mean a number of things.

[Suzi] Or even "*staying* on track."

[Len] Or "staying on track," yes.

[Suzi] Just turning it into a more positive statement: "Help people stay on track."

[Len] Okay, "helping them stay on track, take constructive action, and deal with corporate change." Great.

[Suzi] Yeah. And I like the way you said "deal with corporate change," because that's something that everyone can connect with on some level since change is all around us, and it is something we have to deal with.

[Deb] Speaking of words, and this is just my own personal thing, I get so tired of the word *change*. Is there any other word that we can use that might describe change?

[Suzi] You bring up a good point, Deb, because there are a lot of words that have become so embedded in our language that they lose their meaning, or turn into buzz words. I think that *change* by itself is still pretty safe, because it has contextual meanings for people who aren't in organizations as well. Everyone knows about change, everyone on some level has to deal with change. So I think that one's still okay.

And that's why I like how Len, you said, "*deal* with change," as opposed to coping or even change-management expertise that would be so much more OD-sounding. But I don't know, can anyone else think of another way to express "deal with change" other than using the word *change?*

[John] If you don't like the word *change,* you're going to love mine.

[Len] How about *reorganization.* That's too long, but it's . . .

[Deb] It's kind of like another buzzword: white water, meaning constant change.

[John] Len, I'm just wondering about the phrase "taking constructive action"—that didn't strike a bell with me. I'm wondering if that is necessary?

[Len] Maybe "being effective," but is that a buzzword?

[Suzi] What is it you're trying to say?

[Len] Well, when you have to make plans or you have to organize your team of people to move in a particular direction toward some sort of goal, you need to take constructive action.

[Jeremy] I think you want the people you're coaching, more than being effective, you want them to be excelling. So I think *excelling.* I would prefer *excel* to *be effective.*

[Len] *Excelling* to *be effective.*

[Deb] You're wanting them to make the right decisions to implement certain actions?

[Len] Yeah, meaning that the choice that they make has many more benefits than negatives.

[Deb] So . . . constructive decisions?

[Len] Or, making decisions. What about that? Making effective . . .

[Suzi] Hold on, Len, time out. Because what I'm hearing you doing is wordsmithing, which is very easy to do, and this gets back to the conversation we had last week, about marketing versus selling. So keep in mind that when we spend time wordsmithing this kind of a thing, that's more of a marketing type of activity. And what we really want this to be is the beginning of a sales activity. So we want something that is . . .

[Deb] Powerful?

[Suzi] Not only powerful but natural—wording that's really an easy thing for you to remember and get off the top of your head the instant you meet someone. If I wake you up at 3:00 in the morning, you'll be able to say it right off the bat. It's the kind of thing that you don't want to be locked into so much. So I would encourage you, Len, to think about what are you trying to communicate here about taking constructive action? What are you trying to say? What do you want them to hear in that? What do you want to leave them with?

[Len] I want them to hear that I can help them somehow achieve what they want to achieve, and excel.

[Suzi] Okay, so say that. Say, "what you really want to achieve," and if somebody comes back to you and says, "Well, how do you do that?" you answer, "Well I help them with decision making and taking constructive action," that's how we do that. So what you've done is you've skipped to the *how to do it,* without telling them the *what* you can help them do. And the *what you can help them do* is excel and . . .

[Len] I want them to excel at what they want to achieve.

[Suzi] So that's far more powerful, because then you can say, "I'm Len, I'm a developmental psychologist, I work with executives to get promoted, to keep themselves on track, to achieve what they want to achieve, to excel, and to deal with change."

[Len] Right!

[Suzi] See, that is much more like the cocktail party language that we're talking about than trying to remember exactly the ideal words. So if you keep those core concepts in your head, you can get them out in whatever order they come to mind. And it'll just roll off the tip of your tongue. Now, you know how I was just able to deliver Len's commercial? There are a couple of ways to test the effectiveness of your commercial. One is, if after hearing it two or three times, someone else could give it back to you, as if it were theirs. Another way is to practice it to people who already know you and know what you do. Try your commercial on them, and ask them to tell you what it is that they think you do, and who it is you could help, based on what they heard. Ask for that kind of feedback.

[Deb] Could you say that one more time, Suzi?

[Suzi] Yes. You want to test it out on people in your life who know you, and ask them to tell you, based on only your commercial, what they think you do, and who they think you help.

[Deb] Ask your mother that—she'll never . . .

[Suzi] Parents are great testers! I don't know about you all, but my parents were always saying, "So what is this coaching thing?"

[Jeremy] "What is this coaching thing, I can't understand it."

[Suzi] Yeah. The point is, you keep testing it out. When you get your commercial right (right as you define it), where it rolls off the tip of your tongue, and people get it right away (who you help and what you help them do), then you know you've got the right commercial. Okay, who's next?

[John] Hi, I'm John. I help leaders solve the people problems of change. Ph.D. in organizational behavior and just wrote a book describing a new way to dissolve resistance to change in the workplace. Provide workshops to show managers how to lead organizations into change, particularly when those changes are controversial or unpopular. 70 percent of all planned change projects fail because of resistance to change. I teach leaders how to transform that resistance into commitment and support. I also do executive coaching for leaders who are facing change, or who find their employees struggling with change.

[Suzi] Excellent. John, I like the energy, the way you sound when you say it. Your energy is really positive and upbeat. And I want to see if you can do it without reading it. Because I can actually hear that you're reading it.

[John] Okay. Hi, I'm John. I help leaders solve the people problems of change. Ph.D. in organizational behavior and I've just written a book describing a new way to dissolve resistance to change in the workplace. I provide workshops for managers to show them how to lead change in their organizations, particularly when those changes are controversial or unpopular. 70 percent of all planned change projects fail because of resistance to change. I teach leaders how to transform that resistance into commitment and support. I also do executive coaching for leaders who are facing change, or who have employees who are struggling with change.

[Suzi] Wow! That was good. Here's what I think is effective about yours. You establish credibility right off the bat, it's very clear from the get-go who you help and what you help them do, and then you have a lot of other supporting information that deepens it further. So I think you have a lot of flexibility with your commercial. Let's say you're standing up at a networking meeting and introducing yourself, you can go through the whole thing. If you're at a cocktail party running around meeting people quickly, you might just want to do the first one or two lines. Right off the bat, people know that you're all about helping leaders deal with the people side of change. I think that's very effective. What's other feedback from other folks?

[Len] Um, more emphasis, more emotional emphasis on what's important. Could you . . . there's something about change leading to something, I think the third item. What was that, John?

[John] "Seventy percent of all planned change projects fail"— that one?

[Len] Yeah. And then you wanted to do something. What do you do?

[John] I help leaders transform that resistance into commitment and support.

[Len] Right. Maybe something like this: Try to form that resistance into like a stepping stone so that they could leap toward the change in the support. I'm not sure how to do it, but what you want to do is tell them how you're going to help them use it in such a way that they can launch from there into what they really want to achieve, I think.

[Suzi] Do you mean that in the commercial you'd like him to express more of how he's going to get there?

[Len] Yeah, but not in any detail. Just very briefly, that he's going to try to form those resistances into something that will help them achieve, rather than prevent them from achieving, what they want to achieve.

[Suzi] I think, actually, that he did that. What's the sentence again, John?

[John] "Teach leaders how to form that resistance into commitment and support."

[Suzi] Commitment and support. And, Len, are you saying that there's a step in between that?

[Len] I'm making it more complicated, I think. I take it back.

[Suzi] I think the trouble with 30-second commercials is it's very easy to try to put more meat around them, and to try to make them more complex. Let's face it, everybody in this telecourse is highly intelligent, highly educated, and it's natural for you to want to communicate that right off the bat. But contrary to the way we've been taught to express ourselves, simpler is better for the 30-second commercial. I think while we're drawn to try to make it more complex, to have more complex ideas, and really tell more of the extent of the services we can provide, we really want to make sure that a six year old can understand it. You don't have to get it in the right order every time, just think through the points and don't worry about the order.

[Deb] This is just my take on it: I would use fewer words because I got lost somehow in the words. I was trying to track exactly what it is that you do, and I was really trying to pay attention, and then I forgot what you just said as the first concept. So I don't know, are we supposed to make these shorter or try to give just a hint—is that our goal?

[Suzi] Well, I think with John's it's okay to have all the words that he has, knowing that he doesn't have to use them all the time. The idea is he's got one that's fleshed out so that he can choose parts of it based on whatever situation he's in. He can use it in pieces to stimulate a conversational exchange.

And another thing, John, when you deliver this to people, you'll have to very carefully read how they're hearing you so that you know when to stop—when they're starting to lose you. It's hard to do that over the phone, but you can do that at a cocktail party or a networking party or whatever—you can see when you're getting past the point of when they're interested and listening.

[John] With earlier versions of this, I went to a convention exhibit, and practiced on unsuspecting vendors. And what I found I would do there was say a couple pieces, and they would respond, and then I would say the next piece, in conversation.

[Suzi] Precisely, and that'll be far more effective for you than delivering it like a speech.

And I think that'll speak to what you brought up, Deb. For example, if you met John and you were having a conversation with him, and he said he works with the people elements of change, you would get that, and you would probably express interest or have some response, to which he could then respond with the other part.

Okay, who's next?

[Bill] I'll go. I'm Bill. I'm a corporate coach and licensed psychologist. I emotionally engage senior talent in the financial services and banking industry. We develop a high-impact, intense, supportive relationship that enables us to move forward and achieve breakthrough results in leadership and interpersonal skills.

[Suzi] Okay. Can you do that one more time? I missed some key points in there.

[Bill] Okay. I'm Bill. I'm a corporate coach and licensed psychologist. I emotionally engage senior talent in the financial services and banking industry. We develop a high-impact, intense, professional supportive relationship. This allows us to move forward and achieve breakthrough results in leadership and interpersonal skills.

[Suzi] It's great. And there's an awful lot of description words, so we've got to simplify it even further. What spoke loudest and clearest to me was "breakthrough results in leadership and interpersonal skills." So I got who you're playing with: senior talent in financial services and banking. And I got what you're helping them do: breakthrough results in leadership and interpersonal skills. All that other stuff was just words that I got lost in. "Emotionally engage" is where I got lost. And I think I got lost, not because I didn't understand the words, but because I started wondering how you do that, and what that looks like, and how is that different from other kinds of executive development? It just sort of took me off on another whole thought tangent.

[Len] Precisely. I was thinking from the point of view of a banker or financial expert, "What did he mean by that?"

[Suzi] Right. So I think if you just simplify the phrase "emotionally engage" into "I work with" or "I teach" or . . .

[Bill] But that's the opposite of what I want to do, I want to distinguish . . .

[Suzi] "I support"?

[Bill] No, that's the last thing I want to do. Only if they're good. I want to . . . how's this for a business name, Drill Down Coaching, or In Your

Face Coaching? I'm trying to get the idea across here that this isn't the same old BS, the same old namby pamby stuff. That I'm going to . . . that I come in with dynamite and band aids.

[Suzi] Oh, I like that! Use *that* language!

[Bill] But I'm also professional, I'm not just a nut.

[Suzi] Now I get what you were talking about with "high-impact intense supportive relationship"! Because all those words were leading me to say, "Okay, what's he talking about?" So I think you have to say it more like you just said it to us: "I come in and I work with senior talent in financial services and banking, I come in with dynamite and band aids, and together we create breakthrough results and interpersonal skills."

[Bill] Yeah, that's better.

[Suzi] Because that sounds more like you . . . that's what you want to do, you're getting in there. Just the image of dynamite and band aids gets that across. And I think you're kind of hiding it with "emotionally engage."

[Deb] It sounds touchy-feely.

[Suzi] Right. It sounds like the touchy-feely you didn't want it to sound like. So all those "high-impact professional supportive relationships emotionally engaging"—okay fine, wake me up when he's done. But "dynamite and band aids," I want to play with that!

[Deb] And "breakthrough results": That has more energy.

[Len] Now, what's the response? What would the response of a financial person be?

[Bill] Well, that's why I threw in the "supportive." But I think that kind of waters it down.

[Suzi] But "band aid" shows the support. You know, you blow them up with dynamite, but then you're there with the band aid too.

[Bill] Dynamite and life support. Oxygen and . . .

[Deb] I work in a financial institution, and it's nuts and bolts straight-forward direct. I think that's what would hit them. Just be very direct.

[Bill] That's where I developed the idea, working with the senior vice president, who really likes it between the eyes. They come off the trading desk, and that's the way they're used to it.

[Suzi] Right. So you don't have to soften it. Now, try it again Bill, where your key points are "dynamite and band aids, senior talent in financial services," and then the three things you focus on with them.

[Bill] Okay. I'm Bill, I'm a corporate coach and licensed psychologist. I come into your organization with dynamite and band aids to impact senior executives and major talent, and enable them to achieve breakthrough results in leadership and interpersonal skills.

[Suzi] I think that it resonates much better this way, Bill. It's more your language. It communicates something far more powerful than all the graduate school words, and that's the goal. So continue to practice it on folks, and see if it gets across what you want it to get across.

Okay, Jeremy you're up.

[Jeremy] Okay. My name is Jeremy and I provide leadership-development coaching. I'm a dilemma-expert on the business problems that wake Mr. and Ms. Business Leader at 3:00 a.m. I'm known for being a trusted advisor and an intuitive idea person. I love what I do and I'm relentless in my search to help business leaders and businesses grow to the next level.

[Suzi] I like the imagery, waking people up in the middle of the night. And what's the phrase you use, "dilemma expert"?

[Deb] And "trusted advisor."

[Suzi] Yeah, "trusted advisor" had a lot of resonance.

[Jeremy] Not sure I like the expert part.

[Suzi] Well, that was kind of a derailment point for me. Did anyone else get derailed there?

[Deb] I did. "Dilemma expert"—what does it mean?

[Jeremy] Well, I want them to ask that.

[Suzi] Then you might put it at the end, Jeremy, because I think where you've got it, it kind of derails people from hearing everything else. I got derailed at "dilemma expert" and then you got me back with "trusted advisor." So until you're sure that you want people to ask about "dilemma expert," put it at the end, or stop after you say that, and let them ask you, and then continue on so that they can hear the rest.

[Jeremy] I could say "dilemma resource," but I don't think that has the same effect.

[Len] I think "dilemma" has got to go.

[Suzi] Yeah, I think it's the "dilemma" that derails, because "I'm a dilemma *anything*" is kind of like, "You're a dilemma? What?"

[Deb] What's the word *dilemma* mean for you, Jeremy?

[Jeremy] That I get in between people and their problems.

[Suzi] Well, say that. That's better. I get between leaders and their problems and I'm a trusted advisor and I help them with the stuff that keeps them up at night. And that really fits with your energy and way of speaking too.

[Deb] Can I use it too?

[Jeremy] Help yourself, you're on the West coast, no one will know.

[John] I got lost on the "Mr. and Ms."

[Jeremy] "Business leaders"? Yeah I was kinda wondering about that.

[Suzi] You can just say "business leaders," you don't have to give them genders. Because I think the hard part with genders is we now are so conscious of genders, and representing both genders, that you know, you just get lost in all the he's and she's.

[Jeremy] In my head it went straight to the "Mr. and/or Ms."

[Suzi] Say it one more time, Jeremy.

[Jeremy] It's going to be the same, I just have it in my head that way. My name is Jeremy and I provide leadership development coaching. I get in between people and their problems that wake people up at 3:00 in the morning. I'm known for being a trusted advisor and intuitive idea person. I love what I do and I'm known for helping business individuals achieve their best.

[Suzi] Good. I like it better. I would say "leaders" instead of "people."

[Deb] And I would turn some of the words around and use some more power words earlier on. "I'm a trusted advisor," "I'm relentless," I like those things, I think I would use those earlier.

[Jeremy] I've got to rememorize it in a different order! Okay.

[Bill] People and their problems. I just think you need to be more specific about the problems. Problems are not just problems, they're critical problems or . . .

[Jeremy] That's where I could use dilemmas, "I get in between leaders and their dilemmas."

[Bill] Uh . . . I think that's too vague.

[Suzi] I like that "leaders."

[Bill] I don't think they're paying $5,000 a day for problems. It's like "critical," you know? I don't know the word it would be, but "big time."

[Suzi] Also Jeremy, a three year old knows the word *problem*, but might not know the word *dilemma*. So it's coming back to that really simplistic cocktail party format.

[Deb] "Problems"?

[Suzi] I think "problems" is really strong. The point is to clarify it to be about extreme problems, or leadership problems, or critical problems, or organizational problems, or personnel problems.

[Len] Well, the phrase "the problems that wake you up in the middle of the night"—that image gets to me.

The Sales Process and Bowtie Model

[Suzi] We've spent a lot of time on the 30-second commercial, but I think it was useful in that now you're ready to fly with them, for the most part. As for the sales process, just to shift gears here quickly, there's an actual process that you want to use when you're trying to get business. And again, when I say "sales" I'm talking about a distinct process—distinct from networking and marketing activities.

Figure 2.1:
The Bowtie Model

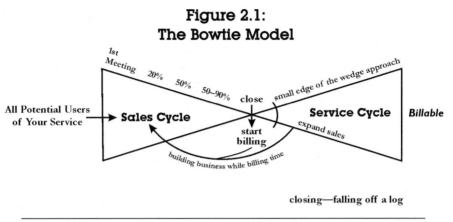

closing—falling off a log

The sales process is one side of a sales and service model called the Bowtie Model (Figure 2.1). It begins with the whole entire universe of potential users of your services, which is why targeting becomes important, which we're going to talk about in a minute.

If you look at the whole potential universe of users of your service, some of those folks are going to engage in a first meeting with you. So whatever networking and marketing you've done that has accumulated in getting a meeting, you're going to get a first meeting with X number of the potential users of your services. That number of the potential first meetings you can get is a much smaller number than the whole universe of people who could potentially use your services.

From there, after you have a first meeting with these people, some smaller number (roughly 20 percent) of that group of targets will move with you to the next step in the sales process, which is, most likely, a second meeting. And then from there, some smaller number of those (50 percent of the second meeting group) will move forward with you to the next step in the process, which may be a proposal, which may be a contract, which may be starting work, which may be a third meeting, which may be bringing you back to meet other people in the organization. There may, on occasion, be a fourth step prior to the close. It all depends.

There's some flexibility in this process, depending on who you're talking to. And then from there some even smaller percentage of those people will move on to the next step, which is becoming your client, which is when you can start billing them, which is when you're actually doing the work. That's the start of your service cycle. In some cases, there may be a step where you start doing the work before you've had permission to start billing them, because you want to hook them into your services. Some people believe in giving away work up front, pro bono, and we can talk about that another time—that's a whole other discussion.

The point here is, the sales process is really a numbers game. And the numbers are that in order to get one first meeting (this is general research, so you're going to have to see where this fits in with your experience), you will have had to talk to 10 prospects. That means that in order to get one first meeting, you will have had to make 10 phone calls, right? And to get 10 first meetings, you will have had to make 100 calls. Of those 10 first meetings, on average only one of them will become a client. So from 100 calls to your 10 first meetings, to someone actually becoming a client takes anywhere from three months to two years, depending.

Part of learning to *Seal the Deal* is to identify what *your* particular sales cycle is. How long does it take you from the first time you meet someone to when they become a client? Or what is *your* hit rate—how many calls does it take you to get how many first meetings to end up with one client? That's how you determine what your sales cycle is. Does anyone have a sense right off the bat of what theirs is? You think about how long it takes you to get clients from the first time you meet them.

[Jeremy] To me it can take anywhere from a week to two or three years. It's enormously variable.

[Suzi] Have others found that as well?

[Len] Well, I haven't done this as a corporate coach, but five years into my practice as a clinical psychologist, I sent out a CD to about 200 EAPs (Employee Assistance Programs), and it resulted in about 10 meetings, which resulted in about four or five good referral sources, which created an enormously successful practice.

[Suzi] Good.

[Jeremy] That's the kind of numbers that Suzi talked about.

[Suzi] And that's the way sales goes. Sales is all about the numbers. It's a numbers game, so it's important to have lots of things in the pipeline at a time, because you're going to be in different stages of the process with different targets at different times. So you want to always be working on business development or sales activities, including always working on your networking and marketing activities, because you're going to be in different places at different times with different targets. Now, where this gets tricky is when you're booked up with different contracts. So you're getting paid to focus on your billable work, but if you don't spend time on the sales work, then you can predict that a good three to six months down the road you won't have any work. Because if you're not focusing on sales and business development continually, the work goes away, and then you have to start again, and you lose momentum.

[Jeremy] Unfortunately, we're up against a clock on this call, so is there something in the next three minutes that we can just wrap up with and come back to next time?

[Suzi] What I'd like everybody to do for homework is start thinking about the entire universe of users of your services, and strategically think about who are the most likely targets for you in that group. To start generating your target list, look at current clients and look at referral sources. You can also look at previous clients, look at your network or databases that you might have, do books of lists, newspapers, trade, or business publications, search the net, look through associations. Do anything you can think of to generate your target list, and then we'll start with that next time.

[Jeremy] Maybe you should spell that out again. In the universe of people who are out there, in your Rolodex or people you know in the business world . . .

[Suzi] No, even broader than that. Take the whole universe of people who could potentially use your services, then narrow that down to a target list. The target list comes from really knowing what you do, who you do it for, who you want to be working with. Who do you want to target? I'll send you a Targeting Worksheet [see page 76] to help focus your efforts.

Homework: Targeting

Start thinking about the entire universe of users of your services, and strategically think about who are the most likely targets for you in that group. To get started, look at current clients, referral sources, previous clients, your network, databases that you might have, newspapers, and trade or business publications. Also search the internet and look through association directories and databases. Do anything you can think of to generate your target list that will make it the best representation of the best targets for your professional services.

Defining Your Services

How do you talk about what you do? How do you define your professional services to people? Well, you have to find your own language for it, but the sample statements below may help you articulate what you do, if you happen to be an executive coach.

If you are another kind of professional or consultant, reading this piece might not be as productive for you as taking a few minutes to brainstorm a list of the things you do and who the ideal users of your services are. Pay specific attention to what's in it for those who want your services. In other words, why would they buy from you? Who are the types of people who want your services and where are they currently seeking them? Practice sharing with people what you're passionate about, what you're committed to, or what's important to you in general. Then, when it comes to speaking about what you do professionally, you'll be more confident in sharing that subject.

Sample Definitions of
Executive Coaching from Different Experts[1]

1. "Executive Coaching is a facilitative one-to-one, mutually designed relationship between a professional coach and a key contributor who

has a powerful position in the organization. . . . The coaching is contracted for the benefit of a client who is accountable for highly complex decisions with wide scope of impact on the organization and industry as a whole. The focus of the coaching is usually focused on organizational performance or development, but it may also serve a personal component as well."

—Summary findings from the *International Executive Coaching Summit*, October 1999, compiled by Lee Smith and Jeannine Sandstrom, and including information produced by 36 coaches.

2. "There are four methodological factors that distinguish the coaching of super-keepers from that of other employees . . . These factors are: (1) holistic approach, (2) deep behavioral insight, (3) the active involvement of top corporate executives, and (4) sustained relationships with the coach and/or trusted internal collaborator "usually a senior human resource professional."

—Karol Wasylyshyn in "Coaching the Super-Keepers" a chapter from the book *The Talent Management Handbook: Creating Organizational Excellence by Identifying, Developing and Promoting Your Best People* (2003). Wasylyshyn's approach to coaching senior executives is a collaborative and pragmatic one, integrating depth psychology and strategic business priorities.

3. "Executive Coaching is a company-sponsored perk for top high potential employees. It is a customized and holistic development process that provides deep behavioral insights intended to accelerate an executive's business results and effectiveness as a leader. This coaching is based on a collaborative relationship among the executive, his/her boss, his/her human resources manager, and an executive coach."

—Karol Wasylyshyn

4. "Executive coaching is defined as a helping relationship formed between a client who has managerial authority and responsibility in an organization and a consultant who uses a wide variety of behavioral techniques and methods to assist the client achieve a mutually identified

set of goals to improve his or her professional performance and personal satisfaction and consequently to improve the effectiveness of the client's organization within a formally defined coaching agreement."

—Richard R. Kilburg in *Executive Coaching: Developing Managerial Wisdom in a World of Chaos*. Kilburg can be summarized as having a psycho-dynamic and a systems perspective.

5. "The essence of executive coaching is helping leaders get unstuck from their dilemmas and assisting them to transfer their learning into results for the organization."

—Mary Beth O'Neill in *Executive Coaching with Backbone and Heart*. O'Neill also writes about how it is vital to be "managing your own challenges" and helping the client transfer learning. Hers seems to be an Organizational Development perspective.

6. "Coaching is a one-on-one development process formally contracted between a professional coach and a management-level client to increase the client's managerial and/or leadership performance, often using action learning."

—Robert J. Lee syllabus for "Change at the Executive Level," Fall, 2002 Syllabus, Milano Graduate School, New School University. Lee's perspective might be summarized as an organizational consulting approach including action learning.

7. "Action coaching is a process that fosters self-awareness and that results in the motivation to change, as well as the guidance needed if change is to take place in ways that meet organizational needs."

—David L. Dotlich and Peter C. Cairo in *Action Coaching*. Dotlich and Cairo also write about self-awareness linked to business results and an action plan put in place. Dotlich and Cairo seem to have an organizational consulting business results, action learning perspective.

8. "A masterful coach is a vision builder and value shaper . . . who enters into the learning system of a person, business, or social institution with the intent of improving it so as to impact people's ability to perform."

—Robert Hargrove in *Masterful Coaching*. Hargrove has also stated, "Coaching is intervening in the drift. You don't need a coach to turn out the lights," in his interview on "Top Coaches in the USA" videotape. Hargrove rejects the idea of calling himself an executive coach or even a coach, preferring to see himself as a "conversation partner." Hargrove calls his approach to coaching transformational.

9. "Coaching is not telling people what to do; it's giving them a chance to examine what they are doing in light of their intentions."

—James Flaherty in *Coaching: Evoking Excellence in Others*. Flaherty's approach has been described as one of personal construction.

10. "Executive Coaching is aimed at inspiring executive leaders to make behavioral changes which transform themselves and the people around them thereby increasing business results and performance. Coaching is about providing inspiration. Consulting is about providing information. Information plus inspiration equals performance acceleration."

—Jeremy Robinson, for e-mail newsletter, Corporate Coach Direct. Robinson's approach is results-oriented and motivational.

11. "Coaching is a learning technology to produce a specific result. Clients care about their results, which are meaningful to their individual situation."

—Ramon Williamson

12. "Coaching is a necessary profession. It gives leaders the gift of islands of potential sanity. Coaching provides executives with time to think. Lack of thinking results in not knowing who we are becoming, where we are going, the implications of our actions, or what are our opportunities for learning. Stress, overwhelm and anxiety reduce our capacity to see patterns emerging. Coaching creates an oasis of reflection that helps people remember that they have brains and inner capacity. Coaches allow leaders to remember what it feels like to be a thinking, sensate being."

—Margaret Wheatley

Moments of Truth and the Service Cycle

Your business is entirely made up of moments of truth. A moment of truth is one instant in which a user of any service rates his or her experience of that service. Your clients have assessments, opinions, thoughts, evaluations of you, your service, your firm, your deliverables, your presence, your effectiveness, your personality, your appearance, your materials, your performance—and the list goes on. There are multitudinous moments of truth throughout every stage of your sales cycle and service delivery. In their critical-to-professional-service-providers-book, *Service America,* Karl Albrecht and Ron Zemke discuss moments of truth as they pertain to a customer's experience of your service:

> One of the obvious places to start thinking about the quality of an organization's service is to take inventory of the moments of truth in that particular business. Think about your own business. What are the various points of contact at which the customer passes judgment on your enterprise? How many opportunities do you have to score points? The cycle begins at the very first point of contact between the customer and your organization. It ends, only temporarily, when the customer considers the service complete, and it begins anew when he or she decides to come back for more.[2]

Albrecht and Zemke recommend that you diagram your particular service cycle to discover the critical moments of truth in your interactions with customers. Start by dividing your service cycle into whatever you might identify as the smallest client experience points. What are the steps a client goes through with you from the first moment of contact through to completion? At each step, what are the potential moments of truth or moments of defining client experience?

For example, when a prospective client looks you up on the internet to find out more about you, and you have grammatical or spelling errors on your website or a lousy navigational system, and he can't find what he is looking for on your site, that is a moment of truth. If a prospective client meets you at a cocktail party and you are drunk, that is a moment of truth. If you have an ethical conflict while serving a client or violate the code of conduct of a client organization, that is a moment of truth.

Moments of truth can be positive, too. For instance, if you are quick to respond and exceed a prospective client's expectations, you have earned moment-of-truth credits. Perhaps you handled a sticky situation with aplomb and demonstrated excellence in your delivery of services—that is a moment of truth. Everything in terms of your behavior, your conduct, your interactions, your materials, your employees, your agents, your deliverables, or any contact between you, your clients, and your business is potentially a moment of truth.

This is a useful exercise to complete prior to thinking about targeting strategic prospective clients for your sales cycle, because you can use your knowledge of your service cycle and the critical contact points (moments of truth) specific to your business to profile your ideal client, thus more effectively targeting those most likely to buy your services. The more attention you pay to these details, the better handle you get on your business and your potential customers. Again, in Albrecht and Zemke's words:

> The service cycle will be unique for your particular business. It may vary from one customer to another, and from one situation to another. At any moment, each customer who is doing business with you is somewhere in his or her uniquely personal cycle. Of course, customers don't usually think of their experiences consciously in terms of a cycle; they generally pay attention to whatever concrete needs they have at a particular moment. But it pays for you to think about this cycle in very specific stages, because it is the very substance of your business.[3]

It takes far less time and energy in your sales process if you are working with ready consumers, rather than with unwilling participants in your sales cycle. Step 10 of this book is entirely about the importance of referrals—the targeted prospective buyers who have already had at least one positive moment of truth with you or your firm.

Branding

Although branding falls squarely under the marketing umbrella, it bears mentioning because it supports your networking and sales. In fact, branding can be a very effective tool for integrating your networking, marketing, and sales. What makes a brand? Integrated messaging focused on sustainable, consistent, recognizable uniqueness. You are familiar with product brands: The most notable examples are when the brand name becomes synonymous with the object (i.e., Kleenex for tissue, Band-Aid for adhesive bandage, Post-It for sticky notepaper) or when the service becomes a verb (i.e., "I Googled it and found the answer"). More relevant to self-employed professionals is the concept of branding around individuals. Consider, for example, Cher, Emeril, Oprah, Martha Stewart, or Donald Trump. These individuals have created empires out of the brand that they are. Whatever you may think about each of them, there is a distinct and consistent imprint that is conjured up. There is something (or several things) about each one of them that is supremely definitive of that person's image, and you will see the markers of that imprint in every appearance, product, performance, or picture you see from that person.

Think for a moment about Bond. James Bond. Yes, I mean 007. A fictional character, yes, but a brand nonetheless. There are distinct elements of Bond that are predictable, recognizable, sustainable, and consistent. So much so that even when played by different actors over the years, there is an essence of Bond that makes him Bond. You've likely heard debates about who was a better Bond, with Sean Connery clearly in the lead over Roger Moore, George Lazenby, Timothy Dalton, and Pierce Brosnan. If Bond weren't such a distinct brand, we wouldn't be able to argue the merits of how accurately he is portrayed by the various actors who've held that coveted role.

How can you start to create a brand YOU? Peter Senge talks about "personal mastery"; Stephen Covey talks about "sharpening the saw."[4] Whatever you want to call the process, it means you have to do some internal work. Until you have clarity about who you want to be in the world, or who you want to be for your clients, or how you want to show up in your industry, you cannot begin to craft an integrated image or imprint for all your networking, marketing, and sales.

What is your unique offering to the market, to the world, or to your profession of choice? What are your distinct quirks, characteristics, areas of expertise, skills, attributes, and successes? What is the look and feel of brand YOU? How can you integrate that uniqueness into all you do, say, write, and create? Once you have defined that unique thing that is wholly YOU, how can you make it recognizable in a consistent and sustainable way? Can you integrate it into all your messages, all your promotional materials, all your writing, all your appearances, all your services? This will take some thought, and many folks rely on the counsel of branding experts and public relations specialists. If you are going to engage in shameless self-promotion anyway (and that's something you must do to build your business), the consistency, recognizability, and uniqueness of your brand will take you farther than if you don't spend any time thinking through strategic branding questions.

Branding Worksheet: Defining Your Brand

1. Who do you want to be in the world? _____

   _____

2. Who do you want to be for your clients? _____

   _____

3. How do you want to show up in your industry? _____

   _____

4. What is your unique offering to the market? _____

   _____

5. What is your unique offering to the world? _____

   _____

6. What is your unique offering to your profession of choice? _____

   _____

7. What unique value do you bring to your clients? _____

   _____

8. What do you want to be known for? _____

   _____

9. What are your distinct quirks, characteristics, areas of expertise, skills, attributes, and successes? _____

   _____

10. What is the look and feel of brand YOU? _____

    _____

(continued)

Branding Worksheet:
Defining Your Brand (concluded)

11. How can you integrate that uniqueness into all you do, say, write, and create? _____

    _____

12. Once you have defined that unique thing that is wholly YOU, how can you make it recognizable in a consistent and sustainable way? _____

    _____

13. What will it take to integrate it into all your messages, all your promotional materials, all your writing, all your appearances, all your services?

    _____

    _____

14. What kind of impact do you intend to have? _____

    _____

15. What will it take for you to align your intended impact with your actual current impact? _____

    _____

16. How can that be boiled down into one bold, powerful, enrolling statement for you to use as your lodestone? Write several drafts until you have one that suits you. _____

    _____

Branding will help you with targeting and vice versa. In order to determine your brand, it helps to know who you are targeting. Use the Targeting Worksheet on the next page to help you make strategic decisions when winnowing down the list of all potential users of your services.

Targeting Worksheet:
Making Strategic Choices

Making strategic choices is a way of narrowing the scope of who might be a qualified prospect for your services. It allows you to identify targets who are more likely to be interested in making appointments.

1. **Know your product/service.** List three to five key reasons why your service adds value:

   * _____

   * _____

   * _____

   * _____

   * _____

2. **Understand users.** Identify and list current successful users of your services: _____

   _____

3. **Identify potential users.** Who has not yet used this service but should?

   _____

   _____

4. **Make a list of targets.** Use multiple resources to generate this list: current clients, referral sources, previous clients or "dead" accounts, networking, databases, book of lists, newspapers, trade or business publications, the internet, associations, the needs of the consultants and practitioners in your office, etc.

   Specific resources I might use to find targets: _____

   _____

   Targets I know off the top of my head: _____

   _____

(continued)

Targeting Worksheet:
Making Strategic Choices *(continued)*

5. **Know the position of the prospect within the organization.** Does the prospect have the authority to buy your services? _____

6. **Know the decision-making machinery.** Who is the decision maker and what is the decision-making process? _____

   _____

7. **Clarify assumptions.** What are my assumptions about each target/ prospect? How can I find out if these assumptions are accurate?

   _____

8. **Know your competitor's clients.** Survey them to determine satisfaction.

My competitors:	Their clients:
_____	_____
_____	_____
_____	_____

9. **Know your own clients.** How/when/why do they most effectively use your services? Survey them to determine satisfaction.

Current clients:	Reasons for use:
_____	_____
_____	_____
_____	_____

10. **Analyze your list of targets.** What are your organization's chances of success with them? If you've already done business with them, what was the outcome? _____

    _____

(continued)

Targeting Worksheet:
Making Strategic Choices *(concluded)*

11. **Identify your point of sale.** Do you know who the buyer is in each target organization?

Target company: Point of Sale:

_____   _____

_____   _____

_____   _____

12. **Ask the right questions of the right people.** Don't assume you know what they need. It's okay to know nothing. Generate a script based on your research of the target company.

_____

_____

_____

_____

_____

_____

_____

_____

You can divide your target list into those you have access to via some connection or mutual contact (warm lead), and those you don't have direct access to. The latter are what we'd consider cold leads, and the best strategy there is to try to find anyone you know who knows them and who could help you by making an introduction or arranging a meeting. Think of them as prospective buyers. The goal is to avoid cold calls and turn any cold lead (aka fantasy) into a warm lead (aka prospect) by finding folks you have in common.

Endnotes

1. As excerpted from *Definitions of executive coaching* on www.executivecoachacademy.com. Permission from Jeremy Robinson, Executive Coach, Robinson Capital Corp.

2. Albrecht, K., & Zemke, R., (1985). *Service America! Doing business in the new economy.* New York: Warner Books, Inc., pp. 31–39.

3. See note 2 above.

4. See, for example, Senge, P. M., (1990). *The fifth discipline: The art and practice of the learning organization.* New York: Doubleday; and Covey, S. R., (2004). *The 7 habits of highly effective people: Powerful lessons in personal change* (rev. ed.). New York: Free Press.

Step 3
Calling Prospects
and
Setting Up the First Meeting

"Sometimes life seems like a poorly designed cage
within which man has been sentenced to be free."
—Sheldon B. Kopp

"As long as a man stands in his own way,
everything seems to be in his way."
—Ralph Waldo Emerson

The telecourse call for Step 3 delves into the process of calling people on your target list to set up appointments and takes a brief foray into the subject of gatekeepers. Calling prospects is an action that falls squarely in the sales column. Remember, networking is what you do continually to meet people and make connections; now it is time to move some of those connections into your sales cycle—into the Bowtie Model (see Figure 2.1). You do this by setting up meetings. These meetings are not for the purpose of networking; these are meetings for determining if the targeted prospect is going to move into your sales cycle or not.

After the telecourse discussion, this chapter explores the concept of phone fear and offers a guided inquiry to help you move through it so that you can pick up the phone and start dialing with confidence. Also included are a couple of worksheets to assist you in making calls to set up appointments and a template for tracking your progress. The chapter wraps up with a list of reminders, suggestions, and tips for making appointments with prospective buyers.

Telecourse Session #3:
Moving toward Your First Client Meeting

The Sales Process Revisited

[Suzi] Let's review the sales process, because we hit it so quickly last time. I want to be sure you understand it as process, a cycle. It is pretty much a numbers game, and there are activities that go into the sales process that are distinct and separate from networking activities and marketing activities. So what I'd like to do is go around the group and review the sales process—what you remember or what you think you heard last week. And don't worry if you don't get it right.

[John] Well, we distinguished between sales and marketing. Marketing is preparation, but sales is implementation.

[Len] In terms of the number of contacts you would make, you can expect to make as many as 10 calls before you would even get together with one person.

[Suzi] Close, you're close. You've got the basic numbers. Again, what the general research shows—and part of what we have to do as coaches in our distinct fields is figure out how this applies to us in our experience—is that **for professional services, it takes 10 phone calls to get through to six people in order to schedule one meeting.**

In the case of referrals, where it's a warm lead—someone you trust has referred you to this person, and someone they trust has referred you to this person—the same 10 calls will actually get you through to more people, more like eight people, and it could lead to three or four meetings. So the numbers get better in the case of referral. What you're trying to get from all your phone calls is a first meeting. It takes 10 first meetings to get 5 second meetings, in order to get one client. So what that means is, you can pretty much count on making 100 phone calls to get 10 meetings to get one client.

In other words, moving through the sales process is a systematic process—you make phone calls to set up meetings, you go to these meetings and interview the client in the meeting, and then you set up the next step. Generally speaking, the next step is going to be another meeting. It could be a meeting where you bring someone else back from your team, if you want to expand the business that way or it could be that you're coming back to meet with other people on their team, maybe the decision makers on their team. It could be that the next step is when you bring back your proposal and deliver that in person. But the goal of any sales activity at this stage of the game is to get a meeting. Later on, the goal of your sales activity will be to get a decision, whether it's about a meeting, a proposal, a contract, a project, etc. So networking, marketing, and sales activities have different goals. Networking activities are about seeking contacts and connections. Marketing activities are about building your image or your credibility. Sales activities are about getting meetings—getting meetings with decision makers.

It boils down to a systematic cycle of making phone calls, setting up first appointments, going to those first appointments, interviewing the client, setting up the second meeting, and asking for the business. Then once you get the business, providing the service is also part of the sales cycle, because once you're in the client relationship, you're still in the sales cycle if you're interested in getting more work or referrals from this person. So providing exceptional service is also part of the sales cycle, because then you come back into the sales cycle much further down into the process. It becomes easier than starting from scratch with someone who's in your entire universe of potential users.

[Jeremy] Suzi, maybe I'm getting ahead here, but I have a technical side question: What's your view on having an assistant make follow-up calls for you after you've scheduled the meeting just to remind the person you're meeting with them at such and such time?

[Suzi] My answer's going to surprise you, I think. **Never confirm your appointments.** I'll tell you why. Because when you call and confirm an appointment, it gives them a back door out.

[Jeremy] A chance to say no.

[Suzi] That's right. It gives them a chance to say, "Oh, something's come up, I want to reschedule." If you don't call to confirm, and you show up for an appointment, and they're not there, suddenly they're going to feel that they owe you.

[Len] Assuming that they have a conscience.

[Suzi] Assuming that they have a conscience, right. But now you have some leverage. What's going to happen if you're there, and they're not? They're at least going to schedule another meeting with you. They might actually give you business if they feel really guilty for standing you up—you never know. I think it was Robert Cialdini who said that there are two times when you have power: When the other person says "sorry" and when they say "thank you."[1]

[Jeremy] Has that happened to you?

[Suzi] Yes, it has. When I show up and the person I'm meeting with isn't there, I wait for 10 or 15 minutes. It's not like I sit there for a whole hour and a half—my time is valuable too. But you never want to call and confirm an appointment, because it gives them a way to wiggle out of it.

[Jeremy] Right, I have a colleague who's just told me he waited an hour and a half for the person who handles the coaching in a major pharmaceutical company.

[Suzi] Wow. The flip side is, if you have something else going on that day, and you want to reschedule it, call to confirm. That's a sure fire way that they'll cancel on you. So rather than calling to reschedule, call and say, "Are we still on?" Then they'll say, "Oh, well as a matter of fact, something came up." Then you can respond, "Oh really, great, when can we reschedule?"

[Jeremy] So you want to set another time when that happens?

[Suzi] Right. Here's another secret about how to set up your first meeting. When you're setting up your first meeting, you're going to be doing calls. You're going to be doing hot calls or warm calls depending on whether you're calling someone you've met, or someone who was referred to you. And when you call, the entire purpose of your call is to get an appointment and then get off the phone. You don't want to spend a lot of time on the phone telling them about your services, telling what you can do for them, or interviewing them over the phone. **The whole purpose of the phone call is to get the appointment and get off the phone.** You introduce yourself—this is a good time to use your 30-second commercial—and then you say, "I'm just calling you today because I want to set up a time to come in and talk to you about the coaching or consulting services I provide and how it might be helpful to your organization. How's Tuesday at 3:00?"

Make sure you say, "How's Tuesday at 3:00," or whatever, at the end. Pick a date and time, and say it right at the end of your spiel: "Hi, I'm so-and-so, the reason I'm calling you is . . . How's Tuesday at 3:00?" And the reason you do that is when you say

"How's Tuesday at 3:00?" or "How's Friday at 1:00?" or whatever, they get out their calendar. Once they've gotten out their calendar, you've gotten one step closer to a meeting. You never want to leave it open-ended and say, "When can we get together?" or "When works for you?" You always want to suggest a specific date and time. And only one, don't give them options. Just suggest one specific date and time. If they say "No, I'm not available then," have another one in the wings: "Okay, how about Thursday at 5:00?"

[Jeremy] A technique I've sometimes used is telling people I'm going to be in the area and I just need 15 minutes of their time; they can kick me out of the office after that, if they choose.

[Suzi] Well, is it true that you only want 15 minutes of their time?

[Jeremy] No, it's not true. It's just a ruse to get in the door.

[Suzi] You don't need a ruse. I'd steer away from that because it somehow diminishes you. It makes you look like "I'm not as important, my time's not as important as yours," and you don't want to get that message across. You want to communicate peer status, and by that I mean, you're a busy executive as well. You do not want to be in the position of a subordinate begging for 15 minutes of the king's time.

[Jeremy] Right, good point.

[Len] Well, if the issue of time did come up, what would you say?

[Suzi] An hour. You deserve an hour. You know, you're offering a legitimate service.

[Len] But you wouldn't bring up the time?

[Suzi] No, I wouldn't. "How's Tuesday at 3:00?" Now, oftentimes they might say (this is where gatekeepers come in), "My secretary handles my schedule, so you'll need to call her." This is good news. This is not a brush off. When they tell you that, and then you get the name and number of the secretary, it's no longer a cold call. Now you're saying, "Sheila, John said I should talk to you to set up an appointment with him. What does his calendar look like at 3:00 on Tuesday?" Be thankful when they refer you to the gatekeeper—it's not just smoke and mirrors trying to get you out the door. There are other tricks when you get the gatekeeper. Has anyone else had trouble getting past the gatekeeper to the person they're trying to reach?

[Jeremy] Of course.

[Suzi] What are some of the things you've run into that gatekeepers have said to you?

[Jeremy] Well, they usually want your whole rap, right then and there. They want to guard the pass.

[Suzi] Which is their job.

[Jeremy] Right, that's their job.

[Suzi] Has anyone found something that worked?

[Jeremy] If you have a contact and you know the person, or you have a warm call and can mention the name of somebody who knows them and wants you to speak to them, that works.

[Len] Okay, but in the scenario we just outlined, you've been told the gatekeeper is supposed to give you the appointment. Now we're talking about when you've gotten to the gatekeeper, but you haven't gotten to the person.

[Suzi] Right. Usually when their boss sends you to the gatekeeper to get on the schedule, they just do it. But other times, you're calling in, trying to reach Marsha CEO. You've reached the gatekeeper, and the gatekeeper is actually trying to keep you from talking to Marsha CEO. What have you found that works to get you past the gatekeeper in that situation?

[Jeremy] Sometimes what works is to establish a relationship with the gatekeeper, to not even try to push by the gatekeeper, just to be very, very warm and friendly. Depending on the person, I just try to mirror the gatekeeper. But if I find somebody with a great sense of humor, then I'm golden, because I know I'm going to get the appointment then.

[Suzi] Good. That's definitely one strategy. There are three strategies for getting past the gatekeeper. One is to befriend the gatekeeper and have him or her schedule the appointment for you so that you don't even have to talk to Marsha CEO to set it up; you just do it through the gatekeeper by befriending them or using humor or whatever. Another strategy is to call when you know the gatekeeper's not there, either early in the morning or after 5:00 or 5:30. Oftentimes, the executives are there, and the gatekeepers are not. Oftentimes, the gatekeepers are 9:00 to 5:00ers, and the CEOs are there at 7:00 a.m., or whatever. By the way, 7:00 a.m. is a great time to reach people.

And the last strategy is to be bold—it's really about speaking from a confident place, as if you are a well-known colleague of the person you're calling, and to use everybody's first names. Use the gatekeeper's first name, and use the CEO's first name, or whoever you're calling. "Hi Mary, this is Suzi, calling for John. Is he there?" In other words, you sound like you know him, you sound like you've got a right to be calling, you sound like you're a friend. You don't sound like you're a salesperson calling to talk to someone you've never met before.

[Jeremy] Is that sometimes experienced as, I don't know . . . inappropriate?

[Suzi] It depends on how you pull it off; it depends on your confidence level and personality style. I have a colleague who's very effective at this. She calls everybody by their first name immediately, and it comes across from her as confidence. But sometimes, depending on the culture of the organization, that might not be appropriate.

[Len] Seems like you'd have to know something about the culture of the organization. It might automatically mean that you don't get another shot at that company.

[Suzi] Could be. . . . On the other hand, if it's a company where everyone uses Mr. and Ms. So-and-So, and you come in with the first names, they might assume that you're a family member, or someone really close to the person you're calling. So it could work in your favor. You just really have to know your audience.

[John] I have a side question for Suzi and Jeremy. You do a lot of this stuff, so how much of the time do you spend doing these types of cold calls?

[Jeremy] Not enough.

[Suzi] I do everything by referrals, that's my preference. I don't like making cold calls.

[John] So this 100-to-1 ratio, you don't have to deal with that?

[Suzi] Yes, I do. You still have to be constantly active, you still have to stock the pipelines.

[John] I'm talking about making 100 calls in order to get one client.

[Suzi] My rate's a little bit better than that. My rate's about 65 calls to one client.

[Jeremy] That's still a lot of calls.

[Suzi] Oh yeah . . .

[John] That's about 55 more than I would have guessed.

[Suzi] Well, it depends. . . . You've always got to be playing the numbers game, there's no two ways around it. It's still a numbers game, even when you're good at it. And that's good news, that's not scary news. Once you know that it's a numbers game, you just keep playing the numbers. Once I figured that out, it was like a constant reminder: "Okay, I've got to be making phone calls, I've got to be reaching out to somebody all the time."

[John] So are these 65 calls to 65 different people, or is this the grand total of all of them?

[Suzi] It depends. Sometimes it's different people in the same organization trying to get to the right decision maker, that type of thing.

[Len] Suzi, what's the average length of a call?

[Suzi] When I'm setting up an appointment, less than 5 minutes. It goes exactly as I told you, literally. It's "Hi, my name is Suzi. Here's why I'm calling today. I'd like to set up an appointment for a time to talk to you. How's Tuesday at noon?" That's it.

[Deb] Suzi, how many sales-related calls do you make each day?

[Suzi] I don't count them anymore . . . I just always make calls every day. I should actually track this better than I do, but I have this really big desk where I can spread out all my papers with my possible leads and referrals and contacts, whatever, and I'm always calling, every day I'm calling people. I don't call the same people every day, obviously—I'd get to be annoying. But if I'm not calling those people, then I'm calling people in my network to find out what else they have going on.

[Jeremy] Do you organize this all via your desk or do you have an organizer or a Rolodex that you use?

[Suzi] No, I do it on my desk and my wall. I'm very visual, and I'm not very high tech. A lot of people do it in their Palm Pilot; I just put notes in my paper calendar.

[Jeremy] So you use a tickler system?

[Suzi] Yes, I put notes in my calendar on when to follow up with people, and when to call people, and I have papers spread out all over my desk to tell me who I'm calling when, plus my files for active clients, or less active clients. I have a huge wall with a whiteboard and newsprint paper where I track my sales process. But yes, you've got to do sales activity every day. And I would say you definitely have to do networking and marketing every day as well. But the thing is—this comes back to one of the things we talked about in our first session together—we don't want to delude ourselves that networking and marketing activities are going to get us the dollars. We need all three: networking, marketing, and sales activities. So what we're focusing on here is the sales activities of making the phone calls to set up the appointments, having the appointments, and asking for the business. And we have not yet talked about having the appointments, but I want to see if there are any more questions about setting up the appointments.

[Len] Is there a good time of day to schedule an appointment?

[Suzi] No. It really depends on your preferences, and what works with the culture of the organization you're calling into.

[Deb] What about the call?

[Suzi] We talked a little bit about good times to call if you're trying to avoid the gatekeeper—call before 7:00 a.m. or after 5:30 p.m. But I've found that almost any time is okay. I would just say don't call at lunchtime, because you know you're not going to get people then—you're just going to get a voice mail. And a voice mail is very easy for someone to ignore.

[Len] What if you're making contact through e-mail?

[Suzi] That's marketing activity, not to be confused with sales activity. E-mail can be useful, just be clear that it's marketing activity. **If you're not in a meeting with a prospect, you're not selling.**

[Jeremy] You've got to be in it to win it, right Suzi?

[Suzi] Right. It's great to send letters and e-mails and then follow up. I would recommend that you observe and chart for yourself how much time you're spending on them. You could actually chart each week how much time you're spending in networking activities, in marketing activities, and in sales activities. And I think you'll be surprised to find that most of us have a natural tendency to avoid the sales activities, because the networking and marketing activities are more comfortable and fun. You'll find, shock of all shocks, that you're spending the bulk of your time on networking and marketing, and then wondering where the dollars are.

[Jeremy] As I'm listening to what you're saying, I'm amazed I do as well as I do. I've got to do better at this, because I've got a lot more to go in terms of potential for selling.

[Suzi] Jeremy, you've been at it for a while. And what happens is, when you've been at it for a while, the networking and marketing does eventually lead to dollars. But if you're only doing networking and marketing activities, the sales cycle is about seven years.

[Deb] What does that mean?

[Suzi] Meaning the time it takes from when you meet someone to when they hire you if you're only networking and marketing. But if you're doing sales activities, the sales cycle is three or four months to three years, depending on the situation.

[Deb] Wow.

[Suzi] Here's an example. I work with a lot of law firms, and what law firms teach their associates about business development is what we know as marketing; they don't teach them networking and sales. And they teach them to start when they're second-year associates, because by the time they get to partner is when they're going to be generating revenue from the contacts they made as second-year associates. They plan for it to take about seven years for them to get the results of their networking and marketing activities.

[Jeremy] So they have that part right.

[Suzi] They have that part right, but when I go in there and talk about sales, they immediately see that they can cut that cycle down if they're doing sales activities in addition to their marketing activities. It's pretty amazing.

Appointment-Setting Tips

[Suzi] Let's move on to some general appointment-setting tips. Remember the goal is to set up the meeting and get off the phone—that's the entire purpose of your call. You don't want to get into long drawn-out discussions, and you don't want to sell to the prospect while you're on the phone to them. Does everyone know what I mean when I say *prospects*?

[Len] Prospective client.

[Suzi] Right. And in your call, you want to give them a reason to see you. One way I've done that, that I think has been effective when you're calling into an organization, is to mention that you've done work in an organization that's similar to theirs. They always want to hear about it. For example, I called the general counsel of Sears, whom I'd met once before at an event. I reminded her where I'd met her, and who I am and what I do, and said, "You know, I've been doing executive coaching work with the VP and lawyers at DuPont for the past five years. I would love to set up a time to come and talk with you about what I've done for them. How's Tuesday at 5:00?" When you talk to a prospect about what you've done for someone else, it's not as threatening to them, and it helps them see how you could be of use to them from what you've done for some other client.

[Len] I think that could also go against you if you're working in a tight area—in a narrow field.

[Suzi] I've had situations like that—where there are concerns because you're working for a rival. A colleague of mine learned this lesson the hard way. She had done some work for Pepsi, and then she went and called Coke. She figured "Well, I've done some work for Pepsi, so I can come and work for Coke." Well, if you know anything about Pepsi and Coke, you know that they are arch rivals. When the first thing she had to say was, "I'd love to tell you what I've done for Pepsi," they didn't want to have anything to do with her! So you have to know your target. And if it's not appropriate to name names, then don't. But you can still say, "I'd love to tell you about some of the work we've been doing in your industry that I think might be relevant to you." You want to be careful and strategic about naming clients. Know when it's going to be of use to you, and know when it isn't going to be of use to you.

[Deb] Suzi, could you repeat that? You called somebody and told them about the attorney thing. Could you just say that again so I could get it?

[Suzi] Sure. I said my 30-second commercial, my name and who I am and everything, and I said, "I'm calling today because I know that you know that I've been doing this executive coaching work at DuPont with the attorneys there for the past five years, and I'd love to come and talk to you about what I did for them."

[John] If you don't have experience with similar organizations, how do you handle that?

[Suzi] This is where it gets a little tricky. I ran into this when I first started because I was coming from school teaching, and I didn't have corporate experience. So I analyzed what I had done as a school teacher and which elements of that experience might be relevant in a business context. I told stories about my "clients," and I just changed the language. They were real stories, right out of my classroom, but I changed the language to be business language. I talked about my third graders as if they were executives.

[Deb] Could you give an example?

[Suzi] This was 9 or 10 years ago. But I remember one example was about dealing with interpersonal conflict, which was really two third graders on the playground fighting over a jump rope. And there was another one about managing . . . what did I call it? Managing simultaneous deadlines, or something like that. I had to think through: "What did I do as a teacher that could be relevant in business?"

The point is, you have experiences in your personal and professional background that you can make relevant in the world of the person you're talking to. It's about taking the time to analyze what those experiences are and translating them into the correct language. The idea is that you can talk about those things in a way that's authentic for you and natural so that you're not lying or making things up, but you're really demonstrating how your experience is relevant to them.

[Jeremy] And if you get stuck, a book I recommend is the *Portable MBA Desk Reference*. It's sort of like an encyclopedia of business terms. You can read it one page at a time and slowly digest business language; it also gives you a feel for what it's like to take an MBA program.

Starting the Client Conversation

[Suzi] Okay, so let's move on. Let's say you've called, you've set up your meeting with your prospect, and you're at your first meeting. What do you do to start the conversation? What do you normally do right now? How do you handle getting the meeting started?

[Deb] I just sort of establish the relationship. If it's somebody I know, we'll just sit down and have a conversation first, just to build rapport. And then I don't know what to do after that.

[Jeremy] I'm similar. I go for making some kind of eye contact, and rather than just blow ahead, I actually go in the opposite direction. I step back a little bit, gauge the situation, make contact, see what the handshake is like. I like to get a sense of the person in slow motion in the room, get a feeling of the room, the tone they want to set, whether they want to tell me first what their needs are, and then I sort of take it from there. I'm very much in a listening mode, ready to listen to them talk about their needs. Obviously that's my preference—for them to talk first about their needs. But if they don't want to, and they want me to set the pace, then I'll do that.

[Len] I haven't done a lot of these, so I think my preference would be to come in and make eye contact. I get the feeling of the other person and I offer a structure if the other person doesn't suggest a predetermined structure. Basically I want to let them know what I expect out of a relationship, and I also want to know what they expect out of a relationship. But I also want to establish some sort of relationship with them, and an understanding; I want to understand the degree of commitment that they have to achieve what they want to be achieving.

[Suzi] Before going into your first meeting, you want to prepare for it the way you would prepare for a coaching call or consultation. You want to come up with a list of questions. The thing that I've found effective in sales meetings is to handle them as a coach, from a coaching approach, because I'm comfortable there and good at it. What I mean is, I'm in the first meeting already coaching the person around determining the outcome of what a relationship with me might look like, what the results might be, what value they might place on the results if we were able to accomplish them effectively.

From what all of you said, you're right on target: you want to get in there, establish the relationship, establish some rapport, but also establish your status as peers as well as lead the conversation. This is a really good time to use your 30-second commercial. This is a really good time to say, "Let me tell you a little bit about myself," because then you're establishing credibility right up front. And then, with your questions, you'll start the ball rolling in a conversation, and you'll start to learn about them. And the 80/20 rule really applies here—you want to be listening 80 percent of the time, and only speaking 20 percent of the time. At the same time, you want to take control of the meeting when you come in. Because if you take the lead, you're saying, "I'm a leader. I'm your peer. I'm not going to wait for you to take the lead because you're the big boss, I'm going to come in and take the lead." In terms of establishing equal status and credibility, I don't think that's anything we need to practice. . . . Do you feel comfortable with that?

[Bill] I don't think we feel comfortable with that. I don't think any of us really feel that credible.

[Suzi] Okay, then let's back up. Let's go back to mindsets.

[Bill] That's what it's all about—mindset?

[Suzi] It really is. And then this contributes to establishing peer status as well. You're coming in, you're talking to a CEO or an executive, or someone who is an accomplished leader. You need to demonstrate that you are an accomplished leader as well, and show that you are equal to them. You have your own business—you all have doctorates, for gosh sake! That's impressive. Not all people selling to businesses have doctorates. You know, most of them come in with MBAs.

[Bill] That's another point. If someone has a doctorate, would you recommend that they use it?

[Suzi] Whatever you feel comfortable with when you're meeting with someone, depending on a number of things: your comfort level, the culture of the organization you're coming into, the atmosphere you want to establish in the conversation. If it's someone you believe is going to be intimidating to you, you might open up with telling them you're a doctor. If you want to be more laid back and comfortable, you can be Bill, and then you can follow it up with, "I'm a doctor of psychology." You know, there are ways to get it in there so that it builds the credibility . . . but if you want them to call you Bill, tell them what to call you. It really all comes back to your mindset.

You've got to set yourself up before going into any of these meetings, because your mindset is what gets communicated loudest and clearest about you. If you're feeling inadequate, or if you're feeling anything less than stellar and spectacular, that's going to communicate in the meeting. So you want to think of an image that you can hold onto that makes you feel like you're boosted up and ready to handle anything. And that image is really connected to your vision. What I mean by that is, think about why you have your business. Think about what you want for yourself in the future. A colleague of mine envisions herself being a retired billionaire lying on a beach. So she thinks of that image before going into a meeting, and it calms her and gets her centered so that she can go into the meeting from a confident place. That doesn't work for me. I think about the image of a million-dollar consultant. And I think, what does that look like? How is that person being, the person who is a million-dollar consultant? And then I put on that cloak, if you will, before I go into the meeting so that that's who I'm being when I'm in there.

Whatever that is for you, you want to come up with your one little thing that you can remind yourself of. It's almost like flicking a switch: It doesn't matter what kind of a day you're having, you can flick that switch and walk in there projecting everything you want to project.

[Jeremy] To me it's a question of mood as well as mindset. I mean, when I'm really feeling great after something has gone well, with a coaching client or some prospect that I've sold or some contract that's happened, even though I feel like going out and calling my friends or something, I try to remember that's the time to be calling prospects. Because I'm really up and that's in my mood and my voice, I want to be calling and meeting with as many people as possible from that expansive place. But that's a discipline that we have to strive for, because most of us wouldn't be doing that at that time.

[Suzi] Another tip is to keep a mirror in your office. I know it sounds kind of corny, but you smile into the mirror before you pick up the phone. You know you can tell if somebody's smiling when they're talking to you on the phone. So if you practice, if you smile at yourself in the mirror before you pick up the phone, that's going to come across.

[Bill] This is very much like acting. . . .

[John] How would that be in an interaction?

[Suzi] You have to have really clear intentions: a clear intention for the call, a clear intention for the meeting. And there's nothing wrong with stating your purpose up front. There's no reason to have a hidden agenda here.

[Jeremy] I usually think of it another way: that I have a facility for turning around a contract very quickly. I think that communicates a service modality to the client—that I'm ready to serve them and do business right away. That's my way of telling them that I take what they do seriously, and I try to match it.

[Suzi] That's great. So to start wrapping up, what I'd like to do is have you all set goals (and be realistic) for how many first meetings you will arrange between now and our next session together. Not how many meetings you will have, but how many you will arrange. In other words, how many calls are you going to make in the next week to set up how many meetings? You can set up the meetings for a month down the road, it doesn't matter when the meetings are set up for. But let's go around and say, "Here's how many meetings I'm going to set up between now and our next session," just so you get to start practicing.

[Bill] We're talking about sales calls? Live ammunition here?

[Suzi] Yes, and let me give you a little more context. Our next telecourse session is about handling objections, so I want you to actually come next time with some of the real objections you've heard from people this week. So you've got to get out there and make some calls to try to set up some appointments. We're getting into action here, we're not just in theory anymore.

[Len] Also we need to know what we need to bring, besides ourselves, to these meetings.

[Suzi] You're talking about marketing materials. Notice your attachment to having them. I wouldn't worry about that. Just set up the meetings for now.

[Bill] Don't let that get in the way.

[Suzi] Right. You know, you don't have to have all your ducks in a row—just set up the meeting.

[Bill] Just quack.

[Suzi] Really. **This is as simple as, "Hi, my name is X, here's who I am, here's what I do, I'd like to talk to you about Y. How's Thursday at 3:00?"**

[Jeremy] I think what Len mentioned is an important point—the rationalization, or the self-talk, that many of us do that ends up being an excuse for delaying and procrastinating.

[Suzi] Well, true, and this isn't rocket science. This is just pick up the phone and make an appointment. You do it for the dentist or a haircut all the time.

[Jeremy] But people who come from a psychology or a psychotherapy background, or maybe also even organizational development, may feel like, "Oh gee, I have to have this great brochure, and I have to have this in place and that in place."

[Suzi] Just don't worry about it.

[Jeremy] You know . . . like I have to have it perfect.

[Suzi] You have all you need already. **You already have everything you need. Really. You have a couple of ears and a mouth and a brain, and you have fingers to dial the phone with. You probably have phone numbers for some people you'd like to meet with. That's all you need. Don't make it harder than it has to be.**

I can just hear the tension. This is amazing—the panic on the phone right now. Look, this is not supposed to be a big scary thing, this is supposed to be set up some appointments. So here's the thing: If you only want to commit to one, just commit to one. We're not going to judge you by how many you commit to doing between now and next week. This is for you. So wherever you want to be in terms of how much you want to get in the game is fine. And what's the worst thing that can happen? The worst that can happen is you call and you speak gibberish and they don't understand you and they hang up on you. You know, you make appointments all the time, you call people all the time. You know how to do this, you already have these skills.

[Jeremy] So let's hear it, gang.

[Bill] I'll commit to making calls until I get an appointment.

[Jeremy] Okay, so that's Bill.

[Bill] However many calls I have to make. I'm not quite clear who I'm calling yet. I think I'll call people who might be hiring coaches.

[Suzi] Go to your Targeting Worksheet [page 76] and look at your targets. So your goal then, Bill, is to set up one appointment between now and Tuesday, is that correct?

[Bill] I'll make a bunch of calls, but I want to set up an appointment.

[Len] I'm similar. I'm going to make a bunch, and I'll set up as many as I can. But I don't know when, it'll have to be down the road. I mean, is there a time frame in terms of the phone call, how far out you should have the appointment.

[Suzi] Well, as soon as possible, but you've got to look at your calendar. I mean, right now, I'm booking people two weeks out, because I don't have anything sooner than that.

[Len] Okay, but that's not a problem? Like if I make it three weeks or more?

[Suzi] That's fine. Just make sure you say, "How's Thursday, April 19, at 1:00?" So, Len, how many . . .

[Len] I'm going to make as many phone calls as I need so that I can have at least three appointments.

[Jeremy] All right, three appointments.

[Len] I'm nervous.

[Suzi] Good. That's a good sign. Feeling nervous is your indication that the activity is out of your comfort zone—exactly the kind of activity that leads to personal growth. That's why I say it's a good sign if you're feeling nervous. By the way, when I first started my business, I actually redefined all those fear feelings. This is one thing that I'm most proud of in starting my business. Every time I felt terrified and nervous, I just reframed it as, "This is how I know I'm alive."

So congratulations, Len, you know you're alive.

[John] Well, I guess I'm alive too, because I'm scared to death.

[Suzi] Good.

[John] I have a big barrier here. One of my problems is that I don't have anyone I know whom I can call. So uncovering someone to call is a big deal.

[Suzi] Yes, and working through your Targeting Worksheet will help you do that. Also, calling people you know in your network already, and asking them who you can call will help you. You already have these skills. You know how to be with people. You all are experts at being with people. You wouldn't be in the field that you're in if you weren't good at being with people. It's really all about being with people.

[John] My biggest skill in college was my ability to handle blind dates.

[Suzi] Well, there you go. . . .

[John] But that's the whole point: The blind date was set up by some-one else. Once I'm there I'm golden, but asking for the date still . . .

[Jeremy] How many appointments, John?

[John] Appointments. If it takes 100 calls to make an appointment, I know I'm not going to do that. I'll try to make 5 calls.

[Suzi] No, it takes 100 calls to *get a client*. It takes 10 calls to get an appointment. And it might take less than that for you.

So John has committed to 5 calls. Does that mean you're expect-ing that 5 calls will lead to an appointment or are you not committing to an appointment?

[Jeremy] Why don't you commit to 10 calls, John? That way we'll call 10 calls one appointment.

[John] 5, 10, if it's 5, 10, 300 . . . In my head they're all the same goddamn thing, so I'll try.

[Suzi] Are any of you *Star Wars* fans? You'll remember when Jedi Master Yoda said, "Do or do not, there is no 'try.'"

[Jeremy] This is a good thing, John. Trust me.

[John] I never believed Vince Lombardi, so I don't know why I should believe that this is a good thing.

[Suzi] I just want to remind you all that you can't do this wrong. No matter what happens in all your attempted calls this week, we're going to have lots to talk about next week. Okay? So even if you don't get the appointments you've committed to, you're still getting lots of useful stuff for the laboratory of our telecourse call here.

[Jeremy] Good way to think about it, laboratory.

[Suzi] Jeremy, are you going to commit?

[Jeremy] Yeah. I'm going to commit to four appointments.

[Suzi] Okay. I'm going to set up three appointments. See? I'm playing too!

Now, as a final thought, I want to say this to all of you: **Have your fear and do it anyway.**

[Len] Right. In fact, I'm going to just head directly toward the fear, and I'm going to do that first.

[Bill] Well, I remember how the hair stood up on the back of my neck when Suzi talked about knowing that she was alive when she felt fear. I guess I'm alive. I have to remind myself of this all the time: **Being successful is doing it.**

Homework

We're getting into action here, we're not just in theory anymore. Get out there and make some calls to try to set up some appointments. Set a goal for yourself (and be realistic): How many first meetings will you arrange in the coming week? The goal is not how many meetings you will have, but how many you will arrange. In other words, how many calls are you going to make in the next week to set up how many meetings? It doesn't matter when the meetings are scheduled for. The important thing is to start practicing making those calls. Also, take notes on the objections you hear from people when you call this week. Later, you'll come up with ways to respond to them. For now, just keep track of what people are saying when they are trying to keep you from having a meeting with your target prospect.

Phone Fear

It is not uncommon to find that you experience phone fear when faced with the idea of calling prospects. It seems like a contrived outreach at first and can be very uncomfortable. This is normal. The only way to alleviate your fear is to practice making calls. After making lots of calls, it will eventually, I promise, start to feel better. Will you completely overcome your phone fear someday? Not likely, but calling does get easier with practice. Good thing, too, since we now understand that the number of calls we need to make to keep and manage a full pipeline into the sales process is pretty high!

The Phone Fear Exercise on the next page gives you some questions to help you see what gets in your way, or what is beneath your phone fear. You can use them to explore these issues by yourself, or you can have a friend or your coach ask you these questions so that you can focus on the inquiry, voice your reactions, and perhaps get some feedback.

Exercise:
Guided Inquiry about Phone Fear

Have a friend or a colleague ask you these questions so that you can process them aloud. If you can't find someone to work with you, you can write your responses to these questions, but you will lose some of the power of the exercise that comes from speaking your thoughts and feelings to a trusted coach, colleague, or friend.

1. What are you really afraid will happen or not happen?

2. What obstacles or barriers get in your way in selling?

3. How do you prepare to call prospects?

4. What is your perception or assessment of the person on the other end of the phone line?

5. How do you view or think about the person you are calling? Who are they for you? What assumptions are you making?

6. How do you think the person on the other end of the phone perceives you?

7. How much importance do you place on creating relationships with the targets you call?

8. When have you had an experience of fun or play when making phone calls?

9. What would make calling fun for you?

10. What motivates you to take action?

11. What actions or risks are you not taking, the taking of which would open unforeseen doors for you?

Practice Script:
Setting Appointments

Write a practice script including a quick introduction of who you are and what your company does, the purpose of your call, and the date and time you'd like them to check on their calendar. Then practice aloud or with a friend by making an imaginary call and asking for feedback.

Identification statement:

_____

_____

_____

_____

_____

Purpose of the call:

_____

_____

_____

_____

Request for the appointment:

_____

_____

_____

_____

_____

Worksheet:
Prospect Contact Log

When making prospecting calls, it is useful to have a quick and easy reference map for yourself. Use this log to track who you spoke to, where, when, what happened, and what's next.

Contact name and title	Company	Date of contact	Result of call	Next steps

Notes:

Tip Sheet:
Appointment Setting

- Goal: Make the appointment and then get off the phone.

- Remember the purpose of your call—getting the appointment. Avoid drawn-out discussions and don't attempt to sell the prospect on the phone.

- Give the prospect a reason to see you and find the reason to see them. "We really should get together. . . ."

- Request a specific date and a time for the appointment. Get the prospect to open his/her calendar. Return to that date and time request (or propose another specific time) after each question or objection.

- Understand the numbers game and set personal goals.

- Use your 30-second commercial and your practice script.

- Be honest: Do not tell the prospect that the meeting will take five minutes when it will take more time.

- Be prepared for objections. Practice your responses.

- Smile! Get a mirror for your desk.

- Remember the O.N.E. rule: Offer No Excuses . . . just set the appointment and get off the phone.

- Don't call the same leads too often.

- Leave messages that allow you to remain the driver of the process: "I'm sorry I missed you, if I haven't heard back from you by next Wednesday, I'll try you again then."

- Ask the gatekeepers for help.

- Use third parties and referrals to get through.

- Always begin with the most senior person who could possibly use your services.

- Ask for the prospect's help to better serve him or to better understand the organization's decision-making processes.

Endnote

1. Robert B. Cialdini is the author of Influence: *The Psychology of Persuasion* (New York: HarperCollins, 1998), considered the most important book on persuasion ever published.

Step 4
Handling Gatekeepers
and
Objections

"We don't get less afraid by being more prepared,
we only get more prepared by being more prepared."
—Suzi Pomerantz

"You miss 100% of the shots you never take."
—Wayne Gretzky

There is a type of preparedness that will make it easier to make the call, particularly if you are prepared to handle the myriad of gates, smoke screens, and objections that will come at you before you get the appointment. Knowing what various realistic kinds of questions, requests, and reactions will allow you to prepare your toolkit of responses to have at the ready. The telecourse material in this chapter will explore how you can be ready to respond to gatekeepers and to the objections you might hear from your prospect.

This chapter also includes strategies for getting past the gatekeepers and handling objections. There's a piece about rejection and a few worksheets for overcoming objections and keeping track of calls.

Telecourse Session #4: Getting Appointments

Appointment-Setting Results

[Suzi] First I want to check in quickly about how it went with the appointments that you set as your goal to make between last week and this week. Then we'll move into objections, working through a kind of coaching process, to cover the objections you've been hearing as you've made these calls, what objections you expect to hear, and then how you prepare your responses for these objections. The idea is to remove some of the fear around making these calls and get out and make meetings.

So let me just check: I promised four, Jeremy promised four, John said he would make five calls in the goal of making one appointment, Bill said one appointment, Len said one appointment, and Deb left before we did that part. So what we had done was everyone promised how many appointments they would try to schedule between last Tuesday and this Tuesday, not necessarily to have the meetings this past week, but just get them scheduled.

So I'll go first: I actually scheduled four appointments.

[Jeremy] Wow.

[Suzi] But I've been doing this for a while, so it didn't take me 40 calls to make four appointments, it only took me 10 calls. So . . .

[Deb] Almost 50 percent.

[Suzi] Yeah, I'm getting there. Who else wants to say how it went?

[Len] I've been very busy, and I didn't meet my goal. But I contacted two different people. One person was out and not returning my call. I got the address of the other person but I still have to make a date to get together.

[Suzi] So you actually spoke to a person and got the address?

[Len] Yes.

[Suzi] What's your observation about getting the address and not getting a date on that call?

[Len] Actually, I was going to call, but I coincidentally met the person in a shop. As we were talking about getting to understand their business and how I might be of some assistance, I got the phone number and address. I still have to call to make the date to get together.

[Suzi] Okay, good.

[Len] So there was no objection I had to overcome in that case. The other person had indicated an interest indirectly, and I have her card. I've called a couple of times, but I haven't gotten a return call. There was a third that I was planning to touch base with, but I actually was a little shy because I've studied the bank—I have to really get to know it better.

[Suzi] Do you know the person you want to contact there?

[Len] I'm not certain. On one hand I want to go directly to the top, to the president of the bank, because he's the one who has really shaped the philosophy of this particular bank.

[Suzi] So this would be a cold call for you?

[Len] That's correct. On the other hand, I'm reluctant to go directly to the president, because I don't want a rejection from the top. You know, I would like to talk first to somebody whose rejection doesn't mean a final rejection.

[Suzi] Does a rejection from the top mean a final rejection?

[Len] Well, it's a heavy thing; it's a heavier rejection if you get rejected from the top.

[Suzi] Is it Len? Is it really? This is a really good inquiry for us to explore for a minute.

[Len] When you talk to a vice president, for example, or an assistant to the guy who's in charge, and that person says to you, "Well, I have to discuss this with the president," it's a better way of being put off than getting shot down directly by the president, I thought. Why? Because how can you overturn that?

[Suzi] I could argue with that . . .

First of all, if you're talking to a vice president who says, I need to talk to the president, that could be a smoke screen. That in and of itself could be an objection, to not give you an answer. So it's not necessarily that they really need the approval of someone else. And also it's not necessarily true that if the top person in the company rejects you that you won't get work in that company.

I had a situation where I spoke to a CEO of a $100 million company, and in this meeting, he wasn't clear about anything that I could do for his company. And he was not interested at all. However, I ended up meeting one of the division presidents of his company through another contact, and in conversations with this division president, he absolutely saw the value and need for our services—and he's the one who got us in, he's the one who sold us internally to the CEO, because he saw the need. He had the need, he had the budget, he made it happen.

[Len] But the president couldn't give you an answer, is that right? And the person he sold, what was their function?

[Suzi] CEO. It was the CEO of the overarching company. They have three divisions, and each division has a division president. So I had first talked to the CEO, who couldn't quite see what was going on because his focus was less on the day-to-day functioning of the divisions, and more on mergers and acquisitions, on handling shareholder value, dealing with the media—you know, the CEO had very different focus. And when I was able to talk to the president of one of the divisions, he very clearly saw what the day-to-day operational and leadership needs were, and where our services could be helpful. So he went through his internal connection, back to the CEO or wherever he needed to get the funding. I think he had the funding and just basically told the CEO, "Oh, by the way, we're doing this."

[Jeremy] It sounds like Len's question to you is, "How did you get passed along from the CEO to the division president?"

[Suzi] I didn't get from the CEO to the division president, it was a separate contact.

It wasn't that the CEO said, "I don't see the point, but why don't you go talk to the division president?" It wasn't that at all. The CEO said "No."

[Jeremy] But you didn't give up.

[Suzi] Right. So the point of this story is: **A rejection from the top isn't necessarily a final rejection.** And it's useful to challenge your beliefs, because as this case shows, the belief that a rejection from the top is final would end the game.

[Len] And how did you know to contact the division president?

[Suzi] I didn't at the time. It came about later on through different net-working leads.

I had continued networking, pursuing different connections, and found out, "Oh, somebody knows this division president, and I can go through that contact that I have"—a mutual contact. So I want to challenge the belief that one rejection from the company, no matter how high up, is a complete rejection. It's not final. And I think a lot of times we get stuck believing that.

[Jeremy] That's a great point. Especially in this day and age of companies that have so many different layers and tentacles, and people don't know everything, and they can't make decisions for the organization.

[Suzi] Right. And I would absolutely encourage you to go straight to the top. Go straight to the top because that's the person who has ultimately the most decision-making authority. One of the key things you want to find out in your first meeting with a prospect is: What is the decision-making process in this organization? Who would be making a decision about whether or not to hire me? So absolutely go to the top, and if you get rejected by the top, don't think it means you don't get work with the company.

[Deb] I thoroughly agree. I had one issue in one of the companies that I do some contract work with that sort of came to a dead-end. And now there's a whole issue in another area, and they're coming to me asking, "What can you do about this? What can you do about that?" Some of the people are the same people who originally didn't want to contract with me in the first place.

[Suzi] Exactly.

[Deb] The work comes in from a different angle.

[Suzi] Also, a lot of this business-activity/sales-activity stuff falls under the category of **"Whether you believe you can, or you believe you can't, you're right."**

You know that saying? Whatever your beliefs are, that actually is what becomes true. Part of the underlying purpose of this telecourse is to bring to the surface the underlying beliefs that get in our way so that we can gain some power over them. If we know what they are, we can choose whether or not these are the beliefs that empower us to get the results we want to get. So thanks, Len, for bringing that up, that was a great point. Okay, who's next?

[Deb] I know that I've been kind of sluggish with all this, it's sort of a pattern, but I'm trying to focus more on this. For example, I have a goal of meeting with this one particular person, and I know it's just a phone call, because he will sit down and meet with me, and he's the vice president of wireless something-or-other with a small local telecom company. And I'm already in the company doing stuff: I help them with their internship project. So I just need to make the phone call and then pick his brain to see what their needs might be.

[Suzi] Good. Is there something in the way of doing that, or is it just about time?

[Deb] It's just about time . . . so I'm going to try to schedule lunch or something for next week. On second thought, maybe I'll just hop up to his office when I'm at the company tomorrow. I could just go up there.

[Suzi] Does he have a secretary who schedules his meetings?

[Deb] No, I think he schedules his own stuff.

[Suzi] Okay. Well, if he's not there, I would encourage you to take five minutes and call. Because really the call can just be, "I don't have time to talk now. I'm just calling to set up an appointment. Can you meet Friday at noon?"

[Deb] That's good too. And the other thing is, Agilent Technologies has a big plant up here, and I met a woman at a local meeting who's doing some of their leadership stuff. We had a very brief conversation about how she's trying to standardize their leadership program. I mentioned some large companies that I work with as a consulting psychologist and Organizational Development person. So she was actually pretty open with me. She asked me for my card. I was very low-key about it that night, and then I sent a follow-up e-mail requesting some time to sit down to talk to her, because she had mentioned she was interested in some outside consulting. Her e-mail back to me was, "Thanks for the follow-up. We probably will be doing some executive coaching, but not right now."

[Suzi] Okay, good—that's an objection.

[Deb] "But keep in touch," she said, "because we might do some sprucing up of our managers with some coaching." So I'm not sure she actually remembered our conversation, because I didn't really talk to her about coaching. I talked to her about helping her standardize her leadership program, because apparently that's what she was trying to do. And she's new on the job, she's only been there a few months, so I . . .

[Suzi] Here's what there is to do with that, Deb. Call her up and say, "I'm just calling because you may remember we met, and we talked about standardizing your leadership program. I'd like to set up an appointment so that we can talk about that. How's Friday at 3:00?"

[Deb] So just be more assertive?

[Suzi] It's just very direct—it's a five-minute call. It's like this: "I'm calling because you wanted to do this." You're not forcing yourself on her. "I'm calling because we talked about standardizing your leadership program. I'm just calling to set up a time when we might sit down and talk about that. Does Tuesday at 3:00 work for you? How's Tuesday at 3:00?" And by the time you say that, she's looking at her calendar.

[Deb] Really?

[Suzi] Really. That's why you always suggest a specific date and time at the end of the call.

[Deb] So then she focuses on that.

[Suzi] Exactly.

[Deb] And that really works, Suzi? Boy, I really have a hard time. I mean I can easily do it with somebody I have a connection with, like this guy, Scott, but I don't have a connection with her.

[Jeremy] Yes, you do.

[Suzi] Deb, you already have a connection with her. You had a conversation, that's a connection. How much of a connection do you need?

[Deb] I think I mean more of a familiarity—that's what it is.

[Suzi] Assume it. Jeremy's right, assume "as if." You had a conversation with her. She wants your help. You're just calling to help.

Okay, Jeremy, how did you do on your four appointments?

[Jeremy] I had a great time making phone calls and playing phone tag, but basically I got sort of one big virtual appointment. It's far away from me, so I can't be there, but I got an offer to bid on a national coaching project for a Fortune 500 company.

[Suzi] That's exciting. And how many calls, Jeremy, would you say that you made?

[Jeremy] I probably made about 10 calls, but I felt I should have made more.

[Suzi] Good. Okay, Bill or John, how about you guys?

[Bill] Well, I procrastinated earlier in the week because I was very busy. There was one prospect who wanted me to work with the CEO and Chairman of the Board, who are father and son, and the present CEO will soon be the Chairman of the Board, and the son will soon be the CEO.

[Suzi] And . . .

[Bill] Uh, he didn't call me back for two days, so I called him, and he said he's still considering it. I was very excited for a couple of days, and then I was disappointed, I mean very disappointed. By the time Monday came around, I said to myself, "You know, you'd better get going on this." So I tried calling the most likely candidate, who was a warm call, someone I know who runs Madison Square Garden, but apparently he doesn't work there any more. It took me about six calls, working with their telephone system, to figure that out . . . so I didn't make a lot of calls.

The interesting thing is the one guy I didn't get an appointment with. I think I know what the sticking point was. When he described the family dynamics at the company, I told him, "This family you're describing is right off the cover of my family business brochure." And it is. He asked, "Is that a family you've actually worked with?" And I said, "No, it's a composite of families." "Have you ever worked with a situation like this?" he said. And I said, "No." I wasn't really ready, but I shouldn't have said no.

[Suzi] No, Bill, there's nothing wrong with that, but what you're telling me, and what I think you didn't hear, is an opportunity to set up a meeting right then and there. In fact, there were a couple of opportunities. Right when he said, "Have you done that before?" one was to say, "I haven't done that exactly, but I'd love to set up a time to talk to you about some similar situations that I think are relevant. How's Friday at 9:00?" The other opportunity is that you might have said, "Well, how about if you introduce me to the Chairman of the Board, or whoever your contact is there, and I will go and set up a meeting with them to talk to them directly about the work that I've done that's similar to the situation they're facing, and see if they're interested in working with me?"

I don't think it's a lost cause at this point. I think you can still call him back and say, "I just had a cancellation in my schedule. I am available Thursday morning at 9:00. I'd love to come and talk to you about similar situations I've dealt with that might be relevant to your CEO and Chairman of the Board family. Are you available Thursday at 9:00?" And if he says no, that he's not, throw him another date and time: "Listen, I really think we should get together, I definitely have a lot of things I could share with you about how we've handled similar situations that I think you'd find would be relevant to this particular case."

[Bill] Okay, that sounds good.

[Suzi] It's very easy to get discouraged, because people don't call you back, they throw you these smoke screens, they try to get rid of you. Don't take any of that personally, take it as, "Okay, I've somehow gotten out of leading this situation, how do I get back in control? How do I reclaim the lead here?" And you've got to figure out how far you want to press it, too. I think there's still an opportunity for you in this situation. There might be some point where they're really not interested and you have to walk away from it, but you're not there yet.

[Bill] Well, you know, I've got to start somewhere, but I'm afraid of doing my practice wrong with companies like that.

[John] Me too, Bill.

[Suzi] A couple of points in what you were just talking about, Bill, that I want to bring up for everybody. One is the belief that you have to have something dazzling to dangle in front of them, to actually impress them and get them to be yours. That's not true. I think that you, in and of yourself, with your skills and talents, are dazzling enough. Now, you do have to have enough examples, anecdotes, and success stories that you can tailor and customize to be relevant to any situation. So you want to come up with a number of success stories of people you've helped, or companies you've helped, that you can talk about in general enough terms that you can get your point across about how you can help any prospect you have a chance with. And if you practice on them and fail, it doesn't mean that you lose them forever, it just means that you've learned something in the process.

So I would encourage you to get out there and not wait. I also heard you say you were working on one opportunity and then you wanted to wait until you had something else. Part of what we were talking about on our last call, about it being a numbers game, is you've got to have lots and lots of irons in the fire at any one time. You've got to be pursuing a lot of opportunities at all times, because as we all know, they don't all come to fruition as quickly as we'd like. So it really is about just pursuing so many leads at once that you don't have time to get depressed or upset about the one that you're attaching so much meaning to that doesn't come through right away. The numbers really help you not be so attached with the particular outcome that you want with any one company.

[Bill] What do you do when they ask you for references?

[Suzi] Don't you have references to give them?

[Bill] Yeah. But maybe not . . . This is a multimillion-dollar corporation.

[Suzi] First of all, you don't know what will impress them. You don't know what they're asking for when they ask for references. It doesn't necessarily mean references from companies exactly like theirs. **Always ask what type of references would be most helpful to them.**

[Jeremy] You can also shape and control the references, Bill. You can say, "Look, I have a recent coaching reference, I think this would be a good guy for you to talk to."

[Suzi] Right, but also consider that they might not *really* want references. That could be another smoke screen to put you off—he already heard you say, "Well, I haven't done this exact thing."

So when someone asks for references, it's useful to find out more by saying something along the lines of: "You know I have a lot of references I can provide for you. Can you tell me a little more about what you're hoping to hear from that particular reference so that I can send you the right reference—someone who will be helpful?" Because then you'll find out whether they want just a character reference, or whether you have ever worked with *anybody*. There are a lot of assumptions that I'm hearing in what you're saying. For example, you're assuming he wants references for the same exact scenario. But you already told him you haven't done that same exact scenario before. So it's okay that you don't have a reference for that.

[Bill] I should send him my brochure, with the family on the cover.

[Suzi] Well, remember your whole purpose here is to get a meeting. So you could say, "You know what, I could give you a whole list of references, but what I think would be better is to get together and talk about what you're really looking for, how I can really help, and who might be the best references for me to send your way. How's Friday at 9:00?"

[Deb] So every time, Suzi, you go straight for the time. And that's been your key, huh?

[Jeremy] Selling that time.

[Suzi] You know, that's the point. You're trying to get a meeting. If you're on the phone, the whole purpose of being on the phone with them is to get a meeting. It's not about identifying their coaching or consulting needs, it's not about sparkling them with all the things you can and can't do—that's not the time for that.

When you're on the phone, the only thing you want to do is set up a time to get face to face. That's it. That's your ultimate purpose.

[Bill] Okay. How do I finesse out his objections?

[Suzi] Okay, before we get to that question, I want to check in real quick with John. John, did you make your five calls? Did you get one appointment?

[John] My goal was to make five calls. Jeremy amended that to make 10. And so, I mean technically, I did. But I'm several steps before making the real calls. Like Bill, I didn't want to waste learning time on anyone; I didn't want to run the risk of calling people I really consider valuable leads because I didn't want to risk messing up on the real deal, so I found a list of people on the web who could be practice people for me. And so I called 10 of those folks.

[Suzi] Great!

[John] But it took me three days to pick up the phone the first time. This is the part that is the big barrier to me. I mean you guys talk about picking up the phone and making phone calls as if that's not the problem. To me, that's the problem. You know, Jeremy, you said you had fun making phone calls. I don't identify with that—I did not have any fun. It was, and is, really tough for me to do that.

[Suzi] Well, then, giant kudos to you for doing it 10 times. That's excellent!

[John] It might be useful for me if Suzi and some of the rest of you would just tape record your end of the conversation some time. I'd like to hear what one of these things sounds like from someone who knows how the hell to do it.

[Suzi] I can tell you right now exactly what it sounds like. Whenever I pick up the phone, it sounds like this: "Hi, my name is Suzi Pomerantz, I'm an executive coach." Then I do my 30-second commercial, and I usually reference how I know them, or where I met them, or why I'm calling them.

Cold Calls, Phone Fear, and the Myth of Preparation

[John] So what if it's a cold call?

[Suzi] Okay, if it's a cold call, I say, "You know what, I'm calling because I recently completed a project with an organization similar to yours, and I'd love to come by and talk about what we did for them, and share with you where it might be helpful to you."

[John] So what if you haven't recently completed a project with a similar company?

[Suzi] Even if it wasn't recent, chances are I have at some point done some work with a company that is in some way similar to theirs. It's just a matter of accessing my memory to find the parallels.

[John] Yeah, but I have trouble lying.

[Suzi] But it's not lying . . . because somewhere in the past I've completed a project with a company similar to theirs, or with a person in a similar situation to them.

In other words, no matter what you've done, you have war stories and success stories you can share. For example, back when I first started years ago, my work experience was being a schoolteacher. I took my experiences with my third graders, and those are the stories I talked about with the business people. They were real experiences, but they didn't necessarily know I was talking about third graders. Don't sell yourself short: You have had experiences relevant to your prospects. Even if it's in your family, you have had experiences coaching people. You've done it.

So, to recap, what all my calls sound like is: "Hi, I'm Suzi Pomerantz. (here's my commercial), here's why I'm calling, I'd like to set up a time to talk to you, how's Wednesday at 10:00?" That's it.

There's a myth in all this: **The myth is that we will be less afraid to pick up the phone or to have the meeting if we're more prepared.** And that's a myth because the reality is we're only going to become less afraid by doing it more often and building our confidence in doing it. We don't get less afraid by being more prepared, we only get more prepared by being more prepared.

[Jeremy] That's one of Robinson's three equations: **What cuts fear is action.**

[Suzi] Exactly, exactly, exactly. The myth is "I'll be less afraid to pick up the phone if I'm more prepared, or I'll be less afraid to have these sales meetings if I'm more prepared, or I'll be less afraid to go out and sell my services if I'm more prepared." This is why the natural pitfall is to spend all sorts of time doing the marketing activities of developing brochures, preparing our websites, writing our 30-second commercials—we spend all our time on that stuff because it feels like getting prepared.

[Jeremy] What about the twiddling-our-thumbs marketing activity?

[Suzi] Yeah . . . like looking on the web for people to call. All of these things are great for preparation. **But by being more prepared, you're only more prepared—it doesn't get you into action.**

[John] When I was making my phone calls, I was struck by a comment Bill Walton made on the Final Four telecast. He was talking about whatever the guys were doing out there and said, **"Let's not confuse activity with achievement."** And I felt like that—I was doing a hell of a lot of activity. But since I didn't have a basic level of preparation, I didn't have the skills built up. Since I didn't have that, I wasn't talking achievement, I was talking making the 10 phone calls.

[Jeremy] But that was good you did that.

[John] Right, but the point is that was still activity.

[Suzi] But it was productive activity in the sense that you were practicing the action of picking up the phone, making the calls.

[Jeremy] And that reduces the fear about that, the inhibition about that.

[John] Not yet it hasn't . . .

[Bill] But, John, by the tenth call, how did it feel to make the call?

[John] Uh, terrible, frightening.

[Bill] As frightening as it had been in the beginning?

[John] Well, it didn't take me as long to pick up the phone, but I was also under time pressure to do it.

[Bill] Well, there's one positive difference!

Dealing with Objections

[Suzi] Okay, back to Bill's question about how to "finesse" his prospect's objection.

There are two different situations where we need to handle objections. One is when we're on the phone trying to get an appointment, and the other is a sales meeting, after you've actually gotten the appointment. There are certain objections that you may hear in each situation, and we have to figure out how to handle them. The first thing to know about how to handle these objections, and the way to be prepared for them, is that there is only a finite set of objections that you will hear.

Let's start with being on the phone. If you're on the phone and you're calling to get an appointment, the purpose of the call is not to identify their coaching or consulting needs. The purpose of your call is to get a meeting scheduled. So what are the kinds of objections that you hear most often from people you're trying to set a meeting with?

We've already talked about some of them. For example, someone says, "Just send me a brochure," or someone else says, "Don't need it, I'm not interested."

[Deb] "Don't have it in the budget for this year."

[Bill] "No time for it."

[Suzi] "I'm not the right person to talk to." "We don't do that here, we don't use coaching (or consulting) services."

[Jeremy] "What is it?"

[Suzi] Or, "We already have a company that provides coaching services." What are others that you've heard on the phone? Are those pretty much the standards?

[Len] "Don't bother me."

[Suzi] Have you *actually* heard that?

[Len] No, but I'm anticipating I will.

[Suzi] I've never heard that. I've made hundreds of calls, I've never had anyone say that. Jeremy have you ever had anyone say that?

[Jeremy] No, but I'm with Len, I'm still waiting for that one.

[Suzi] Again, we're back to the mindset. If you go into a call expecting that outcome, that attitude will color your way of being on that call.

Okay. Once you know the standard objections that you'll hear, you can plan your responses ahead of time so that they will roll right off your tongue, like your 30-second commercial. **The first trick of handling objections is to see it as the beginning of the chess match that is business development.** As you know, part of playing chess is that you plan your move a couple moves ahead, so while your partner is planning their move, you're already planning your move two or three moves ahead. You have to predict or anticipate what the opponent will be doing. The same thing is true with handling objections. If you're predicting what all the possible objections are, what you also need to do is plan all your possible responses. Then you're prepared: When they make their move, you make your move.

This is not meant to be used as a technique for procrastinating for making the call; this should be a pretty quick preparation. So let's talk about the things you can say in response to these standard objections.

Let's go around and have everyone say what you hear most often, and what your standard response is, or what you've said that's worked.

For example, if what you hear is, "Just send me information," how do you respond, remembering that your purpose is to get a meeting? How do you respond to that in terms of the chess match; to get it back to getting a meeting? What are the responses that you've used that worked? Pick one.

[Len] I haven't done this long enough, so it's not based on experience, but I can imagine if a person on the phone said, "I don't want to be bothered with this," I could say, "Well, if we got together on such and such a date I could learn exactly the nature of the difficulties that you've had and then I could provide you with a brochure (if they wanted that), or tell you exactly how we could be of help to you."

[Jeremy] Sometimes, if you've gotten that objection, I could imagine matching somebody's comment and empathizing with them. I might say something like, "Gee, I hate it when somebody calls me up and seems to bother me also," and then still make the pitch.

[Suzi] Yes, exactly. For instance, you could say, "I'm sorry, I'm not interested in bothering you, is it better if I call you at another time?"

[Jeremy] But I would actually say more, Suzi. I might say, "I can relate to your feeling bothered, because when that happens to me, I feel the same way, but I think this might be pretty interesting for you."

[Suzi] In that situation, I've said, "I really think that I have something here that I can help you with. And I really don't want to bother you. Can I set up an appointment? Can I talk to you Tuesday at 9:00? I don't want to bother you, I just want to set up an appointment. Let's do that." Sometimes, if you're bothering them, they'll set up an appointment just to get rid of you. You know? The quickest way to get you off the phone is to give you what you want.

[John] That doesn't feel right to me. I mean Jeremy's notion of empathizing and blah blah blah . . . that's worked on me before, in fact, that's how I bought my website from folks unknown, unseen—that was their response when I said, "I'm not interested." I ended up buying a website from them. But to say, "I don't want to bother you, just let me bother you with a one-hour meeting, so I won't bother you anymore," that doesn't sound like something that would ring true for me.

[Suzi] Well, if you're thinking about it that way, I wouldn't recommend you do it that way. As for me, I don't think about it as "I want to bother you for an hour so I'll stop bothering you now"; it's more like, "I actually have something that I think you're going to be interested in. I don't want to bother you at all, I just want to set up an appointment."

[Bill] Suzi, I know that the goal that you have is just to set up that appointment. But you don't say anything on the phone that you think would be of interest to that person?

[Jeremy] She does her 30-second commercial.

[Bill] And you also modified it with the particular person that you're talking to, to match their company or their particular concern, right?

[Suzi] Right, I do my commercial and I tell them why I'm calling. And the why I'm calling is either "Because so-and-so thought we should get together," or "I got your name from someone who thought that I might be able to help you with something that they told me you were dealing with," or "You and I met at a conference and you asked me to give you a call." **What comes right after a commercial is the *why it's relevant for me to be calling them.***

[Bill] How you could be linked to them somehow.

[Suzi] Right. When a prospect says to you on the phone that they're not interested, here's a quick and dirty that you can say back, which, depending on why they're not interested, you'll tailor to fit. But this is what I've found has worked. They say, "I'm not interested," I say, "You know what? A lot of my current clients said that before they saw X." And X is either "the value of the coaching service," or before they saw "the results we were able to produce with a CEO in the same situation," or before they saw "the ease with which they could increase the morale of the team by working with us," or before they saw "the benefit of the training." You know, you throw a relevant result in there.

So it sounds something like this:

A lot of our clients (I often say "our," because I want to sound bigger than "my") said that to me before they saw (think on your feet to come up with a relevant result). I'd like to come by and talk to you about how we demonstrated that to them. How's Friday at 9:00?

Beyond Objections

[Deb] You were talking earlier about building all the materials related to your marketing stuff. That in and of itself helps me to articulate—to think on my feet what to say to handle an objection. That preparation says to me, "Oh, I can do this." It gives me more confidence in being able to articulate what I can do. Just that process.

[Suzi] Absolutely. It's very valuable. It's like the business-planning process. I'm not saying don't do that stuff—your marketing stuff is very important. It's critical actually, because you have to have a brochure to leave with them, you have to have a website, and it is confidence-building. But . . .

[Deb] . . . you have to take it to the next step.

[Suzi] Right. The next step is where you turn it into dollars, clients, business—those marketing activities in and of themselves don't get you the client. That's the baseline. You know how you kind of assume a baseline of being competent in completing the services? The baseline is having the materials. It doesn't get you the business by itself.

[Deb] No, I was talking more about the internal process that you're trying to project. That you're feeling confident to project something. And that process in and of itself really helps me build my confidence to be able to say to somebody "You know, I can do this."

[Jeremy] Suzi, I want to come back to your comment about the myth about feeling like you need to be prepared before you can make the call. I think actually what is accurate in that is that there is a time where there's a need for a lot of preparation, but that time is not to make the call. The time to be prepared is after you've made the appointment. After you've made the call, and the appointment is set, then you make your preparation. Then you really work like a dog to get to know everything you can about the background of that prospect. But to make the call, you don't need that preparation.

[Suzi] Again, we've got to come back to the purpose. The purpose of the call is to get the meeting. And it's not about persuading them to have a meeting, it's just about asking for the meeting. "How's Friday at 10:00? Oh, that doesn't work for you, how about Wednesday at 8:00?"

You know, your whole purpose is to get the meeting. Okay, so what if they say, "I'm not the person you need to speak to, I'm not the right person." What do you say back to them?

[Jeremy] What I like to do, before I just drop them like a squeezed-out lemon, is to find out what *do* they do? And who is the person to talk to? But I don't want to drop them also.

[Deb] And what makes them say they're not the person?

[Suzi] Perfect. Whenever someone says to me, "I'm not the right person," I say, "Oh really? Well, what do you do?" Because chances are, whatever they do, there's an opportunity for you to say, "Well, we should get together, because I really think that there are things we can talk about. Now that you've told me that, I think you *are* the right person. Why don't we get together? How's Friday at 9:00?" And if you're really convinced after listening to their response that there is no reason to meet with that person, if you can't find any reason at all to meet, then you can say, "Well, who should I speak with, who is the right person?"

[Jeremy] **The more allies you have in an organization who know about you, the better.**

[Suzi] Exactly. It's called building depth in the organization.

[Deb] And it may be somebody useful in the future.

[Jeremy] Everybody's a potential client.

[Suzi] Or they know potential clients for you. Nobody's on the bench, everybody's in the game. Let's try one more.

What do you do when they say, "We don't have the budget for that," What do you say to that?

[Bill] My response would be, "You would have the budget if you had a decent coach there."

[Suzi] I love that! "You would have the budget if I was working with you." Oh, that's hysterical . . .

[Bill] I don't know if it would go very far.

[Suzi] Well, no, but it's amusing. You can always think that and amuse yourself. Here's a real one you can try. If they say, "We don't have the budget for that," you can say (this is going to sound familiar), "You know, a lot of my current clients said that before they saw the cost savings that resulted from the coaching (consulting, whatever) services I was able to provide. I'd love to come and talk to you about how we've helped our clients achieve significant savings. How's Tuesday at 3:00?"

Are you starting to see the pattern here?

[Bill] Definitely. If in that brief moment I can understand what their need is from what their objection is, for example, then I can address that particular need by mentioning other people who had the same need and how I helped *them* address it. And your example was perfect for that: "Well, a lot of my clients said the same thing before they saw how they could be more efficient."

[Suzi] Yes. And the other thing is that part of what happens—and this happens with practice—is knowing how to hear in each objection what they're *really* saying. Because sometimes when they say, "We don't have the budget for that this year," they're not really talking about budget at all. Sometimes what they're really saying is that they don't see the value in what coaching (or your services) can do for them. So what that means is that you have not yet identified what their problem is and how your services can help them solve it. It could be that you're talking to them about leadership coaching, and what's really bugging them is attrition. Maybe they're not making the connection that attrition really is a leadership issue. So part of what to do is to keep exploring to identify what their challenge or issue is. And again, this objection doesn't happen on the phone; these are the objections that happen more often in the meeting after the phone call to set it up, where you really have time to explore these things. On your phone call, your purpose is just to get a meeting.

So, we're at the end of our session, and I just want to make sure that everybody's clear about what the homework is.

[Bill] I shall write down all the objections I can think of and all the kinds of responses I can make, and I'm going to make more calls.

[Suzi] Yes. And keep in mind that the purpose of making the call is to get an appointment. So the responses to the objections ought to be in line with that.

Homework

Write a list of the objections you often hear—or objections you would expect to hear in different situations. Then write out your responses for each one. Use the Overcoming Objections Worksheet on page 140. Remember, there is a predictable and finite set of possible objections. Your power to overcome them comes from exploring them and preparing your responses in advance.

Getting Past the Gatekeepers

Gatekeepers have a difficult role. They are tasked with granting only the right people access to their executive. They have typically developed their own criteria or screening process to help them determine if you are a good risk or not. You must respect the gatekeeper, for he is constantly faced with competing demands. He must limit any interruptions to the executive's day that might be unnecessary or a potential distraction or waste of the executive's valuable time while simultaneously not excluding individuals the executive would want to meet. How well he interprets his own screening criteria could make or break his job. Once the gatekeeper recognizes that, it is in his best interest (or the executive's, or the organization's) to let you in, or if it seems worse to keep you out than let you in, he'll find a way to let you in. Gatekeepers have tremendous power to pave the way for you. Before you chart your battle plan to get past the gatekeeper, consider that this person is not your adversary or foe, but your potential friend. You'd do well to find ways of getting in with the gatekeeper rather than getting past the gatekeeper.

Strategy 1

Avoid the gatekeeper and try to catch the executive. Call when the gatekeeper is not there—early in the morning before normal business hours or after 5:00 or 5:30 p.m.

Strategy 2

Use first names of both the gatekeeper and the prospect and speak from a confident place, as if you are the prospect's well-known colleague, even if you have never met or spoken to that person before.

> Example: "Hi, Mary, is John available?" Or, better yet, "Hi, Mary, this is Ellen calling for John. Is he there?"

Strategy 3

Befriend the gatekeeper and have him schedule the appointment for you. This strategy is extremely beneficial once you've sealed the deal with that client, because the gatekeeper can help you navigate not only the culture of the organization, but the particular nuances of getting things done with your executive client. The gatekeeper who is a really top-notch executive assistant will be your best ally for finding out key information and charting your course through the executive's schedule. Of course, this strategy is the most time consuming because it requires creating the relationship and the associated relational upkeep. It is time well spent.

List the possible universe of gatekeeper reactions to your call. What might he or she say? I've done the first one for you as an example:

- She's in a meeting. May I ask why you are calling? (Often they will say this even if the person is not in a meeting and could take your call. Don't be offended, the gatekeeper is just doing his or her job. They have to balance the right mix of getting things handled and keeping distractions away from the executive they are serving.)

What are some others?

- _____
- _____
- _____
- _____

Now, give your possible responses to the gatekeeper's reactions listed above:

- Maybe you can help me? I'm just interested in scheduling a meeting with her and I'm looking at Tuesday at 3:00. Can she meet with me then?

- _____

- _____

- _____

- _____

Voice Mail Gatekeeping

Sometimes the gatekeeper is electronic in the form of voice mail. Leaving voice mail messages that get returned can be yet another challenge.

Write the message you currently leave with a prospect when you get their voice mailbox: _____

_____

Now analyze your message. Was it too long? Did you try to cover too much ground? Did you leave it in the prospect's hands or keep the lead?

Try to keep voice messages as concise as possible. Do not use a voice message to provide a lengthy introduction about yourself or your services. Remember, your whole goal is to set up a meeting to do that. I use a modular approach. I have six basic bullet points that vary from prospect to prospect, but cover the basics.

Here's an example of the modules of a message I leave that has a high percentage return rate. It is very short; try never to leave a long voice message because you risk that the prospect won't listen to the whole thing if he can't tell early on who you are and why you're calling.

Intro: "Hi, Tim, this is Suzi Pomerantz."

Relevance: "We met at XYZ conference briefly."
Or "Max Newell said I should get in touch with you."
Or "Jane Cash gave me your name and number."

Purpose:	"I'm calling to schedule a time when we might meet in person."
Reason:	"I'd like to find out more about your role and your organization and share with you some of the results we've recently produced for a firm like yours."
Proposal:	"I'm looking at Tuesday at 9:00 a.m."
Promise:	". . . and I'll call you again tomorrow to see if that fits in your schedule."

Literally, that's it. Nothing extraneous. Don't fall into the trap of trying to fully introduce yourself, your business, your services, and sell them all on a voice message. It can't be done. Just let them know you are interested in setting up a meeting and that you'll call back. This keeps you as the leader of the process and you won't lose time waiting for prospects to call you back. It also allows you to build trust and prove integrity. If you consistently do what you say (e.g., "I'll call you tomorrow at noon to schedule something") and you do it (i.e., call them at noon the next day), you are proving you are a person who keeps his or her word. Even if you just leave another message that says, "Hi, Tim, it's Suzi Pomerantz again. It is Wednesday at noon and I mentioned yesterday that I'd call you today at noon to coordinate our calendars. I'll try you again this afternoon at 5:00 or you can simply call me and let me know if Tuesday at 9:00 a.m. works for us to get together." Of course, then you have to call at 5:00 if you haven't heard from him. However you space it, keep yourself in the driver's seat.

Practice Script:
Voice Mail Messaging

Okay, now it's your turn. Take a test run at crafting your own super-short message to leave for prospects whose gatekeepers are their phone mail systems:

Intro (Introduce your name; if you wish, you can include your company name): _____

_____

Relevance (Remind them where you two met, or whom you know in common): _____

_____

Purpose (Tell them why you are calling today. HINT: to set up a meeting):

_____

_____

Reason (Why are you requesting a meeting?): _____

_____

Proposal (Suggest a specific date and time): _____

_____

Promise (Say when you will call again, and then make sure to put it on your calendar to do so): _____

_____

Practice with a partner until you develop a natural message that feels authentic to your style and personality. Seek suggestions from your practice buddy for which messages will most likely motivate return calls.

Write your new message here:

_____

_____

_____

_____

Handling Objections:
The Beginning of the Chess Match

Now that you are masterful at how to get past the gatekeepers, be they human or technology-based, what happens when you actually reach your prospect on the phone and he or she is resistant, or says things that sound a lot like trying to get rid of you?

There are strategies you can use to handle whatever objections a prospect might raise. Part of all of them is about listening for what the prospect is really saying or asking, and part is keeping your focus and being unstoppable. Either way, you have to make the calls to even hear the objections, but as we saw before with phone fear, it is easy to avoid making the calls. Your preparedness to handle objections and know ahead of time how you will respond to a predictable set of possible objections will allow you to make calls with confidence.

Myth: You will be less afraid (to pick up the phone, have the meeting) if you are more prepared.

Reality: You will only become less afraid by making calls more often. You don't get less afraid by being more prepared, you simply become more prepared by being more prepared.

However, you *do* need to be prepared to handle objections in the business development context.

You will need to handle objections in two situations:

1. On calls to get appointments
   Purpose: to get a meeting scheduled (*not* to identify specific coaching or consulting needs)

2. In a sales meeting
   Purpose: to listen for what their problem is, and show how you can help them solve their problem through your services (and get a second meeting or a next step commitment)

There is a finite set of objections: What are they? What do you hear most often from the people you are calling or meeting with? I've started the list for you. Add other frequently heard objections below:

- Not interested.

- I'm not the person you need to speak to.

- No budget for that.

- We already use someone for that.

- We handle that in-house . . . our HR department does that.

- We had a bad experience with an outside consultant.

- Just send me some information.

- I'm too busy, I can't talk now.

- I'm not available (when you suggest a date and time).

- Call me again another time.

- We don't use coaching here (or consultants, or outside trainers, or whatever).

- You're not local; we want someone who is local to our headquarters.

- This is not something we can take on right now.

- You are an unknown quantity to us, you've never worked with us before.

- _____

- _____

- _____

Now, plan your responses. What will you say to each of the objections above? Many of the objections you'll face can be addressed with some version of the following responses:

> "I'm just calling to make an appointment, how's Tuesday at 10:00?"

and

> "You know, a lot of my current clients said that until they saw (fill in the blank)." (See Typical Objections and Responses tip sheet on page 136.)

Remember your objective in each context. Either you are simply trying to set up a meeting, or, if you are already in a meeting, you are trying to listen for what the problem/challenge is that your services can solve. **Keep your purpose in mind.**

Know how to hear in their objections what they are *really* saying. Listen for what they are not telling you:

- **"I don't have a budget for that this year"** or "that seems really expensive" really means that they don't yet see the value in what you can do for them or how you can help solve their problems.

- **"We don't need that right now"** really means that you have not yet uncovered what their problem or hot issue is. You might be talking about leadership coaching or succession planning, and leadership might not be what they see their issues to be. Perhaps they have a problem with attrition and they are not seeing how attrition is a leadership issue. Or perhaps they are focused on talent management issues and don't see the application of coaching as an intervention into managing and developing the organization's emerging leaders or current leadership bench strength.

- **"We already work with someone who does that"** really means they don't yet see how your services are distinct or unique from what they believe they already have. You should explore this further. Offer examples of how your services complement other coaches/ consultants, or share how you've worked in partnership or collaborated with other consultants within organizations like theirs.

- **"Can you just mail me a brochure?"** really means "I have no idea what you can do to help and I need to get off the phone." This is your cue to set up a meeting and get off the phone. You might say, "I'd rather bring it to you in person and talk to you about the work I've done with N firm (as long as N firm is similar to them either in industry or size) and how I was able to help them produce X results or solve Y problems. How's Monday at 11:00?"

In a meeting, people won't often come right out and tell you that they don't find value in what you are trying to sell them; they instead will couch it in terms of budgets or timing or another smoke screen. Talking about coaching or consulting is abstract and hard for them to understand, and even when they are savvy users of coaching or consulting services, they do not always see the link. You have to find a way to talk about results in terms of anecdotes of how you helped someone (or some company) like them resolve a situation or a problem they are also facing. Couch your message in how you can help them solve their problem based on how you helped someone like them handle a similar issue.

So what do you say when faced with these objections and you have already ascertained the meaning behind the objection? Here are a few sample responses for you to try. Play with these, try them out, and see what shifts or opens up for you. Ultimately, the goal is to get fluid enough with your ability to handle objections on the fly so that you won't need to use something scripted like the examples on the tip sheet on the next page, and you will allow your natural personal style to shine through.

Tip Sheet:
Typical Objections and Responses

If They Say:	You Might Respond With:
Not interested.	A lot of our current clients said that before they saw the value that our service brought to the communication issues in the firm. I'd like to come by and talk with you about a few relevant examples so that you can see if it would make sense for your firm. Are you available Tuesday at 9:00?
I'm not the person you need to speak to.	Really? What do you do? (Listen to their reply and look for your opportunity to say, "We really should get together. How is Tuesday at 10:00?")
I'm not the person you need to speak to (reprise).	With whom should I speak? Can you introduce me?
We use a competitor of yours.	A lot of our current clients also use competitors. Our services complement theirs and I'd like to come by and talk to you about how we've worked with our competitors to jointly serve our client's needs. Does Tuesday at 3:00 work for you?
We don't use coaching services.	A lot of our current clients said that before they saw the 500 percent ROI that executive coaching generated for them. I'd like to share those results with you. Can I come by Tuesday at 9:00?
We don't have a budget for that.	A lot of our current clients said that before they saw the cost savings that resulted from using our services. I'd like to come by and talk with you about how we have helped our clients achieve significant savings. How's Thursday at 11:00?

(continued)

Tip Sheet:
Typical Objections and Responses *(concluded)*

If They Say:	You Might Respond With:
We had a bad experience with an outside consultant.	We really should get together. Are you available on Friday at 1:00 so that I can come by to hear about your experience and to demonstrate how we will provide you better service in the future?
Just send me information.	I would be happy to do so, but there is so much that I could send, I'd like to make sure I have a better understanding of which of our materials would be most relevant to you. Why don't we get together to discuss it on Wednesday at 2:00?
I'm too busy to talk now.	I'm just calling to schedule an appointment. Can you and I talk on Thursday at 3:00?
I'm not available then.	Is (a specific date and time two weeks later) better for you?
Call me another time.	That won't be necessary, I'm just calling to schedule an appointment. Can you and I talk on Thursday at 3:00?

Always follow your response to any objection with a proposed date and time to meet. It will encourage the prospect to consult his or her calendar. If the date and time you proposed is not an option, counteroffer another: "Is Monday at 3:00 better for you?" "Does Thursday at 9:00 work for you?"

And don't forget to thank the prospect for his or her time.

At some point, you will encounter somebody who just keeps throwing you objections. After responding to two or three of these objections, you might discern that the prospect is really not a good prospect for you, at which point you can choose to hang up and try another person on your target list. It is okay to be willing to walk away from these calls . . . remember, it is all a numbers game. Don't spend too much time being attached to any one prospect. Keep on calling for other appointments. Don't take it personally if they don't want to meet with you. It could be an issue of timing. Keep them on your target list and try again in a few months if you still think they are a good prospect.

Handling Rejection

Rejection, and the accompanying emotional hit, is yet another form of objection. If you are actively keeping your pipeline of prospects filled via your networking activities, and if you have a strategic target list full of warm leads, you will be inviting people into your sales cycle at a good clip. If you have a lot of people in your sales cycle at one time, you will not have time to get attached to any one prospect or to any desired outcome. This helps you stay emotionally separate from the sales process. For example, if you are only pursuing 5 leads, you will probably have more emotions vested in whether or not they progress along your sales cycle. However, if you are pursuing 125 leads, you will not have time to get emotionally attached to any one of them, and it will not matter so much if one doesn't go forward with setting up a meeting or even with hiring you because you have lots of others to focus on.

If 1 of 5 leads falls through, it is a bit more devastating than if 1 of 125 doesn't work out. Having higher numbers of prospects to target and higher numbers of folks in your sales process takes out the desperation and neediness of business development, and gives you access to having it be a game. This is important because you cannot win in this game if you are at any level communicating desperation and neediness. The minute you *need* a deal to close, you've as good as killed it. Release the need to get the business and stay unattached to any specific outcomes with specific targets. Simply focus on taking the steps necessary to keep your pipeline filled. Keep moving people through your sales process one step at a time. Keep your attention on serving your prospects and clients and not on your own need to seal the deal.

The Overcoming Objections Worksheet is for you to use in your own practice. Thinking through how you will overcome the objections you most often hear will help you sail through the sales process with grace.

Worksheet:
Overcoming Objections

Objections are part of the journey. See them as evidence that you are making progress. They are a natural part of getting to "yes." If you are prepared in advance to handle and overcome them, you will sail smoothly through the call. There is a predictable and finite set of possible objections. Explore them and prepare your responses in advance. Identify and expect the various "no's" you could possibly run into. They are likely to be some variation on the themes below, but please use this worksheet to capture the objections most relevant to your particular business. Then plan your responses to each one.

Not interested:

_____

_____

Too busy:

_____

_____

Wrong person:

_____

_____

No money:

_____

_____

(continued)

Worksheet:
Overcoming Objections *(concluded)*

Not available:

_____

_____

Relationship with competitor:

_____

_____

Send me information:

_____

_____

Call another time:

_____

_____

Others:

_____

_____

_____

_____

_____

Keeping Track

Research shows that you need to make 10 calls to get through to five or six prospects to set up one appointment. One in 10 appointments leads to a sale. Given these facts, analyze your own statistics. How many calls do *you* need to make each week?

Every sales cycle is different. In order to best understand your own sales cycle, you need to keep track of how many calls yield how many qualified appointments (see the Prospect Call Analysis Worksheet on the next page for an example of how to figure this).

Worksheet:
Prospect Call Analysis

Date	Number of Calls	Number of Connects	Number of Appointments

Step 5
The Client Meeting
as a
Chess Match

"Luck is what happens when preparation meets opportunity."
—Darrell Royal

"Risk-taking, trust, and serendipity are key ingredients of joy.
Without risk, nothing new ever happens. Without trust, fear creeps in.
Without serendipity, there are no surprises."
—Rita Golden Gelman

You will be leading the client meeting, and that will take some preparation. Many successful sales practitioners consider the client meeting to be part of the networking process, and they use it to go fishing. They are fishing to uncover a specific need that they can help address, or a specific problem that they can solve. Where does networking overlap with sales? Technically, that fishing expedition is part of the sales process, so be clear in your own mind where you are in the process! It is hard to be the leader of a process if you are not aware when you are in it. Networking happens all the time, and sales happen when relation and preparation meet implementation. There are lots of fish in the sea. If you wait until someone asks you for a proposal to begin the sales process, you might miss a lot of bites.

Telecourse Session #5: Into the Client Meeting

Experiences with Objections

[Suzi] Okay, your homework was to come up with objections and how you would respond to them. What objections did you hear most often? The Overcoming Objections Worksheet is to assist you in determining the finite set of possible objections so that you can brainstorm responses for each. Some of the objections we commonly hear when calling to make appointments are "I'm not interested," or "I'm not the right person to talk to," or "We don't have the right budget for that," or "We do that in-house, in our HR department," or "Last time we hired a consultant it was a bad experience," or "Just send me some information." Others are "I'm too busy, I can't talk now," "I'm not available on such-and-such a date," or "Call me again another time." What did you come up with?

[John] Well, basically, what I got was, "not interested," but it's unclear to me whether the model is then to counter with logic, or whether it's to empathize, or whatever. So . . .

[Suzi] Let's back up. What is the purpose of being on the phone with this person?

[John] To get a meeting.

[Suzi] Exactly. So if empathizing gets you the meeting, go for it.

[John] What I was interested in was the types of things that you have done on these objections that have worked.

[Suzi] Yes, with that particular one, if they'll tell me why they're not interested, great. But if they won't, if they just say we're not interested at this time, then I always counter with, "You know, a lot of my clients said that before we could talk to them about the value of the coaching, and I'd love to come by and talk to you about some of what I've been able to do with them. How's Tuesday at 5:00?" or whatever. So it really is as simple as that model, and it sounds a little foreign when you first try it.

[John] What about, "We don't have the money for it"? How do you handle that one?

[Suzi] I would say, "A lot of my clients said that before they saw the cost savings that resulted from using our coaching service. I'd like to come by and talk to you about how we've helped our clients achieve significant cost savings. How's Tuesday at 9:00?" Again, the purpose is to get a meeting. It's not about telling everything you have to offer.

[John] "I've had a bad experience with a consultant." How do you handle that one?

[Suzi] "Well, you know what, we really should get together to talk about that. I'd love to find out what your bad experience was, and see if there's something that we can do to improve on that experience with you. Are you available Tuesday at 3:00 so that I can come by and tell you how we can provide you a better experience than you've had in the past?"

[Jeremy] What's fascinating about your style, Suzi, which I think is incredibly effective, is it's like you listen, but it's almost like you don't completely listen. You're so motivated, and so what a client of mine used to call "one-pointed," the objections seem to bounce right off.

[Suzi] Right. And it's foreign to us as coaches or counselors, because we really want to listen to the meaning behind their objections.

[Jeremy] It's really about a different mindset.

[Suzi] It is. Because the time to actually be a coach is once you've got the contract. Otherwise you get stuck—it's really easy to get sucked into providing all kinds of free coaching to people you're trying to get a meeting with. Because then you start asking more questions, and you want to find out more information, and you start really listening, and that's not the point—the point is to get the meeting.

[John] Something like, "I'm too busy, I can't talk now." How do you deal with that?

[Suzi] "Would Thursday at 9:00 be better for you?" If they say, "You know, really, I'm too busy," I say, "I'm just calling to set up an appointment, I don't want to take a lot of your time. How's Tuesday at 9:00?" And then, "Oh that doesn't work? How's Thursday at 3:00? I just want to set an appointment."

In other words, I'm saying I don't want to take up a lot of their time. I just want to set up an appointment and get off the phone. That's all I want to do. I mean think about when you call a doctor's office receptionist: They're so crazy busy, all they want to do is make an appointment and get off the phone.

[Jeremy] That's a good analogy.

[Suzi] You're calling to schedule an office visit. You don't want to get into lengthy conversations with these people about your symptoms, or your issues, or what you're trying to get into. Because chances are, you're talking to a receptionist when you call for a service provider, and you don't really want to talk to them, you want to talk to the specialist. So think about it that way too. You don't really want to get into the content of the issues on the phone. You just want to make the appointment and get off. The time for getting into content is in the meeting.

[John] But what about when the secretary says, "What's this concerning?"

[Suzi] "It's concerning setting up a meeting with so-and-so about the work we've done with so-and-so about XYZ company, and how we may be able to help you."

[John] I said that to a secretary once, and she said, "Well, we don't need any of that." What do I say to the secretary who tells me they don't need any of that?

[Suzi] Well, what happened there is you're stuck with a gatekeeper. So that goes back to the lesson about getting past the gatekeeper. The trick is you don't want to get into a whole lot of that with the gatekeeper. You know, the trick is to get directly to the decision maker.

[John] Yeah, that's true. And some calls can be made at 7:00 in the morning, and the calls I made after 5:30, no one was ever there, so every call I made I was talking to a gatekeeper.

[Jeremy] Try 3:00 on Friday. 3:00 on Friday is a great time to sell.

[Suzi] Yeah. I also wouldn't leave it at what a gatekeeper says. If a gatekeeper says, "We don't need that," just say thank you and get off the phone, and keep trying to call a person who's not a gatekeeper.

[John] Okay.

[Suzi] The gatekeeper is just doing their job by trying to get rid of you. That's what they're there for. I can tell you one thing, John, when you run into a gatekeeper and they want to know what it's about, the responses that you want to give the gatekeeper are to make a point that the person asked you to call them directly. Or you want to get across the point that you need to talk to that person directly. So you want to either say, "We met at such-and-such a meeting or such-and-such a conference, and he or she suggested that I give him or her a call," or "I'm calling about the executive coaching matter," as if it's something that you've already been discussing with that person, because then they can't say it's a cold call . . . they're trained to pick out if you're calling to sell them something.

So if you say, "Oh, I'm calling to talk to Jim"—and I would definitely use their first names—or "I'm calling to talk to Mary about the executive coaching matter," as if, matter of fact, you've already been talking about it with them, you're just calling to follow up. You could even say, "I'm calling to follow up," because then, the dutiful gatekeeper will take a message, "John is calling to follow up with you." Then of course you might get a confused executive who wants to know "follow up from where?"—they've never heard of you, but they're not going to say that to the gatekeeper.

[John] I had one gatekeeper say, "Okay, I'll be right back," and she went and talked to the executive, and she came back and said, "No, he doesn't want that." So . . .

[Suzi] I would say in that case you gave the gatekeeper too much information.

[John] Oh yes, I would say so.

[Suzi] No, there's nothing wrong with that when you're learning. But this is all part of learning, you know. You get to the point that you realize the gatekeepers are there to keep you away, so don't give them too much information. Don't give them enough information to keep you away.

[Jeremy] And—this is hard sometimes also—don't take it personally. Just keep on moving ahead.

[Suzi] They ask, "What is this about?" You answer, "Well, I'm just calling to make an appointment with John. Is he available Thursday at 3:00, or do I need to talk to him directly? Does he do his schedule or do you?" Because by then, you've got them thinking about scheduling, or they've forgotten that they've asked that. You say, "I just need to set up an appointment with John. Is he available Tuesday at 3:00? Oh, you don't do his schedule, great, can you put me through to him? Can you put me through to his voice mail, I'll talk to him directly."

[Len] If you got through to his voice mail, then what message would you leave there?

[Suzi] That depends . . . is this a person you have a referral to?

[Len] Well, actually, this is a cold call.

[Suzi] A cold call, and you've gotten through to the person's voice mail, great! "Hi so-and-so, this is Len. I'm calling to talk to you about executive coaching. I want to set up a meeting with you to discuss the work that I've been doing with other clients that might be useful to you. Here's my number (give your phone number). I'm calling to see if you're available Tuesday at 3:00." I would keep it as straightforward as possible. Why? Because it makes it less confusing for you, there are fewer things to try to remember at once, and you're really not getting into coaching at this point—you're just trying to set up a meeting. Now, I also wouldn't be offended if they didn't call you back, I would just keep calling until you get them live.

[Jeremy] Keep calling. Keep dialing those numbers.

The Power of Persistence

[Suzi] Be persistent. And even if you think too much time has passed, I would still persist. Here's a story: A person I met at a talk I gave January 31st gave me his card at the end of the talk and said, "I'm interested in talking to you." I started calling him, and the first conversation we actually had was February 9th. Just yesterday, April 9th, was the first time I was able to meet with him. I had to persist all the way through. There were times when he didn't call back, and I just kept the stance that he wanted to talk to me. One response to his not calling me back after I left three messages might have been that he didn't want to talk to me anymore. But I just kept assuming that I was here to provide a service to him, and he was too busy to talk to me. And that ended up working.

[Jeremy] Now I'll tell you something interesting from another point of view—from somebody who's gotten those persistent calls. My experience usually, at first is, "Gee, that person is a colossal pain." But

there is a sense of appreciation when I've had the experience of a person calling and calling and calling, and a feeling that I've got to meet with this person because they're unbelievably persistent. Like even if I meet with them for five minutes, I've just got to congratulate them on their persistence.

[Suzi] Right, but not everybody values that tenacity.

[Jeremy] Do you all feel you can relate to being this persistent, or does it feel like "Oh man, this is a big stretch"?

[Len] Well, I'm kind of stretching mentally, listening to this. I know one of my clients, one of my therapy clients, is a very successful salesperson. He sells network television to local affiliates all over the country, and he'll call 20 times before he gets a meeting, and then meet with the person as if he isn't offended. And he doesn't have a problem with it at all. I guess I shouldn't either.

[Deb] You know, I think it bothered me, but Suzi, you just said something about you have something to offer—that you have something of value that you can provide for him—or he needs this. I think when you have that kind of attitude, for me anyway, that there's something I can give to you, then that other stuff goes away.

[Suzi] That's exactly right, Deb. Your whole attitude is what really comes across on the call. And if you're leaving messages coming from an attitude of "Hey, you know what? I'm just here to help, I'm here to provide services, I've got something of value to offer, and I'm just calling to help you," then it's going to communicate that—as opposed to, "I'm calling to sell you services. I'm calling to sell you stuff. I need your money. I'm trying to sell you. I need a contract from you." Whatever place you're coming from is what's communicating.

You've got to find what feels comfortable to you. I can't feel good about what I'm doing as a salesperson if I'm coming from a place that's all about getting the contracts and the appointments and the money and all that. I can't feel good about it because I'm a coach, I'm a helper, I'm really here to make a difference with people. So my attitude is, "I'm calling to help you. If you want my help, great. If you don't, I'm sure you know someone else who does, and let's talk about that."

In other words, my philosophy is, there is nobody on the bench in this sport. This is not a spectator sport. Everybody's in the game. So if I can't help you, and I can't help anyone in your company, chances are you know someone I can help, and let's talk about that. No matter what, we should get together; I firmly believe we should get together. But if I can't help you, even if I can't help your company, even if there's no budget, even if you've got 62 gatekeepers lined up to keep me out, we should still get together, because chances are there's still some connection that we have with each other, and I'm going to find it.

[Jeremy] There's definitely a religious zeal that helps with this.

[Suzi] It's about being open to possibility, which is what we do as coaches anyway.

[Len] I think my problem is that I've been coming from a place of "I need this meeting because I need to bootstrap myself into a place that I'm not at now, and I'm not comfortable at now, but I'll be comfortable later"—and this is like totally twisted. I really need to be in the mindset now that I'm going to be in a year from now.

[Suzi] The whole "fake it 'til you make it" really works too. Act "as if." You are there to help, and if they don't need your services, you don't need them, and you don't need their contract. They could be the last target client on your list, and you don't need them. And you know what else? The truth is, they don't need you. They've survived all these years and succeeded on their own all these years without you. The trick is to let go of all that need on both sides. You don't need them, they don't need you. Now let's see what's possible. Nobody needs anybody, let's see what's possible. What can we create?

[Deb] I like that. But how come they don't need us? Oh . . . because they've survived however long without us.

[Suzi] Yes, you take any average CEO, someone in their 40s, 50s, or 60s, they've been alive that long, they've succeeded in business without you. Somehow they've managed without you. They've succeeded without you up until now. And, yes, you can help them, you know you can help them, but truly, they don't need you. And truly, even if the company is going down the drain, and you're the only person who can save it, truly, they still don't need you.

[Deb] So then what value can we add?

[Suzi] You can help. You can support, you can listen, you can provide guidance, you can coach them to come up with their own answers. There's a lot of value you can provide, but they don't *need* it. It's that need, we get so attached to the outcome.

[John] They can use us, but they don't need us.

[Jeremy] Now we're into Buddhist selling, right?

[Deb] Letting go.

[Suzi] Yes, letting go. You've got to let go of attachment to the outcome. This is why it always comes back to numbers. We've said over and over that it's all about numbers, which is why you need to be setting up meetings and making calls—because none of these people needs you. So you've got to have 20, 30, 40 in the pipeline at a time, because you don't know what's going to happen, how long each sales process is going to take with each one, when something's going to pop—you just want to keep the numbers going. And that only helps you, because it's much harder to be attached to the outcome if you've got 40 things in the pipeline than if you've got just one. If you've got one, you really want that to come through. You've really got to have that contract, you really want to work with them. But if you've got 40 things you're pursuing, you don't have time to be attached to any of them.

[Jeremy] And you know what else? I really believe people can smell that.

[Suzi] There's like a desperation—it's kind of like dating.

[Deb] That's exactly what it sounds like. . . .

[Suzi] It's all in your attitude. If you don't need them, you're going to be much more attractive.

[Len] I wonder, Suzi, have you ever experienced the impact of a person saying that you are like a pushy salesperson, someone who rubs them the wrong way?

[Suzi] No, I've never had that. And if I did, I would be mortally wounded.

[Len] You would?

[Suzi] I would, because I hate that concept of a pushy salesperson. I don't think of myself that way. And if I get to the point where I start to think I'm being pushy, I have that conversation with them. I say, "I think I've left you six messages in the past week, and I really don't want to be pushy. So if I'm being pushy, just leave me a message and let me know to back off, and I will. But I really think we have something to talk about. I'm just calling to set up a meeting."

[Len] Okay.

[Suzi] I come from a very genuine and sincere place. Yes, I want a meeting, but I don't want it at all costs. And if I've got 40 things going in the pipeline, yes, I'm going to be persistent, but I don't need to make a pain of myself, because that's not going to help them or me. And if I get any read from a potential client, I talk to them about it. "I really don't want to be pushy. . . . Are you starting to feel like I'm being pushy here?" Most of the time they'll say no, but if they do say I'm being pushy, I'll say, "Okay, let me know what's a better way to work with you on this. Should we set up a meeting a month from now, should I call you two months from now?"

[Len] So there's always a meeting.

[Suzi] There's always a meeting, because I really value the face time.

[Jeremy] The end of the story you're always going to end up with a meeting.

[Suzi] Right. That's always the goal.

[Deb] In terms of that desperation feeling, is there a way not to come across that the meeting isn't so desperately needed?

[Suzi] Well, I won't sound desperate for a meeting, because I don't *feel* desperate for a meeting. I just truly believe, whoever I'm talking to, there's a reason we should get together. I might not know what it is yet, but I know that if I meet with anybody in the world, and talk to them enough, I'm going to find some connection. Either I know a book that they need to read, or they could use my services, or I know someone else who's even better for them. Or let's say they're looking to hire someone, and I know someone who's looking for a job in that arena. I know, if we talk long enough, I'm going to find some connection, I'm going to find some way to help them or work with them, or maybe they have a referral for me, or maybe I have a referral for them. And this comes down to part of what you're doing when you're in the client's meeting too: you're being a connection-seeker. That's what you're doing in the meeting. You're not looking to be a salesperson in the meeting.

[Deb] A connection-seeker.

[Suzi] You're looking to connect them up, you're looking to identify and assess their needs and to connect them up with something that meets their needs, whether or not it's your services. But part of what you're keeping in mind in the meeting is that you have something to offer, and you have something in mind that's going to create some results. That's going to have some value for them. Now it's just a matter of matching all that up. It's opportunistic matchmaking: do their needs and your offer, and the value of the results that can be produced, match up? If not, then what are their needs, and where is there some connection you can help them with?

[Bill] I think this is very true. I think one of my earliest and best referral sources was the head of an EAP whom I interviewed to get into. And she referred me to another EAP as well.

[Suzi] Isn't that great?

[Bill] I contributed something totally non-professional, but I contributed something.

[Jeremy] That's a great point, Bill. I think that's always been my approach to any referral source. Not even to look for the referral, just to look at the person and find out who they are and what their needs are. It might be completely personal between us. Nothing might happen from that. If you don't get attached to that, then you have a relationship with that person, and a lot of things can happen.

[Suzi] I have a colleague who tells a great story to illustrate this. He and his wife have four kids, and in a meeting with a CEO prospect of his, he discovered the CEO needed a babysitter. And this guy, with his four kids, knew a lot of babysitters. So he ended up connecting the CEO with one of their babysitters. Four years later, the CEO ended up calling to give him work as a coach. Four years later! Because he remembered that he had connected him up with a babysitter when he needed one.

[Jeremy] It helps them come back to you when you're out there making the calls. That puts you out there in front of them when you're making the calls, and it's a reminder, because people will forget. But if you're always out there reminding them, you leverage what you've done before.

In the Meeting

[Suzi] So moving on, let's assume you've handled all the objections, you've set up your meetings, you've gotten your appointments. What do you do? You're in a meeting with a client now, what do you do?

[Jeremy] I think what you do first is prepare for a meeting with a client.

[Suzi] Yes, of course.

[Jeremy] To me that's a big deal.

[Suzi] Let's talk about that. . . . How do you prepare? What do you do to prepare for a meeting?

[Jeremy] One of the things I do is try to find out as much information as I can about that person and their company, and really spend a lot of time doing my homework. And the more detailed information, and the more different sources I consult, and the more stuff I get, the better. So I want to come across to that person, when I get there, as somebody who's really done their homework and really knows stuff about them that might even surprise them: Stuff about their company, in terms of their needs, what they've done, in terms of my sources.

[John] What sort of sources do you access?

[Jeremy] It could be people who I know who are colleagues, who have worked there, or if I know people who currently work there. It's a lot of phone calls. I'll spend hours doing that stuff, for one meeting, to be really well prepared.

[Suzi] And to give you another alternative, I don't do that. Because I can spend hours doing that stuff, researching, and that's not billable time. I can overwhelm myself with information, and I stress myself out when I do. So my slogan is: **"Be prepared enough to wing it."** I want to do a little bit of research: I probably go to their website, I get a feel for their company, I get a feel for the person I'm going to be talking to. I take a few notes, and I may use that information to create the questions that I'm going to ask, and then I file that away. Then I guide the client meeting the same way I guide a coaching conversation, with questions. So my preparation is to design the questions I'm going to ask.

[Deb] And how do you design the questions you're going to ask?

[Suzi] Well, it depends on what I want to know. And it depends on what I already think I know, because a lot of the questions are about checking out assumptions. And then, just like Stephen Covey says, you start with the end in mind: "Okay, where do I want this meeting to end up?" Well, at the end of this meeting, I either want them to know there's an opportunity for me to do work, or that there's some other connection that we have. I ask myself, "So what questions do I need to ask this person to get there?" Chances are I want to know more about what they do. I want to know not only about their company from their perspective, but I want to know about their job from their perspective. I want to know: What are their challenges? How did they come to be here? How did they get here? You find out really interesting things when you ask that question.

[Len] How's this for an example? In a couple of days I've got the guy who's the lead salesperson for a major financial services firm . . . how do I prepare for this kind of meeting?

[Suzi] What do you want to accomplish?

[Len] Well, I want him to think about me when he thinks "coach." He's got other people.

[John] Be unique.

[Len] Well, how I positioned myself is with other coaches present. I positioned myself against the other coaches present, making sure I stood out. I have an impact, and I'm an impactful person, that's how I see myself as being.

[Suzi] The real chess match strategy of the client meeting is less about positioning yourself, and more about listening to them.

[Len] That I can do on the fly.

[Suzi]Yes, you can. And there's something really powerful that happens when you design your questions ahead of time. You might not even use the questions that you've designed ahead of time, but just the process of thinking through the chess match of the client meeting and designing your questions ahead of time helps prepare you. In other words you envision a series of moves: I want to ask this question, and depending on how they answer, I either want to ask this next question or this other question. And depending on how they answer that, I want to take this route and ask this series of questions, or I want to back up and ask this follow-up question.

So thinking through that chess match prepares you in a different way from being in the meeting and really being present and coming up with questions, which is what you'll do anyway, because that's who we are as coaches. We get in, we get present, and we ask the questions that are there to ask in the moment, based on intuition or signs we're reading, or whatever. But the process of thinking through "What do I want to ask? What do I want to find out? Where do I want to go? Where do I want to lead this meeting?" gives you access to deeper listening. Because the moment you stop leading the meeting is the moment you start wasting your own time.

[Deb] Say that again.

[Suzi] The moment you stop leading the meeting is the moment you start wasting your own time. And *how* you're leading the meeting is by letting them talk.

[Jeremy] I agree. The idea of having designed questions is like having a script, which you can then improvise from. But having the designed questions gives you the structure to give yourself the confidence to lead the meeting and to go where you want to go with a client. It doesn't mean you don't listen 80 percent of the time.

[Suzi] Right, you must listen at least 80 percent of the time. And having the right questions will allow you to do that. There's another thing to prepare, too, and this I would actually spend a lot of time preparing initially. You want to prepare stories and anecdotes that demonstrate accomplishments and skills that you have. Eventually you'll have these in your back pocket; you won't need to spend a lot of time preparing them.

You want to own these stories—you want to practice these stories as if you were standing up on stage telling them to people. You want to practice telling them in a natural way. You want to have a beginning, a middle, and an end to your story. You want it to make a point, you want it to be concise, you want it to demonstrate something tangible about you, because what happens is rather than positioning yourself as a uniquely separate coach from the other coaches who are present—rather than saying, "The benefits of working with me are X, Y, and Z," or "The unique things that I offer are X, Y, and Z"—you can tell stories. And those stories demonstrate what those benefits and unique contributions are. Even having just one or two stories in your back pocket to pull out at relevant points in the conversation will give your prospect a clear view of you. He will be able to see relevance of your services to his scenario within your story.

[Deb] Can you give an example?

[Jeremy] Everybody in this class has client stories. Now they might not be a coaching or consulting or professional services client, but they have been some kind of client of yours. They've been a client of yours as a student, they've been a client of yours as a patient, they've been a client of yours as a colleague. We all have interesting stories that in our moment of fear we forget, and then we become inhibited. If we just unfreeze those stories and start to remember. . . . Some of them are funny stories, and some of them illustrate what you've done well or what you've helped uncover with a client. Just try to pull them out, and even write some of them out so that you can tell them easily.

[Suzi] You don't even need to write the whole story down, but just jot reminders to yourself.

[Jeremy] Whatever helps you remember.

[Suzi] So if you're going into a meeting with some specific topics in mind, you want stories to prove how your coaching was effective on those specific points. Let's say you know going in that the prospective company is interested in cost savings or retention issues; you want to come up with stories that demonstrate your effectiveness in helping other clients solve those particular problems. And the stories are something that you want to practice telling so that they actually have a beginning, a middle, and an end, and you're proving something. Because what happens when people listen to your anecdotes is they see themselves in them, and rather than your saying, "Here's what I can do for you," your story allows them to make that leap and participate with you in a different way. They start to see, "Oh, he or she did that for these people and that's exactly what I need. I can see what he or she can do for me."

[Jeremy] It's interesting, Suzi, because it's the same advice that writing teachers have given to writers for centuries—maybe not centuries—for decades: Don't just tell the story, show it.

[Suzi] Exactly. Your chess match in the actual meeting is not only planning two steps ahead what's the next question to ask while still listening—I mean you still have to really be present and listen. It's also about figuring out, "I really want to use this story in this meeting. When is the appropriate time to throw it in?"

[Jeremy] Yeah, you've got to get to the storytelling part.

[Len] I'm thinking this is like hypnosis and suggestion in a way. Because if I go in and tell a story about how once I was coaching somebody and suddenly that company wanted a whole bunch of extra services from me that I didn't originally go in for, I don't even have to allude to the fact that that's exactly what they're trying to do.

[Suzi] Right.

[Len] So if they want to use coaching to get job placement contracts, and if I tell a story about going in and providing one service, and then they wanted me to provide other services, it can be imputed, or it could be inferred, that this guy knows how to shake loose the money.

[Jeremy] Yeah, exactly.

[Deb] And that you also understand what they need.

[Suzi] Right, you definitely want your stories to be relevant. There's nothing worse than telling a story that's not relevant, because then they're looking at you with this funny look on their face.

[Jeremy] "Who is this guy?"

[Suzi] That's why the stories take planning, just like the questions take planning. And there's so much that you're focusing on in the meeting. First of all, you're leading the meeting. Second, you're thinking about the chess moves two moves away. Third, you're thinking about what questions you want to ask. You're really focusing and being present and listening to the person and what their needs are and what they're not telling you. So you've got all that going on. If you have your questions and stories planned ahead of time, it's much, much easier, because then you don't have to think about them. If you take the time to think about them in the meeting, chances are you're missing half of what the client's telling you.

[Deb] I have a meeting Friday with a company that's using me a lot right now to do some team building. They called me again to help them do some facilitation—they're having some problems with one of their managers—and I would really like to get into the position of coaching the plant manager. So I have a meeting with him on Friday to talk about some of his engineers who don't trust his manager. They already have trust exercises and things like that that one of their HR people came out to do, and so we're going to sit down and look at a survey they have to fill out. This guy's constantly telling me inside information, but I'd really like to get in a position where I'm just coaching him on this, because I think the manager he's having problems with really needs some management training and leadership assessment. I don't really know how to position myself in the meeting on Friday. Maybe it's just to help him with this tool or something. . . .

[Jeremy] What if you thought about your practice, and other areas you've worked in business, and were able to come up with a story about helping a guy like him? Would that break something? You know there's nothing like being able to tell somebody that you've worked through an experience like this with somebody else and something got created out of it—that's really powerful.

[Suzi] Jeremy's right on target. If you can, think of a story that's going to paint the picture for him. Rather than just saying, "I can do this for you," it's a different way of showing your experience.

[Jeremy] That way it's not like you're boasting—the story gives you credibility.

[Deb] Right, and I think that's where I went wrong with him before. I was going to help with their redesigns for the plant, but he wanted an HR consultant to do more of it. He's a guy who sort of has specific ideas about what the situation is. I think he just needs a lot of education on how I could provide him that value. So you're recommending just a story. . . .

[Suzi] Deb, this goes back to the 80/20 rule. If he has all these ideas in his head, and you actually draw all those ideas out of him and write them on a flip chart so that he can see them, he's going to think you are brilliant. And all you have to do is simply show him his ideas. I'm serious.

So I think your tack with him might be something like this: I would definitely keep your talking to a minimum, and in your talking, if you can share one or two stories that will help him make that connection, you're going to be golden. But by designing the questions ahead of time that are going to draw his ideas out, asking the questions, and then showing him his ideas, you become his partner.

[Len] Suzi, given the information that you have right now, how would you go about designing those questions? What would those questions be?

[Suzi] I would ask him what he wants to do. I would start as open-ended as that: "So what is it that you think you want to do?" Or I might even start with the partnership language: "What are we going to do? What are we going to do about the situation?" And I'd actually get out the flip chart, ask follow-up questions to each of the things that he says, and start pulling the ideas out of him. "How would we do that? And what result would we get if we did that? And how would we know if we got that result? And what are the criteria that we'd be looking for to let us know that we got that result? How long would it take us to get that result?"

[Len] If I'm picturing this correctly, Deb would have a tablet with big sheets of paper, and she would ask, "What do you want done here?" And he says, "Well, I want to coordinate my teams, and I want to get them responding appropriately." And she would write down on this chart "Having the teams respond appropriately."

[Suzi] Well, I'd use all of his words. First I'd write "Coordinate teams," and then I'd add, "Have them respond appropriately." You're taking his ideas, and you're just putting them on a flip chart to show him. These are his ideas. However, he thinks you've done it, because it's in your handwriting.

[Len] And would you follow up with, "How would you go about doing that?"

[Suzi] Or "How would we know when we got there? What would be different? What would look different about your teams if they were doing that?"

[Len] So that would be like a way to measure it?

[Suzi] Yeah. "What would it look like? And what would the value of that be for the company?" Or you might ask, and this is a good way to get more information, "How does it work now? How's it working now, and what's wrong with how it's working now that you want to fix?"

[Deb] I like that idea! He might think I'm wacky, but I like that idea because we can go into his conference room and I can say to him, "Let's get a little more structured about it, and I'll write down your ideas so that we can look at them." I also like what you're saying about using "we," because then I'm partnering with him, rather than saying, "What do you want? What are you looking at? and How can I do this?" So I like the joining. . . .

[Suzi] Now, at the end of that meeting, Deb, you have to be very strategic about whether you leave those notes with him, or whether you take them with you. It all depends. If you can create an opportunity for some follow up that requires you to take the notes, by all means do it. Otherwise you've got to leave them with him, because they're his notes.

[Deb] That's easy because he wants me to continue to facilitate the rest of the people doing their thing. So, and I've done this before with him, I tell him I will type up the notes and then e-mail them to him.

[Suzi] Perfect. So then you've got the notes, and you've got content for proposals for later. I mean the whole flip chart is a really valuable thing.

[Deb] And I like that because what it does is it has both of you looking at the same thing together.

[Suzi] Exactly. And you can also clarify. Using the flip chart removes doubt and assumptions from the conversation, because you're writing it in his words, and you can ask about what you don't understand. Or if he sees it in his words and meant something else, he can clarify at that moment.

[John] And it's important to use his words, even if they're awkward. Write the awkward words.

[Len] Then he would also have an opportunity to modify it if he wants to, and then you can rewrite the modification that he says.

[Suzi] Or if you think you know what he means, and it was awkward, ask him before you write it. "Do you mean this? I'm not quite sure how to capture what you just said."

[Deb] Yeah, I'm good at that. Sometimes what I'll do is I'll write down what he says, and ask, "This is what you're saying?" And then he says no and I can cross it off or whatever. So that part's easy. . . .

Elements of Successful Client Meetings

[Suzi] This would be a good time to overview the six elements of a successful client meeting. I'll break these down for you a little further, but here's the list:

Six Elements of
Client Meeting Success

1. Rapport building

2. Trust building

3. Asking pre-designed questions

4. Listening (follow the 80/20 rule)

5. Storytelling

6. Getting the second meeting

Rapport building, number 1 on the list, is about how you open the dialogue. You want to establish peer status, and by that I mean you're an equal of this person—you're not a subordinate coming in to grovel for the opportunity to deal with him or her. And you're not coming in as better than him or her. You're coming in right at the same level. It's also an opportunity to find connections. And it's an opportunity to get the client talking about themselves. You're trying to build rapport, so I would steer clear of some of the things that people do when they meet someone for the first time and they're in their office. The tendency is to try to connect with them and build rapport based on pictures they have in their office.

[Jeremy] Yeah, to use as simple ice-breakers.

[Suzi] Don't do that. In fact, a colleague of mine tells a wonderful story about how she got trapped doing this early in her career.

She walked into someone's office, and there was a giant stuffed marlin hanging on the wall behind the desk. And so, of course, she starts commenting on the marlin. "Oh my gosh, are you a fisherman? That's really a cool thing, I love to fish. Did you catch that yourself?" The prospective client just starts laughing. Then he looks her straight in the eye and says, "Nope, that's just there for salespeople like you to ask me about." So you want to be very careful about trying to reach out to people like that.

Now, number 2: Building trust is where you're confirming your competence, modeling your integrity, and demonstrating some of your basic mindsets. A lot of rapport building and trust building happens in your 30-second commercial. And I definitely recommend you start off the meeting with that, especially if you're meeting the person for the first time. "Let me tell you a little bit about myself. . . ."

[Deb] Can you talk a little bit more about building trust?

[Suzi] When you're demonstrating your competence, you're building trust. . . .

[Deb] So confirming credibility. . . .

[Suzi] Demonstrating competence and modeling your integrity helps with this—also storytelling. It's not like you're doing the six elements in 1-2-3-4-5-6 order. I have listed them here in a linear fashion, but it's an organic process—you're weaving all these things into the meeting.

[Deb] So demonstrating competence would be something like we talked about earlier, in terms of starting the meeting like you would a coaching process. I mean, you basically start in right away.

[Suzi] Sure. You give them a little taste of it. So the third element is questioning. You're finding out as much as you can about what they do and how they do it, asking them questions about the past, about what's currently going on, and about what they want for the future. You are looking for ways you can be helpful to this person. Asking questions is the way you find out what their needs are. This is where you find connections to how you can help them. And all the while you're keeping open to what's possible—exploring what's possible.

[Deb] So the questions are about the past and what they want from the future. . . .

[Suzi] And what the current situation is.

[Jeremy] You want to get with their hopes and dreams also, I think.

[Suzi] Oh, yeah.

[John] That's where I always want to be.

[Deb] And what wakes them up at night.

[Jeremy] Well, yeah, that's the fear part. But you mainly want to get to what they're looking for, in terms of a win for themselves and their company. That's such a great question.

[Suzi] Yeah, what's their ideal? Now, the fourth element of a successful client meeting is listening, and so you want to predict and prepare for what might be your obstacles to listening, especially if you're the kind of person who sort of checks out at that question about ideals. Have all your questions written out beforehand so that you can listen fully. When you're listening, you should be engaged in the following actions: confirming what they're saying, clarifying what they're saying, and taking notes on what they're saying.

[Len] You'd be writing down notes?

[Suzi] You can be writing notes, yeah. You can be asking follow-up questions. And you also want to plan what to listen for so that you know what to pay attention to.

[Deb] How do you do that then?

[Suzi] That's part of designing your questions; it depends on the purpose of your meeting. Are you listening for an opportunity for a second meeting, are you listening for who the decision makers are, are you listening for what the coaching or training needs are in the organization, are you listening for the current hot issues of the day in the organization? Are you listening for the problem you can help them solve?

[Jeremy] And that's not different from developing any kind of relationship. For example, one thing I always listen for is a chance to tell my stories, because I know by the time I have told my stories, I should have some sort of a relationship with that person. And then they're going to be asking for the second meeting, not me. I mean, if possible, I want them to ask for the next meeting. That's much more powerful.

[Suzi] Exactly. That leads us to the fifth element: storytelling. So you want to plan ahead. What types of stories do you want to tell, and when do you want to use the stories to move the conversation forward? You want to develop powerful and relevant stories, and know when to tell them for greatest effect.

And then the last element of a successful first meeting is getting to the second meeting. So you're looking for reasons to get back together. You may actually have to request what you want. You either have to ask for the business, ask for another meeting, ask for the opportunity to submit another proposal, ask for an opportunity to meet the members of the Board, or whatever's next—you want to ask for it.

[Jeremy] That is, by the way, a famous cliché in selling. What is it, Suzi, 65 percent of salespeople don't make a sale because they never directly ask the person for the business?

[Suzi] That's right, you have to ask. In fact, this comes back to what you did when you were setting up the meeting in the first place. Whip out your calendar or turn on your Palm Pilot or whatever you use, and say, "You know what? I think we should get back together to talk about this in a month and I can bring you the proposal at that time," or whatever the next steps are. Schedule that right at the end of the meeting. Don't leave the meeting without doing that because then you have to go through calling them again.

[Jeremy] I don't like to go that far out if I don't have to. I mean my ideal is to make a proposal then and there. I say, "I would love to send you a proposal, I would really like to work with you," and just tell them how excited I am to be working with them.

[Suzi] Also, a great thing you can do in that meeting is have them help you design the proposal. I've actually said to prospects, "What would be useful for you to see in the proposal I'm going to submit to you? What do you need in this proposal?" Most of the time they have someone else they have to take the proposal to—they have to take it to the Board, show it to the executive committee, or convince their colleagues, or whatever. So really you're saying, "Well, what do we . . ."—again I'm back in the "we" mode—"want to put in this proposal so that we can effectively communicate it to the Board? What do they need to see? What are they going to ask you? What do you want me to make sure I cover in here for you?"

In one sense, you're already helping them. And then the best thing for you is when they say, "Here's what you should put in the proposal: You should have a purpose, you should have this, you should give us these things." You know, they'll tell you exactly what they want to see. They'll write the proposal for you, basically, and then you just go put the content in.

[Jeremy] I like that, but I like also that I can lead with a proposal and then I can stand a modification. I think a lot of clients like it when you can whip out a proposal and show that you're ready for them. That's very assertive; it tells them that you're ready to do business with them. And they can modify the proposal, I don't care—I've already put it together and I just want them to sign it.

[Suzi] Do you do that in your first meeting?

[Jeremy] Yeah, I'll do that right away.

[Deb] What is it you do again?

[Jeremy] I'll go and send them the proposal right away, based on the first meeting.

[John] You have the meeting, you leave the office, you go back home, you write the proposal, and you send it in the next day?

[Jeremy] That's right. I turn it around right away. It's my way of showing them I really listen to them, I'm serious about it, I'm ready to start, this is the kind of service they can expect from me. I'll turn something around right away, and they know this is how it's going to be. They want something, I will give it to them. Right away, very timely.

[Suzi] I think whether you do it Jeremy's way or not really depends on what your client situation is, what their corporate culture is, and what their needs are.

[Jeremy] Yeah. I mean they might have to bat it around for six months, but I'm showing them in that moment I'm ready to go.

[Suzi] And the other thing I can tell you, too, from my work with a lot of attorneys and law firms, is that if you turn something around that fast, sometimes they don't value it, because they assume that you've prewritten it, and that you're not giving them something that's based on what they said to you. In fact, the attorneys actually expect lots of pages, so they expect it to take you time to write it.

[Deb] But that's what they do. It's matching the culture really.

[Suzi] Exactly, it's knowing your audience—knowing who you're working with—and if they're going to be inspired by a quick turn around, absolutely, get it to them right away.

Homework

Create strategic questions for the client meeting. Use the Elements of Successful Client Meetings on page 174 as a guide. Think about your success stories for your business and how you might work those into a sales meeting.

Keeping Your Focus in a Client Meeting (Keep Your Head in the Game)

Three Keys to Client Meeting Success

1. Establish peer status and credibility.

2. Interview your future client, using strategically designed questions.

3. Explore the value proposition.

There are three key guidelines to keeping your focus in a meeting with a client—I prefer to call them *client meetings* instead of sales meetings, because one powerful mindset is to act as if your prospects are already clients. First you want to establish peer status and credibility. Then you want to interview your future client, using strategically designed questions that you have already prepared. Then you want to explore the value proposition with them.

Take the lead at the outset, and lay out an agenda with possible outcomes so that both you and the client can engage in the conversation free of the what-ifs that can distract your focus. Give up any attachment to sealing the deal or getting the sale so that you are free to unhook yourself from the conversation and end it if the client is not willing or ready to walk through the process with you. Also, if at any point you become certain that you are not the right fit, be willing and able to say so and propose alternate means of supporting the client to address his organization's needs.

Establish peer status and credibility through your 30-second commercial and by taking a leadership posture for the meeting. Mentally place yourself as an equal to whomever you are meeting with. You are, after all, the CEO of your operation, and if you are a solopreneur, you are also the CFO, the CIO, the COO, the CAO, and the head of HR all in one. No matter who in the organization you are addressing, you can genuinely be their peer.

The client meeting is a chess match, and the interview format allows you to focus on the game and listen for the opportunities that might arise two to three moves away. If you have prepared your interview questions ahead of time, you will have a map to follow as you lead the conversation. (At the end of this chapter, there is an example of the questionnaire I use in initial client meetings.)

The value proposition involves asking questions to have the client clarify for themselves and for you what outcome or result they are hoping to achieve by working with you, and what impact that could have on the organization. Typically they talk about some kind of cost saving measure or talent management solution (succession planning or retention). You then explore with them what dollar value that would represent to the organization, and how much they would be willing to spend to get that result. In other words, you ask: what is that outcome worth to them or to the organization? Typically this number is fairly high—several hundred thousand dollars, perhaps. So, if that's the case, isn't it worth it to them to spend X percent of that amount on your fees to help them achieve that result?

The client meeting is about opportunistic matchmaking based on three things: assessed needs, your offer, and the value of the results as measured by the client organization. In a client meeting, you will need to be a connection-seeker, listening for opportunities to demonstrate your credibility, establish peer status, and share your experience and expertise through strategic storytelling. As in your prospecting calls, where the goal was to get the first meeting scheduled, the ultimate goal of the client meeting is to get to the second meeting—or whatever might be the next step in your sales process.

Listening in the Client Meeting

Apply the 80/20 rule—where you are listening 80 percent of the time and talking only 20 percent of the time. To do that, you need to focus on the questions you will be asking to lead the conversation. Lead a discussion that is relevant to the needs of the client and the organization so that you can quickly assess what the business is going through and where help is warranted. Don't be afraid to make bold comments, share your observations, or ask bold questions. This will allow you to stand out, particularly if you hit the mark. You will be remembered for your skill in quickly analyzing the problem, and if you can also demonstrate your credibility by suggesting solutions as well as sharing anecdotes of how you helped others overcome similar scenarios, you will be well on your way to moving the sales process forward.

One key listening skill is to be genuinely, authentically interested in the other person. It is far more powerful to be interest*ed* than interest*ing*. When you are truly interested in the person you're listening to, they know it and want to continue the conversation. Then if you can effectively make the link between what they want or need and what you have to offer, that's enrollment at its best—no gimmicks, no manipulation, no tricks, no techniques . . . just great selling skills.

Strategic Storytelling

A good tale can deliver your entire message, so spend careful time preparing your stories. That way, they will be ready and available to you when you hear opportunities in the client conversation to work them in. Stories make information meaningful by creating an emotional context around the facts and information. Attorneys do this all the time at trial. You've all seen trial scenarios where regardless of the defendant's innocence or guilt, the attorney with the most convincing story wins the case. Stories hook us in and allow us to see ourselves as part of them. You want your clients to see themselves in your stories, particularly as you craft them in a way that demonstrates your previous wins, your capacity for results, and your skill in your profession.

Paint a word picture that shows what you can do or have done, rather than just listing your accomplishments or competencies. Your success stories about how you have helped clients achieve specific goals are valuable tools in your sales process. Your stories will establish credibility, prove your effectiveness, and allow your client to make the analogy between your tale and how it might apply to their situation. If you have partners or colleagues who work with you to deliver services, think of how you can share their success stories as well. In some cases, you can demonstrate a point about how coaching can be a strategic solution to the client's need by sharing a colleague's story about how she used coaching to effectuate change with a client organization. Even though it isn't your success story, it can work to educate a client about the potential uses and applications of your services.

Be sure that your stories are aligned with and relevant to the client's needs. Don't fall into the trap of telling stories just to brag or drop names, because it will be taken as unnecessary posturing and could work against you. Connect the dots for your client—share stories that link to or build upon information you have gleaned from listening to the client share his current needs.

Don't be shy about sharing your observations about what you hear your client saying about the company. If you foresee how the current scenario could unfold based on previous clients in similar situations, share stories that your client can see himself in and show that you provide the service he needs to handle his situation. Take care of your client, too: Respect his time, value his position in his political landscape, and be his ally in collaboratively designing next steps. How can you support him in proposing these solutions to the Board or to his boss? There are often other decision makers who need to be involved. Do you know who they are? Can they be invited into the conversation? Maybe it would make sense to come back next week to meet with all of them.

Brainstorm your stories ahead of time. Make a list of clients with whom you've had brag-able results. Who was the client? What *specifically* was that client trying to achieve? How did you help them do that? What was the result? What problems did you help solve? What are some wins that you can brag about? For which clients have you exceeded expectations or in some way especially delighted them? If you do not already have a habit of collecting testimonial letters or written, quotable accolades from clients whose expectations you exceeded, please begin to do so immediately! It's as simple as asking clients to write you a letter or put their thoughts into an e-mail.

Often, the best time to capture these things is right when they say it . . . just ask, "Can I quote you on that?" and then put it into writing and have them sign off on it.

Your past successes are a great source of stories. Fine-tune them into quick anecdotal examples you can easily weave into the conversation during client meetings. Practice these conversations so that you know the purpose of the story and so that you don't saddle the story with too much detail.

Getting a Second Meeting

Based on the client's responses to your interview questions, where is your opening to return for a second meeting? Several reasons to come back include bringing a partner or colleague to meet with them, bringing in partners or colleagues to do a presentation or demonstration, meeting some-one else or other decision makers in the client company, or presenting a proposal or co-designing a proposal with the client to support him or her in presenting you to the boss. The trick is to hear the opportunity and store it away so that you can return to it at the right moment in your meeting. We often jump on the opportunity too soon—we take the bait and start steering the conversation into the domain of action ("Sure, I'll write a proposal") before we've fleshed out a clear strategic direction for that action and others. Know when to integrate the opportunity into the meeting in a way that keeps you in the driver's seat. If you are leading the meeting, you can keep it consistently unfolding along the path of your sales process.

Let the client know you have heard them. Be sure that you design your interview questions to elicit information that will allow you to quickly grasp the client's situation, issues, problems, struggles, goals, or vision for what they want to accomplish. Demonstrate your credibility in ways that are relevant to their particular circumstance.

Partner with clients as their guide and support to co-design several options that align with their needs, and make bold suggestions about how and where you might help. Explore for yourself some conversational and natural ways to subtly suggest that you meet again to continue the conversation in a way that makes sense to everybody, and then open your calendar and suggest a specific date and time. Be a helper, a problem-solver, a partner in collaboration with your client, rather than a salesperson.

Checklist:
Elements of Successful Client Meetings

I. Rapport building (beyond the handshake and eye contact)
   A. Opening the dialog
   B. Establishing peerage: conducting yourself as a person of equal status
   C. Seeking and finding connections
   D. Getting the client talking about themself
   E. Communicating expectations
   F. Confirming the agenda for the meeting

II. Building trust
   A. Confirming your credibility
   B. Demonstrating your competence
   C. Modeling your integrity
   D. Operating from essential mindsets
   E. Leading the conversation by explaining how the meeting could go and what actions might come of it
   F. Seeking collaboration and agreement from the client

III. Questioning
   A. Finding out as much as you can about what they do and how they do it
   B. Integrating past-, present-, and future-based questions
   C. Seeking how you can be helpful to this person
   D. Exploring what's possible

(continued)

Checklist:
Elements of Successful Client Meetings *(concluded)*

IV. Listening

    A. Overcoming obstacles to listening

    B. Confirming, clarifying, taking notes

    C. Knowing what to listen for

        1. Listening for various opportunities

          • to make connections

          • to tell stories

          • to seek information

          • to suggest next steps

          • to come back

V. Storytelling

    A. Using stories and knowing their purpose

    B. Analyzing what kinds of stories to tell

    C. Assessing when to use stories to escalate the sale

    D. Understanding how to develop powerful, relevant stories

VI. Getting to the second meeting

    A. Articulating reasons to come back

    B. Requesting the meeting and scheduling the meeting

    C. Escalating the sale

    D. Designing presentation and proposal

Sample:
Client Meeting Interview Questions

I use this form to guide my initial consultation with new coaching clients. It is not meant to be used as a questionnaire that they fill out. In fact, the client does not see this form. Its purpose is to help me recall questions to shape the project and scope of work. I consult this list to prepare for my first meeting with a new client so that all my attention is then directed at listening— listening to their responses, to their issues, to the opportunities, to the layers beneath what they are saying.

Client (or prospect) name:
Title:
Company:
Date and time of initial meeting:

What is your vision for your company?

Describe your company. What does it do?
What is the mission? What are the core values?
Any recent organizational accomplishments?
Current organizational problems or concerns?
What's it like to work here?

Describe your industry. How would you define the culture? Demographics?

Describe your job. What do you do? What is your personal mission? What are your core values? How many direct reports?
What are the toughest issues you currently face in your work?
Are these common to the organization or unique to you?

What are your areas of greatest confidence/strength?
In what areas would you want to increase focus?
What are your expectations, interests, wants, concerns?

What is your vision for your career?
What are your major commitments/specific projects? By when?
What are the obstacles or roadblocks to achieving those commitments?
What do you really want?

(continued)

Sample:
Client Meeting Interview Questions *(concluded)*

Value: What will you have to have gotten at the end of X months to know that your money was well spent/invested?

Why do you want a coach?

What are you hoping I can do for you?

What coaching style suits you best?

Determine: What we'll focus on, structure, payment preference (pre-purchase or billing), homework, purpose, objectives. Protocol for billing your company/getting paid?

How can I best serve you?

Calendar: How long are we initially going to work together? How frequently should we talk by phone? For what duration? How often should we meet in person?

What particular skill(s) do you want to focus on for your personal growth and development?

What do you want to do that you currently avoid doing?

How will you measure your results in this coaching arrangement? In other words, how will you know if you learned anything/created what you wanted after this coaching period?

What are your goals for leadership coaching? What specific outcomes are you striving for in this partnership?

Checklist:
Client Meeting Reminders

Just keep in mind when you are in client meetings:

- Frame your intention for yourself and the client.

- Set context.

- Establish peer status to create trust and rapport.

- State your intended outcome.

- Listen for and handle their objections.

- Align for value/clarify the value proposition.

- Ask for the business.

Step 6
Following Up
and
Tracking

"Success is to be measured not so much by the position that one has reached in life as by the obstacles which he has overcome."
—Booker T. Washington

"Man is condemned to be free; because once thrown into the world, he is responsible for everything he does."
—Jean-Paul Sartre

We've all heard the saying that "what gets measured is what gets done." Well, the same is true for your business development. It is important to create a methodology and a system that works for you, with your particular likes and quirks and style issues so that you can follow your own progress and track people who are in your sales cycle. This chapter is all about how to follow up and keep track of what you're doing because, to paraphrase Jean-Paul Sartre, once thrown into this world, you are responsible for everything you do.

Telecourse Session #6: Follow Up

[Suzi] Last time we spent lots of time talking about elements of a successful client meeting, what you do when you're in the client meetings, and how it's a chess match. You're trying to think two steps ahead, but you want to come prepared with not only the stories that you're going to weave into the conversation, but your questions, so that you can really focus on listening in the meetings. And we talked about how important follow up is, because the sales cycle is a numbers game, and you want to have lots and lots of possibilities in the pipeline so that you can relieve yourself of any attachment to making one of those possibilities come to fruition.

The topic today is follow up. What I'd like to do today is to explore what follow-up approaches you have found that work for you and also what you've tried that hasn't worked. Then we'll coach each other and have an open forum on how to make follow up more effective. We'll just talk about it. Because, really, there's no one right way to do follow up. It varies as much as personality styles and work ethic. What matters most is what you're comfortable doing.

[Jeremy] Suzi, before we do the follow up, I just want to tell one little coaching story that's an example of getting the appointment, and also relates to a follow-up question I have. Yesterday I met with the managing director of a large HR company. We've been playing telephone tag for the past three weeks, and he's been dutifully returning my phone calls, even though he's never met me, and I've never met him. He has a very nice assistant who I've been talking to on the phone. So finally—after really listening to Suzi say, "Get the appointment, get the appointment, get the appointment"—I just said to the assistant, "Look, it's established that he wants to talk to me and I want to talk to him. . . . Why don't we just set up a time, and if it's not good for him, you can let me know, but here's a time I could meet with him. . . ." And so she did that.

[Suzi] The end?

[Jeremy] I got the appointment, and I met with him yesterday. We didn't have to keep circling and circling around, and the meeting went fairly well. But my point was, by closing on the appointment, I was able to get to that next step.

[Suzi] Yay! Good job!

[Jeremy] So sometimes we don't even have to speak to the person to get the appointment.

[Suzi] Right. I have a story about that, too. There's something about people not returning calls to me lately. I don't know what's going on, but these are clients I've already worked with. So I've been meaning to meet with two different people in a client corporation, and I've been calling them and e-mailing them for, I'd say, three weeks. And they're not only *not* returning my calls, but *not* returning my e-mails—they've just been completely out of communication. So I decided, "Forget this, I'm just going to go through their secretaries," and I e-mailed their secretaries, and the very next day had a meeting scheduled with them. So my point underscores yours, Jeremy: When you can work their system, it can work to your benefit.

Working Strategies for Follow Up

[Suzi] Moving into following up, we spent a lot of time on the last call talking about making calls and getting the appointment. Follow up is part of that, especially if you're having to leave messages for people. In addition, there's follow up at different stages. There's follow up in terms of getting the first appointment. Then there's follow up if you've already had the first appointment—you're following up to get the work. So what have you found to work, in terms of following up, when you've had to leave messages for people, when they call back, and also when they don't call back? For example, suppose you've been making calls to set up appointments. What's your follow-up success rate?

So let's just take it one step at a time. What strategies have you found that have worked for you in follow up in order to get appointments? Jeremy just shared one example, where he was persistent in calling the guy and the guy was calling him back, and then he finally called the assistant and set up a meeting. I'd say that was a follow up that worked. He said after three weeks, "Enough of phone tag, I'm going to end the phone tag and set up a meeting."

[Bill] I haven't been making that many calls, but I'd say I did two for two. I didn't leave a message, I just asked when the person would be there. I called back and I got appointments in both cases.

[Suzi] Great!

[Bill] I tend to follow up on Monday because I have to report something in our telecourse call on Tuesday. So last Monday, I called a guy from an outplacement agency to get together to have lunch, because this outplacement agency wants to use coaches to get into corporations. He said, "I'll call you in a couple of days and we'll have lunch." I waited until the end of the week, and he didn't call me. I was hating myself on Friday, and I still didn't call him. I finally called yesterday and the secretary wasn't in. I didn't leave a voice mail; instead I got his direct dial number from the routing system, and I got through to him. We talked, and he said, "You know, you should come in next Monday because I'm having a guy from the financial services company come over. You work with financial services people, so you've got to come in because we're talking to them about providing coaching." And I had called about lunch!

[Suzi] Well, you got right in! And there's also a follow-up tip in what you just said. This guy from the outplacement agency said he'd call you in a couple days to do lunch, and then he didn't call. Another strategy that might be useful for all of us with somebody who says, "I'll call you in a couple of days to do that," is for you to say, "You know what? I'm actually running around so much, it would be great if we could just schedule it now. How's Friday at noon?"

[Bill] I did something similar with another guy. This is my accountant who approached me six months ago to put together a package for consulting his clients, and I would be the business psychologist. I even created a brochure called Family Business Solutions. But he kept blowing off meetings, and I got disgusted. So I decided that I would call him and get an appointment. He said, "How about after May 1st?" and I said, "Fine, let's pick a date." He wiggled around a bit, but we made a date. We're going to meet on the 5:10 train to Greenwich, and we're going to talk on the train. I don't know what his resistance is, but I don't care.

[Suzi] You might open the conversation exploring that.

[Bill] Ask him, "What the hell's going on?"

[Suzi] Or, "Well, I kind of get the feeling that you're not really into this idea any more." You want to give him a back door out, because you don't want to pressure him.

Okay, what are some other strategies or follow-up stories to share? What have you all been doing in terms of calls—how's it been going?

[Len] I've made repeated calls to a brain injury center that has facilities around New Jersey that needs coaching for their staff. And I've made repeated calls to the person who's in charge of coordinating the services in the community, but I haven't gotten a return call. I know that she's interested in having me coach their staff, but she hasn't returned the call. So I don't know what to do . . . I must have left about five messages with her.

[Suzi] And you know she's interested in talking?

[Len] Correct.

[Suzi] And are you certain that she's getting your messages?

[Len] Not really, except I know she has a voice mail greeting that comes on, and it's identified as her, so . . .

[Suzi] Does she have e-mail?

[Len] If she does, I don't have the e-mail address.

[Suzi] Is there an assistant or somebody you could call to get the e-mail address?

[Len] That's what I'll have to do.

[Suzi] This is a really common scenario, Len. You leave messages, you leave messages, you leave messages, and nobody calls you back. Here's one strategy I've employed in that scenario: I just wait a few weeks and then call again, depending on how time-sensitive the thing is. I may just let them not hear from me for a few weeks, and then try again and say, "You know, I really don't want to be a pest. I know I've already left you lots of messages, but I was just calling to see if maybe your schedule has loosened up a bit and we can get together and talk?" Leave that kind of a message. And I might also leave a date—for example, "I'm going to be in your neighborhood, near your office, Tuesday at 3:00. Are you available?"

[Jeremy] Yeah, I've used that one.

[Suzi] Say this whether you're already going to be there or not, because if you get a meeting with them, you will be there, so it's not a lie. Another useful approach in a number of different situations is the apology call. The apology call is, "You know what? I don't know what I've done or what I've said, but I feel I need to apologize to you, and I'm not sure what for. But I must have offended you terribly because I haven't heard back from you."

[Deb] So it's the guilt call.

[Suzi] It's the apology call. "I'm so sorry—could you please just let me know that you've gotten this message and you understand that I'm trying to apologize to you, and could you let me know what I've done? I'd really like to apologize to you in person, and whatever it is, I'm so sorry."

[Deb] Does that work?

[Suzi] Oh, it's amazing. People who don't call you back for three months will call you back the same day and go, "No, I'm not mad at you." It's human nature: people don't want other people out there thinking that they're upset at them when they're not. So I've had people call back immediately and say, "Listen, I've been putting off calling you back because we don't know what we're doing yet." They call you and tell you the truth, rather than just not calling.

[Jeremy] Well another good thing about the apology call is that it models vulnerability. It sort of allows them to be more honest also.

[Suzi] Also, it's not a "technique" that I use. It is an authentic communication. I get to the point in not getting called back that I actually start to get a little neurotic and wonder if I've done something to upset them.

[Jeremy] So it is based on something.

[Suzi] It is based on something real—it's not that I invent an apology out of thin air. When you've done work with a person who wants to talk to you, and you're just trying to set something up and they're not calling you back, you get to the point where you start to wonder, "Did I do something to offend this person, did I overstep some bounds, what have I done?" And if that's the case, it's authentic to call and say, "Whatever it is, I'm sorry. And please let me know what I did so that I can apologize in person, because you're important to me and I don't want to go on thinking that I've upset you in some way."

So what about other follow-up strategies that work, or don't work? One that I've found doesn't work is calling in every day. Calling to follow up every day, I have found, doesn't work.

[Jeremy] I agree. If I let some time go in between, that's better.

[Suzi] What have you found to be effective time frames for follow-up calls?

[Jeremy] You mean after you've had an initial contact with somebody, or after you've already met with them?

[Suzi] Well, all of the above. Let's say you've called, whether you've met them or not. How long do you wait before following up?

[Len] Doesn't it depend on the individual you're contacting, and also the corporate culture? Like Suzi mentioned before in terms of turn-around time for proposals to lawyers and the impression that, if you do it so quickly, they think it's canned. But if you do it slower, in that particular case, they know that you did a job catered to them. And Jeremy's experience with other people, when as soon as they've discussed something and ironed out the details, he's going to have that proposal right to them.

So, isn't it dependent on whom you're working with?

[Suzi] To some degree that's true, but I think follow up is more about you.

[Len] Say more about that.

[Suzi] Well, think about it in terms of the numbers game. We talked about how it takes 10 calls to get through to six people to get one meeting. And it takes 100 calls to get one client. Well, if you're doing 100 calls, you're following up on all these people. You're going to make yourself nuts if you're trying to figure out what all these different cultures are and what the time frame or frequency is for follow-up calls into each of these cultures, unless of course all the people you're calling are in the same industry, in which case it gets a little easier.

So I think that developing your follow-up strategy is really about you and what's going to work for you. Because if it doesn't work for you, you're not going to do it, and if you're not going to do it, you're going to leave money on the table. You're going to miss getting business that's there for you to get if you "drop the follow-up ball." So I'd recommend developing strategies that fit with your life style, with your work schedule, and with your comfort level. For example, John shared with us that even though he made his 10 calls, it was uncomfortable for him all the way up until the last call. So for John, it might be more comfortable to make calls one day a week, where he can just set one day aside and he can prepare mentally for it and make all his calls on one day. That way, he knows that he's off the hook for calls the rest of the week. But somebody like Jeremy, who's comfortable doing it and does it often, could set up a follow-up schedule for himself of making 10 calls a day or 20 calls a day or 50 calls a day, and be just fine with it.

Follow-Up Support Systems

[Jeremy] I find that what I need for follow up is a support document that's like a spreadsheet for following up. Whether it's something that I do on the computer or something I do by hand, I need to refer to that document every single day. It's basically a tickler system and something that gets me organized.

[Len] That's exactly how I was conceptualizing making a series of phone calls like that—to have some sort of ledger or something.

[Jeremy] What something like that does for me is it gets me out of the box of having to think about follow up—it's just on automatic. So I get in, I look at my schedule, I look at this thing, and I say, "This is when I'm going to plug this in today."

[Suzi] Yeah, that's great. It's critical to have a tracking system and practices to support the action you're committed to taking.

[Jeremy] It's a must. Because otherwise you start to go nuts. And it's like, "Oh geez, I called them on this day and this day," and I just look at my list and dates when I called them.

[Suzi] I must admit, I'm not so thorough at that. It's a style thing: I'm going in so many different directions at once, I'm happy when I just get to make calls. I know I should track them better, and it's one of those things that I'm not always so good about doing. I do think you have to have some kind of a system that works for you, but my system is not as organized as Jeremy's. What I have is a white board on my office wall that I stare at all the time. It has a list of all the people and leads that are in my pipeline—not only pipeline things, but clients too. And there are 50 organizations on that list. And what I do is, every day, I reach out to folks on that list. I found that when I give myself a number, say I'm going to reach out to five of them each day, then it becomes a pressure and a stress thing that just works against me. So in learning how to work with myself, which is on some level what this is all about . . .

[Deb] Coaching yourself.

[Suzi] Yes, in learning how to work with myself, I've discovered that I do much better if I have identified the most urgent follow-up calls—the ones I should do immediately. I just write them in my calendar. My calendar's a good, old-fashioned, paper, Month-At-A-Glance calendar, and I write in when I want to follow up with them, and I spread the calls out however I want to spread them out. I just write out, like Jeremy said, a little tickler on my calendar.

[Jeremy] Another thing that I sometimes do is ask myself, "Which would be the most fun? Of all these people on my list, who is going to be the most fun to talk to?" So that's not necessarily doing what's the most urgent, but rather it is calling the people I enjoy talking to the most.

[Suzi] You might want to have people listed in categories and tiers so that you have more than just a sense of priorities, but rather a category of people in your network who could be referral sources you would want to be in touch with. For me, it's a list of people who are prospects from my strategic target list that I want to pursue. And this is a list of people who are already on my target list who I want to follow up with. So if you keep people organized in categories—and you could color code them too—it might be easier to do it that way instead of keeping separate lists. Again, it all boils down to figuring out a system that works for you, one that *really* works for you, not anything that has you feel like you're trying to force yourself into doing. Does that make sense?

So let's do some brainstorming together about what some of your systems might look like so that you can come away from this call with something that you're going to try or that you want to at least experiment with for the next week.

[Len] Well, for the ledger, the left-hand column could be the names of companies, and then underneath, the names of individuals in companies.

[Suzi] Sure.

[Len] And across the top, you could label one column "Referral Source," and then another column "Prospects," and then another column "Follow Ups." And then underneath those captions you can put in your contact time or something—like when you're going to make a phone call. So you would know that at such-and-such a time, you'd be contacting XYZ company, and you're going to be speaking with somebody in particular at that company, and you also know that it's a prospect call.

[Suzi] That's great. Also, using a spreadsheet on Excel makes a lot of sense because you can sort the information by date, client, status, or anything else that you want to track. Any other ideas?

[Bill] I'm thinking I could get really obsessive about it, based on my experience when I knocked on the door of every private practice office at St. Agnes Hospital. I had to develop a system because I can't remember things like that. I had a separate sales slip page in my 7-ring binder for every doctor I spoke to, and then I made notes on every doctor I spoke to. But I didn't have a system for getting back—it didn't plug into my Week-At-A-Glance, and that's what needs to be done: That's the action part. So I would need not only to log the call and other information about when the call's going to be, but I would need to log it into the Day-At-A-Glance for when that is going to happen. I don't know if there's a more streamlined way of doing it, but that would certainly cover the basics.

[Suzi] I was just coaching someone this week who has to make a lot of sales calls to develop business, and he said what works for him is Outlook. Apparently in the Microsoft Outlook software, there's a reminder system that pops up automatically, and if you don't do it and clear it, it keeps popping up until you do it.

[Bill] Every time you turn on your computer?

[Suzi] I guess so. You know I'm not the most technically oriented person. . . .

[Deb] I think Outlook has some really good organizing stuff, but I haven't used it either.

[Suzi] This guy told me that in Outlook, there's a good way to do everything we've been talking about. He said there's even a place to add notes about what you talked about with that person. I'm not proficient with that software, but if it's something that appeals to you, that's another possibility. There are tons of contact management software tools out there if you're so inclined. I like my white board!

[Jeremy] The key is, whatever you do, it should be something that you will look at every single day. That way, you continually have reinforcement, and there's a continual feedback loop, whether it's a computer or something that you write down, or something you write on the wall—it's something you have visual contact with every day. Without it, your follow up will fall through the cracks.

[Suzi] I think that's true. And again, understanding your own sales cycle will create some urgency around this. If you understand in your experience with the companies you're pursuing or the clients you're pursuing that it takes you six to eight months to go from first contact to actually starting work for them, then you've got to have several things in the pipeline, otherwise you're going to be doing nothing for six months.

[Jeremy] Right—we can't say that enough, because most people coming from a clinical background just don't have enough experience with that. And we get very impatient when we don't have a high batting average. I was talking to a guy who has a recruiting business. He's just put in a whole new division in his agency; he hired five people and put them all in place last January. And it was only last week when I talked to him that he had made his first sale. So these five new people in his office have been on his payroll for three months, and he hadn't made a sale yet. But he knows through his past business experience that that's what it takes to load up the pipeline. And he knows it's going to be another three to six months before that really starts to bear fruit.

[Suzi] It sounds like he understands that it's a numbers game, which is why you want to be in constant activity and why it's essential to have a follow-up system. Having something to remind you to be in constant activity or to support you to be in constant activity—strategic activity, not just shooting from the hip—will allow you to drastically reduce the amount of time it takes to make a deal.

[Len] Suzi, I have a question about follow-up calls. When you're calling, do you find your success rate is better or the same when you make a call to an unknown, or when you make a call to somebody who's seen you make a presentation or talk or something?

[Suzi] Oh, there's no contest, it's far better if they have some experience with me. I hate the cold calls. I'll do them if I have to, but I would much rather build my business through referrals and with people whom I have had some kind of contact. When there's a connection—even if there are five other people in between us—I can say, "I know so-and-so who knows so-and-so who told me that you know so-and-so." Even if it's that remote, I have a much higher success rate with that than if I'm just calling someone as a stranger. That goes for initial calls as well as follow-up calls.

[Len] So as long as there's some sort of connection that's visible . . .

[Suzi] For me. Yes, that's what I'm comfortable with. My strategic list is all people who've contacted me because they've seen my work, or it's people who have said, "You know, you should really talk to so-and-so," and I can follow up as a referral. Or it's someone I've met at a conference or through networking or whatever. So, yes, my follow-up strategy is to really work the referral side of things and not pay so much attention to the cold-calling side. But I work with lots of people who love cold calling and find that they're more successful in that area.

> ### Homework
>
> Create your tracking system and review your proposals and contracts.

Checklist:
Follow-Up Strategies

- Work your client's system: Use voice mail, e-mail, going through others to set appointments.

- Instead of accepting "I'll call you back later," ask to schedule an appointment.

- Leave a message to say that you'll be in their area on a specific date and time and ask, "Will you be available?"

- Make an apology call: "I haven't heard back from you, and I don't know what I've done or said that offended you. Whatever it is, I'd like to know and apologize in person."

- Fine-tune your strategies to fit with your life style, work schedule, and comfort level. For example, some people work best making calls one day a week; others do better scheduling X calls per day.

- Develop systems to support your follow-up activities: prioritized contact lists, tracking logs, calendar ticklers.

Following Up and the Mind Games We Play

"There is always an inner game being played in your mind
no matter what outer game you are playing. How aware
you are of this game can make the difference between
success and failure in the outer game."

—Tim Gallwey

We can play a lot of tricks on ourselves and get in our own way very easily. One of the easiest places in our sales process to do that is in following up with prospects. Often we make up stories about ourselves based on a lack of response from folks we're trying to get hold of. In *The Power of Full Engagement,* Tony Schwartz and Jim Loehr put it this way:

> We deceive ourselves by assuming that our view represents the truth when it is really just an interpretation, a lens through which we choose to view the world. Without realizing it, we often create stories around a set of facts and then take our stories to be the truth. Just because something feels real to us doesn't make it so.[1]

You may be familiar with the model often used in coaching where you separate What Happened (the facts) from the meaning you ascribed to it, or The Story About What Happened (the interpretation). The co-mingling of fact and perception is automatic and often invisible in the sales process. By stepping back and observing our automatic ability to make up meaning, we can be more objective and avoid getting sucked into emotionally charged reactions along the way. When we can step aside from our own attachment to how it should go, we have access to choices, actions, and interpretations that otherwise wouldn't be available to us.

A prime example is a consultant I coached who had a fabulous initial client meeting and left knowing that the right decision makers were in the room. It was just a matter of bringing back the proposal they had requested and then he could easily seal the deal. He was confident that the clients were clear about the value proposition and were ready to move forward. He took the notes from the meeting and created a winner of a proposal and felt encouraged as he called the client by the end of the week, as promised, to set up a second meeting where he would bring back the proposal. The client wasn't there, so he left a voice message. He didn't hear back from this client after several days, so he sent an e-mail. The e-mail did not yield a response, so after a few more days, he called again, and felt deflated as he left a second voice message. After a week, he had still not heard a response, and felt certain that he had misread the cues in the meeting—the client must have either not been as keen to move forward as he thought or the client had changed his mind.

Knowing the importance of persistence when it comes to following up, the consultant determined to try one more time. He left a third and, in his mind, final voice message and sent yet another e-mail. Again, no answer. He was ready to walk away from it, until I asked him if there was a familiar pattern to this unfolding of events. There was. He admitted that when he gets discouraged about a lack of response, he assumes two things: (1) that he was wrong about his original interpretation of how things went and the prospect really isn't interested after all, and (2) that he must have done something wrong or missed some cue or upset one of the decision makers in that meeting.

The consultant not only stopped trusting himself, he ascribed self-sabotaging meaning to the lack of response from the client. I explained to him that until you know otherwise for sure, why not choose to assume that the client is still enthusiastic and some life-event has gotten in the way of his responding in a timely manner? Why choose to assume the worst? We discussed strategies for one more follow-up attempt. The consultant determined that it made more sense to go for one more follow-up call, from a mindset of assuming the energy and positive feelings after the meeting were still there, rather than trying the apology call. He wanted to save the apology call for later if there was still no response. We rehearsed a voice message he might leave that would get returned.

After our conversation, the consultant called the client again. He was surprised when the client answered the phone. He was surprised a second time when the client greeted him with the same level of excitement he remembered after the meeting nearly three weeks ago. It turned out the client had been called out of the country to handle a business crisis for two weeks, and although he'd been entirely focused on putting out that fire, his eagerness to move forward on the deal with the consultant had not waned. They set up a meeting for the following week to review the specifics in the proposal, and the consultant sealed the deal.

You don't know until you know if the prospect is not interested. How often have you left money on the table and walked away from something because in the vacuum created by no information, you made up something negative that you chose to believe as truth? People disappear without communicating all the time. They go on vacations, they have babies, they leave to treat a family member who has been hospitalized, they go overseas to handle crises, they get busy and things fall through the cracks, or sometimes they simply get overwhelmed and prioritize to whom they will respond as a survival strategy. Just because someone isn't getting back to you during your follow-up attempts doesn't mean they are not interested. It might mean that, but it might not mean that. And you get to stay the leader of your own sales process if you choose interpretations that will empower and motivate you to stay in action.

Tracking Your Progress

Jay Conrad Levinson—the father of "guerrilla marketing"—reports that 68 percent of all sales are lost due to poor follow-up methods. It is critical to have a tracking system, but it has to be one that works for your business and your personal style, and it has to be one that you will use. Determine for yourself what type of follow-up system will work best. If you are a technology junkie, use Outlook or find one of the many contact management software products on the market. There are even fabulous software products available now that are specific to managing your coaching business. If you prefer paper and pen, there are a number of templates for tracking in this book (see, for example, the Prospect Contact Log at the end of Step 3), or design your own. Just be sure that you have some way of following each prospect's progress through your sales process, plus a calendar for plugging in the follow-up points with each person/organization.

Ultimately, if you are remembering that sales is all a numbers game, you will have so many leads and prospects in your pipeline that it will be impossible to keep it all straight in your mind. Set up your files and system now so that as you get busy, you will be ready to handle your success. You can always revise your system later as you increase your competency. If it gets measured, it gets done—so track your progress!

Endnote

1. Loehr, J., & Schwartz, T., (2003). *The power of full engagement.* New York: The Free Press, pp. 158–159.

Step 7
Proposals, Pricing, and Contracting

"Integrity without knowledge is weak and useless, and knowledge without integrity is dangerous and dreadful."
—Samuel Johnson

This chapter covers more of the nitty-gritty tactical elements of being in a professional service business. It starts with a couple of sample documents from my coaching business: a sample coaching proposal cover letter and the coaching portion of a proposal that included both coaching and training. I usually share these examples with the participants on the telecourse, and we will refer to them in the telecourse dialogue that follows.

The last part of the chapter includes a look at the purpose of proposals in general, which is followed by various models for proposals that might be useful to you if you are newly self-employed or if you wish to improve or re-design the formats of your current proposals. Many coaches and consultants find pricing to be a challenge, so there also is a section on pricing as well as guidance on how to shift your money conversations, ask for what you want, and get into contracting. The chapter wraps up with a couple of sample coaching agreements and resources about coaching return-on-investment (ROI).

Sample:
Coaching Proposal Cover Letter

April 23, 2001

Ms. Law Firmleader
Managing Partner
Savvy Sharp and Smart, Inc.
101 Law Firm Way
New York, NY 10023

Dear Ms. Firmleader,

Innovative Leadership International LLC (ILI) is pleased to submit this proposal for new attorney orientation coaching and support. We appreciate your receptiveness to seeking outside experts for help in these important areas, and we are confident in our ability to produce valuable, lasting results should you choose to retain us.

In this proposal, we address our process as well as our understanding of the issues facing Savvy Sharp regarding retention issues and the firm's commitment to improvement in this area. We set forth a range of options to choose from that offer the firm concrete results from three different investment levels, and on page xx, we provide our recommendations. We review a variety of specific approaches in four areas:

1) Assessment/Analysis
2) Training
3) Evaluation
4) Coaching

and on page xx, we highlight our substantial experience working with law firms and corporate law departments. In addition, we make several suggestions for marketing a coaching initiative within the firm, including how to overcome resistance and how you might sell the idea to the Board and other partners using our calculation of the return on the firm's investment (ROI formula is on page xx). Finally, we include our team's individual qualifications. In short, we aim to provide a comprehensive view of how we can serve Savvy Sharp.

I welcome the opportunity to discuss our proposal with you in further detail at your convenience. If I can provide any additional information, please contact me. I can be reached by phone at 301-601-1525, by fax at 301-528-9501, and by e-mail at suzi@innovativeleader.com anytime.

Warm regards,

Suzi Pomerantz, MT, MCC

Sample:
Coaching Proposal

PROPOSAL FOR COACHING
PREPARED FOR Savvy Sharp

❖ Process

Savvy Sharp is interested in a new associate program that will begin to foster a culture change within the firm to allow for the greater success and retention of minority attorneys. Below we present several ideas for how ILI can help you achieve your vision. We customize all of our programs to your specific objectives and issues; therefore we involve you and the participants in the development of the specific content. Our process involves four steps:

Analysis → Design/Customization → Implementation → Evaluation

In the *Analysis* stage, we will meet with select attorneys at your offices for the purpose of conducting interviews that will allow us to most effectively customize your program and tailor the coaching to Savvy Sharp's specific objectives and issues. We generally spend approximately two to five days working with you and interviewing the key participants of the program. If you require a written report of our findings from this stage, it would take an additional two to three days to compile the report.

In the *Design/Customization* stage, we will synthesize the data we gathered in our interviews and apply it to the distinctions of our programs' content to design your custom program. This design process may require follow-up conversations with you and the participants. We estimate three to five days for this work, which takes place back in our offices.

The *Implementation* stage involves coaching. Our coaching initiatives are individual, customized training programs based on the particular interests and selected areas for development of each attorney we are coaching. The rates are based on the number of attorneys participating in a coaching program and the number of coaching sessions needed.

The *Evaluation* stage allows us, and you, to determine the success of the programs. We generally conduct our final evaluation through a series of interviews a few months following program completion. We have found that these evaluation interviews allow us to check in with the participants regarding the actual transfer of learning from the training and the integration of new skills back into the workplace.

❖ Issues

Based on our meeting with you in X Month, we understand that Savvy Sharp wishes to improve the experience of minority attorneys at the firm, specifically addressing the following:

(continued)

Sample:
Coaching Proposal *(continued)*

- Recruitment of minority attorneys
- Retention of minority attorneys
- Firm culture that better supports and encourages diversity, the success of minority attorneys, and the opportunities for advancement of attorneys of color
- Dynamics between lawyers of color and support staff of color
- Acclimation to firm life for all new attorneys (i.e., all first-year associates and lateral hires, including those of color, focusing on different issues with each), with diversity consulting if needed
- Senior management development: Sensitivity coaching for partners who recruit, mentor, or supervise minority attorneys

❖ Commitment of the Firm

Savvy Sharp recognizes the value that diverse talent brings to the firm's clients. In order to get new clients, keep certain current clients, and increase bottom-line profits, Savvy Sharp wishes to improve its recruitment and retention of highly skilled minority attorneys. The firm is also committed to supporting its attorneys of color and creating an environment that will enhance their ability to succeed at the firm. Ultimately, Savvy Sharp would like to see a series of minority summer or first-year associates who "grow up" in the firm attain partnership status and contribute significantly to the firm's revenues.

While the firm is committed to a positive and productive working experience for all attorneys, there are leaders in the firm who recognize that great strides can be made to further improve the experience of attorneys of color. Currently, there is a lack of in-house expertise in this area, and by seeking outside expertise, the firm is publicly declaring its genuine commitment to proactive change. Furthermore, recognizing the potential negative response to providing coaching for only the firm's attorneys of color (e.g., the possibility that singling out the minority attorneys would incorrectly be perceived as punitive or remedial), the firm is committed to providing coaching services for a cross-section of attorneys.

❖ Options at Different Investment Levels

The three options are summarized below to give you an overview idea of investment levels. More detailed specifics about the coaching program follows. The investment levels are estimates for budgeting purposes, and we will be able to submit to you a more exact budget once you have had a chance to review the options presented herein and select what the firm wants. The levels below are designed to give you a sense of the rates and time involved for each potential solution. Actual time involved will vary based on your choices. In the event that we have over-budgeted the required time below, the firm would not be billed for the excess time. We will bill hourly at the rate of $300 per hour per consultant for coaching.

(continued)

Sample:
Coaching Proposal *(continued)*

A: Basic investment level: $37,500 as depicted below for services up to six months. Cost will vary based on your actual choices.

Access to Coaching: Customized, individual training delivered one-to-one. New lawyers (both new associates and new lateral hires) would have coaching services available to them and they could self-select involvement in the coaching program. We would hold an orientation meeting for new lawyers and new lateral hires to explain the format and benefits of coaching and to give them the opportunity to sign up. Generally, the individualized training (coaching) would cover working with individuals on the issues of concern to them, but might include working with them on how to negotiate the Savvy Sharp culture so that as a new associate (or new lateral hire, minority associate, woman, etc.), they can succeed in the firm's environment. We are assuming, for the sake of creating an estimated budget, that five people would choose this option. This would involve coaching each one for one hour per week for six months with unlimited brief access to the coach by e-mail and phone. Initial coaching meetings would occur in person, the majority would be conducted over the phone to save on travel costs. Estimate 125 hours at $300 an hour, or $37,500.

B: Middle investment level: $105,000 as depicted below for services up to nine months. Cost will vary based on your actual choices.

All of the above ($37,500) plus the following:

Access to Coaching: Customized, individual training delivered one-to-one. Offer coaching (individual training) for mentors, supervisors, managing partners, and leaders in the firm about how to best manage diversity. This coaching would be offered to anyone who participated in the diversity awareness training to further enhance the key learning from the workshops. This would give individual attorneys a chance to work one-on-one with the trainers to apply the content from the training to real situations they are facing. Assume five people sign up for this service for a nine-month period of time, or assume 5 hours a week for 45 weeks. Estimate 225 hours at $300 per hour, or $67,500.

C: Highest investment level: $183,000 as depicted below for services up to one year. Cost will vary based on your actual choices.

All of the above ($105,000) plus the following:

Access to Coaching/Diversity Resource Consulting: Make coaching available to all attorneys of color, women, or anyone in the firm who wants to take advantage of individualized training and mentoring regarding diversity issues, leadership skills, or personal growth and development. Individualized training/coaching about diversity issues and/or general acclimation to the firm and/or practice of law for:

(continued)

Sample:
Coaching Proposal *(continued)*

- All new lawyers hired
- Lateral hires new to firm
- Mentors and supervising partners: diversity management
- Recruiters
- Culture change in firm regarding diversity, encouraging a diverse environment, creating a place where minority attorneys can grow and succeed; may include sessions with senior management, partners, associates, as well as support staff and legal assistants
- Diversity coaching for management and partners
- Coaching for new lawyers and lateral hires of color: both diversity-specific and acclimation to the firm/practice of law

Assuming five people select coaching services for one year, figure 52 weeks, 1 hour per week per person, or 260 hours at $300 per hour: $78,000.

Note: Account/Project management hours billed in addition are estimated at 1 to 3 hours per week at the same hourly rate. Additionally, out-of-pocket expenses will be billed for reimbursement at cost. These may include travel, lodging, ground transportation, meals, mileage, printing/reproduction/binding for training materials, supplies, shipping, postage, telephone/fax.

❖ Our Recommendation

We recommend starting with the basic investment level depicted above, with strong consideration given to expansion toward the middle investment level if our initial results are well received. The cost and scope of work can be scaled to meet your budget. For example, the estimated hours for coaching work could be reduced, which would reduce the overall costs by $300 per hour.

We strongly recommend targeting the key decision makers or those who directly influence the new associates and attorneys of color for training first. For the coaching programs, we recommend providing access to coaching and allowing attorneys to self-select rather than having the firm select participants. This allows for maximum success in the coaching process and removes any possible interpretation of coaching as a punitive or remedial action on the part of the firm. This is particularly relevant for minority associates, who might feel singled out in a negative way if they are the only attorneys targeted for coaching support.

Having worked with many organizations on creating a culture change in their workplace, we have learned that many issues with diversity are due to the automatic, current culture of the organization. For this reason, we advise not aiming your diversity-related intervention at the associates coming into the firm, but rather focusing on the people who created and

(continued)

Sample:
Coaching Proposal *(continued)*

contributed to the existing culture. In our experience, training the new attorneys entering the firm teaches them to handle a culture that is not set up to support them to succeed, which is at best an effort in futility. The best approach is to intervene in the culture and shift it to one that supports the success of ALL new attorneys and new lateral hires.

Below in the Coaching Approach section, we have included other options for coaching that would extend beyond diversity training. These options are not priced as part of this proposal, but rather are included to give you food for thought for long-term planning for the firm. Coaching, which is really one-on-one training, is a powerful vehicle for leveraging attorney time and development. We can train attorneys during times that work with their individual schedules, rather than requiring many attorneys to set aside regular billable hours for group training sessions.

❖ Coaching Approach

Coaching is individual, customized training that allows for each attorney to work on developing or enhancing skills that are most relevant to him or her. We propose holding an orientation session for new hires, during which we would explain coaching and how it will make their employment at Savvy Sharp more productive and successful. We would discuss how coaching can better help the firm meet the bottom line and how coaching supports overall productivity. This type of individual training is often focused on making associates into rainmakers and is an effective commitment from the firm that makes rainmakers stay with the firm. At the conclusion of the orientation session, the interested attorneys will have the opportunity to sign up for individual coaching.

We promote change in individual attorneys and in the firm through executive coaching and training. The coaching process typically begins with an individual needs assessment conversation and a discussion about confidentiality. Coaching does not formally begin until there is an agreement between the coach and the individual client about information sharing, if any, with other members of the firm. We then assist the client in determining realistic and specific objectives for change. Such goals may include enhancing any or a combination of the following: leadership, decisiveness, collaboration, conflict resolution, communication, presentation style, dealing with a difficult partner or associate, or managing stress, productivity, networking, marketing, business development, job motivation, acclimation to the firm, and job satisfaction, among others.

We adopt a direct approach in the coaching process that requires regular feedback from the attorney and we make adjustments in goals and/or techniques as necessary. People often function below their optimal level in part because they hold onto mistaken beliefs about themselves and the world around them. Our certified coaches consequently help clients

(continued)

Sample:
Coaching Proposal *(continued)*

acquire more success-promoting beliefs via such techniques as rational disputation, logical analysis, visualization, perceptual shifting, inquiry, and confrontation. We additionally employ role-playing, self-monitoring, and assertiveness exercises as necessary. Our coaches incorporate humor strategically in meetings to facilitate the attorney's personal mastery of challenging situations. We promote attorneys' acquisition of knowledge and skills in leadership, management, business development and communication that are directly relevant to their workplace, and they often report that they are able to apply what they learn to relationships and activities outside the firm. Our no-nonsense coaching approach is professional, conversational, intuitive, and results-oriented.

Our primary commitment is to the success of our clients, closely followed by our deep commitment to confidentiality and strict adherence to ethical principles. Acting from a philosophy of partnership, we guide our clients to exceed their performance through questions, dialogue, calculated risk, and the fundamental belief that each person has his or her own answers within. Our coaching methodologies allow each attorney to find those answers for himself/herself and design actions that are aligned and consistent with that clarity. We then provide structures and practices to support the implementation of those actions and the realization of each attorney's goals.

In this era of continual change and increasing competition in the legal marketplace, our coaching programs are designed to solidify what is already working within your firm, and to introduce new steps toward maximizing overall productivity and profitability. As part of improving the bottom line, as well as a separate benefit, the coaching results in increased job satisfaction and decreased stress at all levels of the firm hierarchy.

❖ Other Options

As you know, the legal industry continues to face critical changes that impact every law firm. Corporate clients are increasingly demanding top-notch representation at reduced or alternative fees, and they are expecting outside counsel to participate in quality and cost-management initiatives such as Six Sigma. The competitive starting salaries for associates have jumped dramatically, and retaining top performers has become a more difficult challenge than in the past. Today's associates have a new batch of mindsets and expectations that are often contrary to the expectations of senior partners/shareholders in the firm. These realities generate a myriad of complex internal issues that attorney coaching is designed to address.

Many firms want their associates to be more efficient and productive, and their junior partners to improve in the areas of generating revenue, building and sustaining lasting client relationships, and mentoring associates. We work with them to grow in those areas as well as others. We also work with managing partners and management teams to improve

(continued)

Sample:
Coaching Proposal *(continued)*

management skills, succession planning, mentoring and coaching skills, and leadership problem solving. In addition, we work with the entire firm to design and implement a firm culture that values all members of the firm, and focuses on interpersonal and inter-departmental communication effectiveness. Finally, we work with senior partners ready to transition out of the practice of law, particularly addressing their issues associated with letting go and leaving behind a positive legacy. Using the power and effectiveness of executive coaching, we transform your law firm at the levels of individual attitude, individual and team performance, and overall sustainable growth for the firm.

Below is a comprehensive look at the coaching we can provide to four key target groups within the firm. We recognize that your focus is on new associates and lateral hire attorneys and that Savvy Sharp might not be interested in providing coaching in all four areas. However, we believe that targeting multiple, simultaneous results across the firm is the key to success if the intended outcome is firm-wide culture change.

Associates	Senior Associates/Junior Partners
❖ Transforming attitude	❖ Providing exceptional service
❖ Improving performance and productivity	❖ Exceeding expectations
❖ Enhancing retention	❖ Identifying new opportunities
❖ Increasing effective networking	❖ Generating referrals
❖ Providing exceptional service	❖ Asking for new business from existing clients
❖ Exceeding client expectations	❖ Achieving depth with corporate clients
❖ Soliciting feedback	❖ Creating mentoring relationships
❖ Understanding the goals of internal clients	❖ Building relationships with prospects
❖ Engaging in internal marketing activities	❖ Understanding distinctions between sales and marketing in revenue generation activities

Managing Partner and Management Team	Senior Partners
	❖ Designing life after the law firm
❖ Reducing stress	❖ Redefining skills
❖ Honing mentoring and coaching skills	❖ Transitioning career
❖ Developing exceptional management skills	❖ Leaving a meaningful legacy
❖ Planning for succession	❖ Re-inventing oneself as a former attorney
❖ Identifying, designing, developing, and sustaining a positive firm culture	❖ Creating and achieving new goals for next phase
❖ Hiring and retaining qualified associates, including women and minorities	❖ Serving as mentor

(continued)

Sample:
Coaching Proposal *(continued)*

The results produced from a coaching relationship are observable and measurable, commensurate with the firm's requirements for the performance of the person being coached. In general, coaching is considered a perk or benefit provided to star performers in an organization or to those with the potential for stardom. Coaching gives Savvy Sharp the chance to demonstrate how it values its attorneys and how it will invest in their career development at every level.

❖ Our Experience Working with Lawyers

ILI offers a highly selective team of professionals to provide coaching and training services to attorneys. Our unique package includes independent coaches and trainers of diverse backgrounds brought together to provide expertise to the attorneys with whom we work. We have conducted training and coaching programs for attorneys in law firms such as Shook Hardy & Bacon, Schwabe Williamson & Wyatt, Young Conaway Stargatt & Taylor, and in corporate law departments such as DuPont, Sears, Goldman Sachs, Welch's, and General Motors. We have designed training that was delivered by members of our team not proposed herein to firms such as Morgan Lewis & Bockius and Sutherland, Asbill & Brennan, and we have been asked to provide training and coaching proposals to firms such as McGuire Woods and Duane Morris. It would be unethical for us to reveal details about our clients to you, which presents a challenge in providing examples for this proposal. In order to protect the confidentiality of our clients and respect for their privacy, we are unable to elaborate on the specific nature of our work in each firm and law department mentioned above, and we know that Savvy Sharp would expect the same level of respect for its privacy. It is our intention, by providing you with the firm and law department names, that you will see the breadth of our experience working with attorneys. You will find our biographical statements at the end of this document in the section headed, "Qualifications."

❖ Marketing Internally

You raised a concern during our meeting about the potential negative response to providing coaching only for the attorneys of color; the fear being that singling out the minority attorneys would be perceived as punitive or remedial, which is not the intention of the firm. You also expressed the probable need to overcome resistance among attorneys in the firm to bringing in outside experts (i.e., "we don't do consultants"). There was also some question about the best approach for selling a coaching program/initiative to the Board/partners, and how to calculate and communicate the ROI to the firm management. Below are our suggestions:

(continued)

Sample:
Coaching Proposal *(continued)*

Return on Investment (ROI)

Perhaps the most effective tool for selling coaching services to the Board and other equity partners in the firm is to demonstrate the ROI the firm can expect. We use a simple formula to calculate this numerically:

$$ROI = \frac{\text{Benefit of Coaching} - \text{Cost of Coaching} \times 100}{\text{Cost of Coaching}}$$

The bottom-line benefit of our proposed training and coaching program contains a number of major components. It is likely that at least some of the attorneys who choose to receive coaching will focus on and substantially improve aspects of their job performance such as time management, client relations, and marketing, all of which can result in a significant bottom-line boost for the firm. However, the most likely and biggest benefit of our overall program will be in the area of attorney retention (in particular, minority retention). So in calculating the expected ROI below, we will focus exclusively on the benefit resulting from increased retention.

Studies have shown that the level of attorney attrition that many large law firms now experience is extremely uneconomical, impairs client service and client relationships, disrupts collegial relationships within the firm, breeds cynicism and discouragement, and ultimately promotes further attrition. In fact, it has been shown that, on average, it costs law firms over $300,000 to replace one junior associate. This total cost includes the costs associated with recruiting and hiring a replacement (e.g., attorney time devoted to recruiting and interviewing, advertising, recruitment agency fees); lost time/productivity of the exiting attorney (e.g., time spent locating new position, transferring work, not working); the initial transition period of the replacement attorney (e.g., getting oriented to the firm, training time, "getting up to speed" on matters handled by the exiting attorney); and the impact on others at the firm who must duplicate time previously devoted to training, mentoring, and supervising the departed attorney. Not included in the $300,000 calculation is the damage to ongoing client relationships caused by turnover in the attorneys who are servicing them.

A groundbreaking 1998 National Association for Law Placement (NALP) study revealed that associates' decisions to stay or leave their law firms often form during the first year with the firm. We believe that it is reasonable and conservative to assume that the implementation of our middle investment level program would result in retention of at least one attorney of color who otherwise would leave the firm. Plugging this one component of benefit into our ROI formula (assuming a modest $300,000 in attrition cost savings):

$$ROI = \frac{300,000 - 105,000 \times 100}{105,000}$$

(continued)

Sample:
Coaching Proposal *(concluded)*

the ROI comes to an impressive 186 percent. Moreover, there are likely additional long-term benefits associated with your firm retaining a minority attorney. It's reasonable to assume that if—as is one of your primary purposes of seeking our services—a new attorney of color ends up remaining with the firm all the way through to becoming a partner, over the years that attorney (either on his/her own or as part of a team) will attract a substantial amount of business to the firm. It's certainly not unreasonable to assume that this benefit will total at least $250,000 (at present-day value), added to the assumed $300,000 in attrition cost savings, thus resulting in an ROI of 424 percent. That is:

$$\mathbf{ROI} = \frac{550,000 - 105,000 \times 100}{105,000} = \mathbf{423.8\%}$$

Of course, if our program ends up resulting in the retention of two attorneys of color, the actual ROI would end up being over 947 percent. Furthermore, it should be kept in mind that we've calculated these ROI figures without inclusion of the likely significant bottom-line benefits of our program beyond retention. In short, what the preceding analysis shows is that our proposed program clearly makes bottom-line sense for the firm.

❖ Qualifications
Bios attached here in the actual proposal

Telecourse Session #7:
Dialogue on Proposals

[Len] Suzi, I notice that in your proposal example, you covered only coaching, item number 4 in your cover letter, and not the other items, assessment, analysis, training, and evaluation.

[Suzi] I took those out because I wanted it to focus on coaching for our purposes in this telecourse. Frequently, I don't do just a coaching proposal. Often it's for coaching coupled with training. And so most of those other elements are usually in there.

[Jeremy] One nice thing about the proposal that you posted, Suzi, that I think is very important for all of us to take a look at, is that you're proposing multiple coaching engagements for the client. It's great to be working in an organization to be doing one thing, but if you can leverage your efficiency in terms of what you know and how you're known to them, you can reduce the learning curve. So why not sell that from the outset, or at least help them think about that? Sometimes a proposal is a way for an employer to think about what we offer . . .

[Suzi] Right. I always like to propose a lot more than they say they want because it gives them food for thought for the future. And it gives me the opportunity to expand the sale later on. Meaning, once you close for a smaller amount, you get in, you prove yourself, and then you turn it into something more, or you carry it further.

The Offer

[Jeremy] I'm curious, though . . . it looked like what you do in terms of training is to offer initial training before the coaching, is that correct?

[Suzi] Well, sometimes I do and sometimes I don't. It depends on what the organization's looking for. Sometimes what makes sense to them is training, and they don't really understand coaching. So I can offer an initial training, but I always talk about how training is a valuable methodology for disseminating baseline information up front and that it doesn't really get to the heart of causing cultural change—causing individual behavioral change. It doesn't even always fulfill what training is intended to fulfill, which is integrating new knowledge and new skills into the workplace. So I often talk about how training is a great way to get a lot of baseline information to a group of people at once. However, what most organizations are looking for is "Well, this guy's at this level and this woman's at this level, and this group needs this focus," and they often want more individualized things, so I define coaching as individualized or small-group training that's tailored to the specific needs of those individuals.

[Jeremy] When you do a training piece, with the coaching piece, obviously it differs depending on the organization and their needs.

[Suzi] Right.

[Jeremy] So can you give us an idea of what that looks like, where you do both?

[Suzi] Sure. I just did a proposal for a law firm that wanted diversity training; they didn't want coaching at all because they didn't think about it or know it. So in the proposal, I talked about the diversity training, which is what they wanted and what they came to us for, but I also built in all that stuff about coaching to show them what it could do. I was saying to the law firm, "Your attorneys have to be billable most of the time, if not 125 percent of the time, like it is for some firms. So if you're taking a number of them out of billable time for training, not only does it cost the firm the cost for bringing us in to do the training, but it costs the firm lost billable time for however many attorneys you've got in the training at once. And *voilà*, coaching is the perfect solution because we can tailor that to the multiple schedules of the different attorneys, we can work around their billable time, and we can tailor the issues to what they want to focus on, rather than assuming that everyone's at one level and going from there."

[Jeremy] So how many hours for them, or how many days of training, will you be proposing?

[Suzi] Well, knowing the realities of the law firm market, we proposed half-day training, which would be a way to talk about some of the baseline issues of diversity that the firm is facing, but really not get into depth on any of them.

[Jeremy] So how many, like four or five?

[Suzi] We proposed four half days, spread out over time.

[Jeremy] And then the coaching coming off that?

[Suzi] Right. And the coaching happening in between that as well. And we also proposed that if they wanted to have more control over cost, we could do coaching instead of training. We could just offer coaching for anybody who wants to take advantage of it on diversity issues.

About Fees, Value, and Giving Work Away

[Jeremy] Right. I have one more question for you: When you're providing this volume of coaching services, do you get pushed to reduce your hourly rate?

[Suzi] I don't get pushed to, but I offer it.

[Jeremy] You offer a volume discount?

[Suzi] Absolutely. If they're willing to sign up for a year, minimum, I'll offer a 15 percent discount, and that's just a straight discount on hourly fees. I have one client where I've been coaching different people in the organization for six years now, and they've had a discount from the beginning.

[Jeremy] Right. And now they got a real discount, now that your fees have gone up.

[Suzi] Well, I've raised my fees with them too, but I still give them a discount. I raise my fees with everybody, because it got too confusing not to do that.

[Jeremy] How do you handle that conversation?

[Suzi] I do it in a letter. Every November, I send out a letter saying my rates will be increasing effective January 1, and here are the new rates. And we're interested in continuing to serve you. And usually I haven't had a problem.

[Jeremy] So you do it in a very similar way that law firms do it.

[Suzi] Exactly. You know? I think that's what gave me the confidence to do it—my clients are mainly attorneys and they raise their rates all the time, willy nilly, for no apparent reason. I can at least do it once a year.

I tried to keep people at different rates as I was growing in the business, but it was an accounting nightmare. I couldn't keep it all straight in invoicing. I couldn't remember who was at what rate and why and for how long and what their discounts were. It really cost me a lot of time every month.

[Jeremy] So John, how was your conference? Give us a two-minute version of your experience.

[John] It was an e-learning conference in D.C. on how to dissolve resistance to change. I had talked with Jeremy before, and he suggested I do a little marketing thing, which was to tack a tear sheet on the last page of the handout asking them to identify some of the goals that they plan to do in order to resolve their resistance back home, and also give me their contact information, then tear it out, leave it with me, and I'd call them back. There were 50 or 60 people who showed up for the thing, which was a surprise—it was 5:30 in the afternoon on the last day.

[Suzi] Wow, that's great.

[John] Even greater, I got about 15 folks to leave me tear sheets. So, a week later, I sent a little e-mail thanking them and basically letting them know that I'm here and wanting to follow up on their issues. So, yeah, I came back with 15 folks who have some follow-on interest in what I'm doing.

[Suzi] And do you know what your next steps are with them?

[John] Well, the first step was I offered to talk with them on the phone and give them help, encouragement, and coaching on the next step on the list of things they were wanting to do. My initial thought was to just establish a relationship with them. And then the next step, the follow-up step, as that starts to play out, is that we'll have a conversation about moving from informal advice into a consulting relationship.

[Suzi] John, I'm going to play devil's advocate with you for a minute if that's okay?

[John] Okay.

[Suzi] So if they're going to call you for coaching advice over the phone, are you not going to bill them for that? Because you said it would be informal.

[John] Well, the initial step is a non-billable thing, right?

[Suzi] Why?

[John] Uh . . . to establish the relationship with them?

[Suzi] Well, let me ask you something. If you've established a relationship with someone where they are giving you advice/coaching/counseling for free, why would you want to start paying them for the same thing?

[John] Um, because they haven't . . . they haven't taken me the full . . . I could use some help here, guys.

[Jeremy] You're on your own, John—I want you to make money.

[Suzi] Well, let me just talk about that idea for a minute, because this is a very common thing, one that coaches do all the time. Many coaches give a free sample coaching session. And in fact I know that several of the coaching schools actually teach students to do this, to give it away for free, and then turn it into a paying gig later. And I want to tell you, from experience as a salesperson, that never works. The reason is, if you're getting services for free, and suddenly people start charging you, you're not going to want to pay, because you've gotten it for free, therefore the **value** that you have attached to it is zero. So if you charge people right up front, that shows that you value what you're providing, and that they should therefore value what you're providing. They'll treat you very differently if it's a professional relationship that they're paying for right up front.

And so, I think it's great that you have these tear sheets and these 15 people—these people are now 15 hot prospects on your target list. And what do you do with hot prospects on your target list? You pick up your phone, you call them, you make an appointment. In that appointment, you start talking about what their interests are, what their issues are, how you might be able to help them, and you move them forward in the sales process. I think you've got 15 people ready to jump into your pipeline—into your sales process. And if you wait for them to call you and start doing this informal coaching over the phone, not only do you not get paid, but they get something for nothing, which isn't going to have them value you or want to come to you with dollars. And we want you to get dollars. They've heard you speak. You're already an authority. You've already got the credibility. They wouldn't have given you their information if they didn't want you to contact them and follow up.

You've set it up beautifully, absolutely perfectly, to jump into the game with all those people and plop them right into your sales cycle.

[John] Well, if I set them up so perfectly, we wouldn't be having this conversation.

[Suzi] I don't think it's too late. I think you're in the perfect place, because you sent them an e-mail thanking them for their interest, so now all you have to do is start calling them one at a time. I mean if you want to make 10 calls a week, call these people.

[John] That's a good idea, I have one call already set up.

[Jeremy] Suzi, for background information, to help John out a little bit, many of these people are out of town, so he's going to have to do phone appointments with them.

[Suzi] That's fine. You can do phone appointments, or you can go see them. Either way, whatever works for you. Are they grouped together in a place where you could maybe go for a day and set up a couple of meetings?

[John] Uh, no—Minneapolis and Las Vegas.

[Suzi] Okay, so set up phone appointments. Just call them and set up phone appointments to talk about what their issues are.

It's just like we've talked about: You call them up and make an appointment, and that's all you do with the first call. And then if your second call is the appointment, it's as if you're going to see them in person—you plan for that the same way. You ask them the questions about what they want to accomplish, you figure out what stories you're going to weave in, and you ask for the business. And you just start moving them through your sales cycle, just like that. Assume that they're interested in buying your services or they wouldn't have given you the tear sheet.

[John] I have no trouble assuming they're interested in my services, that's not the problem. The problem is I created a fuzzy boundary, by telling them I was willing to talk to them to help bring the workshop experience full circle—to closure. When you go to a workshop, you get all these neat ideas, you go home, and it's real difficult to apply them. So I offered to give them encouragement, coaching, whatever, to help them bring it full circle.

[Jeremy] So you can do that, John, and not be violating what you said . . . you're just bringing it back to what Suzi's suggesting here, bringing it back to a coaching concept, but also a sales concept, where you make the next appointment. Talk about what they want to accomplish, help them clarify, and spend some time—maybe that's two or three calls. But then it's understood that after that, succeeding calls are at your rate, which is going to be in person or on the phone in such-and-such time over such-and-such period of time. And you make it clear how people can access you for what fees.

[Suzi] I absolutely agree that you don't have to go back on your word at all here, because you can weave in the follow up to the training and the personalization of the training with a sales call. That really is a sales call.

[Jeremy] It's even better that way.

[Suzi] Yes, absolutely. Because what you're doing is you're finding out in that call where the training session hit for them, what's missing for them, where they need assistance in bridging the gap between having the training and integrating it back into their work situation, and what their specific scenarios and issues are that they're dealing with. All of that is perfectly appropriate to find out in a sales conversation.

And then at the end of the conversation, and I would do it in one call, I'd say, "Great! It sounds like we need to spend about three coaching sessions together (or six coaching sessions together) and I can help you with this. And we can set up your coaching conversations next week, and here's the billable rate, and I'll send you a letter of agreement." And then you've just closed the sale over the phone.

[Jeremy] John, you still there?

[John] Yeah, I'm still here. I'm . . . I'm hearing the words.

[Suzi] You're providing value in the sales conversation and you don't have to give it away beyond that.

[John] Oh, I realize that. I'm just trying to integrate it. Because you're preaching to the choir when you tell me not to give it away, because that's been a sort of a pattern for a long time, going back 30 years. It's been like, I need the experience, so here's a way to get the experience.

[Suzi] But why not get paid to get the experience?

[John] Well, like I say, you're preaching to the choir here. It's just going to require a different mindset for me to do.

[Suzi] Well, think of it as a paid internship. If you still want to think of it as getting the experience, it's a paid internship. Think about what law firms do—I'm going to use a law firm model again because that's what I'm familiar with. Associates are hired as summer associates. They get paid for that summer, and they're learning; they're learning about the culture and about the profession, they're providing value, and they're getting paid. There's nothing wrong with it. This is something I see all over the world with coaches: We are drawn to coaching because we really want to help people. We are in a helping profession, especially if you come from a psychology background, you're a helper, and you want to help people. Well, that's wonderful, and that's what makes the coaching community such a wonderful place to play, but we keep wanting to give it away because we're so helpful, and that doesn't help us.

[John] For me it's not a matter of wanting to give it away. I know that the way we exchange value in this culture is to exchange resources. But there's a part of me that says some of these folks, maybe all of them, will say "no." And then I'm sort of back to square one. Right now I can revel in this list of prospects and feel good about that.

[Suzi] But, John, it is in that mindset where you are getting in your own way.

[John] I know, I agree.

[Suzi] Why would they say no? They've heard you speak, they value what you have to say, they know that you've got something that they want, and they gave you license to contact them.

[Jeremy] They know they're going to have to pay for something, John.

[Suzi] They know. Now, if you find it an ethical issue to charge full rate while you learn, then you can offer a discounted introductory rate or a reduced rate so that it feels more like a paid internship to you, but I really think they already get the value proposition and you can charge your full rates.

So if they say no, it's not about you. If they say no, it could be any number of things going on with them—it doesn't mean anything about you, and they're still in your list.

[Jeremy] You know what? You're going to sign up a couple of people, and you might have people who say no now, but yes later.

[Suzi] Exactly.

[Len] John, just to put my two cents in here, I have the feeling that when you gave your presentations, you were organized and you knew exactly what you were doing. And now in terms of making the phone call, it feels unstructured, it's not planned enough, and it's not as organized as your presentation. But in terms of making these phone calls, these are not cold calls, as were the ones you made at the beginning of our telecourse. So it's not the same problem in terms of picking up the phone this time.

The problem, it sounds like, is that you were going to offer something without being concerned about the dollar cost or whatever, and now you need a format of some way to integrate it into conversations when you're talking with them. So, Suzi, what I've heard, since they know him already, he could begin the call itself by saying, "Well, on this initial call, we're going to talk about your issues, what you want to address, and your expectations of what you want to have happen. And we're going to talk about costs that would be involved in coaching."

[Jeremy] Give it a headline is what you're suggesting.

[Len] Exactly.

[Suzi] Yeah, you consider it the initial meeting.

[Len] Exactly. You outline on the telephone what you're going to be doing in the call. And then at the end of the call, you'll sell them, and you would like them to say one of two things: "Yes, we're committed, we want to get involved in the contract," which you've already outlined in the earlier part of the call, or, "No, this is not for us." And then everything would be clear, so you'd have it very structured.

[Jeremy] How does that sound, John?

[John] That's helpful.

[Suzi] I think that there's a money taboo that we all run into when we start performing a new kind of service with clients. And, the only way to get over it is to have experience defying the taboo. And as you have experience defying the taboo, it will have a lot less hold on you.

[Jeremy] It's just like going through any type of anxiety: It will go down every time you have an experience. And the experience is not necessarily getting paid for the work; it's telling the client these are the fees for the work, and then it is getting paid for the work or not getting paid for the work. But it's continuing to be out there, as Suzi's outlining for us. It's saying, "This is the value that I provide," and as Len said, "If you want to go ahead, this is what it's going to look like in terms of the service and what it'll cost, and this is my estimate in terms of the time for the initial phase of our contract."

Proposal Basics

[Jeremy] Okay, this is a good segue into proposals. Why don't we move along into the proposals you came up with from your homework assignment?

[John] The main difference between my sample proposal and the ones I saw of Suzi's is at the front end. The next day, I send them a letter that has a paragraph summarizing my understanding of what their perception of the problem is, and then in the second piece, I'll list out the set of mutual things that got raised in the conversation. Like, "I understand that you want me to do X, and the flip side is I want you to do Y (provide access, commitment, etc.)." So that's my thing. It's a bit different from the ones you sent to us.

[Suzi] Okay. So, what about Len? Can you tell us when and how you used the sample that you sent around to us?

[Jeremy] That thing you sent to the venture capital company?

[Len] I had a phone call indicating an interest, and I had called back several times, and finally spoke to the person who was interested in coaching services for the executive offices of a venture capital firm that managed 44 other companies. That was the original message, something like that. And when I called, and finally got hold of her, she was in a rush to go to some other meeting, and simply said, "Just send in something because I just want to know. . . ." I forget what it was she wanted—a list of my clients and information about me or something like that. And she said they were just inquiring in the area—they just were going to put it away in a drawer, whatever I sent them. I didn't want that, but then I couldn't get hold of her again. So my proposal letter to her basically just itemizes the company, the scope of the engagement, and the testing we would be doing, plus levels of confidentiality, the fees, and business arrangements, things like that.

[Suzi] Now is this one going to get kept in a drawer, or is this one actually going to be taken into some consideration?

[Len] Well, I'll be calling them back.

[Suzi] Well, to me, that's rude—that she expects you to put time and effort into writing something to sit in a file. My response would be, "Well, what would your file be interested in reading?"

[Jeremy] You could play with it, like you're suggesting.

[Suzi] Yes. Well, you'll do what you want, but if it were me, I wouldn't waste my time writing something that's never going to be taken seriously—that's just going to sit in a file.

[Len] Well, I haven't gotten a response from her, but I have done my research on the company, and I know who the main partner is. So I'll be calling the main partner.

[Suzi] That's good. I mean see if you can turn that into a conversation, rather than another, "Sure I'll send you something to file away." If there's an opportunity, I'd much rather say, "I'd like to sit down and have a conversation with you about it. How's Tuesday at 5:00?" And get back to getting an appointment, because then you can judge for yourself whether it warrants spending your valuable time and whether they actually want to do something some day with it or not. They can go to your website for generic materials about your services. You only want to spend time writing targeted proposals based on specific discussions you've had.

[Len] Well, that's absolutely correct. But I think that something must have happened at the firm. A number of the companies they had launched on the Nasdaq were losing tremendous amounts of money. The value of their companies had gone down to be one-tenth what they were worth before the drop, and there was a lot of very high anxiety and panic. They were looking for something to help them out . . . I'll be calling them and we'll see.

[Jeremy] What Suzi is suggesting, Len, and I think it's a good suggestion, is let's think of other places you could be calling also, because this is not . . .

[Len] Right.

[Jeremy] This is a long-term prospect, at best.

[Suzi] And there's nothing wrong with long-term prospects, but think about what we talked about at length a few calls back: how much time it takes to be actively involved in marketing activities, networking activities, and sales activities. And if it takes tons of our time to be involved in all three of those activities, and we want the majority of our time to be billable time, then we really start to price our time differently for ourselves—what do I want to spend my time doing? For me, where I prioritize proposals that are going to sit at the bottom of a file is at the bottom of the list, because there are probably things that are going to yield a faster return than doing that exercise. Unless of course you just want practice writing proposals, in which case it's fine.

[Len] There's another thing. In terms of time, what John just did—making a presentation and meeting people face to face—that's far more economical than making cold calls to all those people. And far more economical in terms of time and money. So when you do finally make the phone call to them, that call has a higher value and a higher potential for a positive outcome.

[Suzi] Right. It's called a warm call.

[Len] And to make room for more warm calls, I'm designing some lunch-and-learn workshops. I'm going to go around to different companies, financial organizations, and associations in the area, and arrange to make presentations there. And I'm also planning to have a type of raffle.

[Suzi] Yeah, I do that, too. You collect everyone's business cards, and you raffle something off at the end. I do that all the time.

[Len] Exactly. So also during the raffle, I'll be able to tell the people what the cost would be for the services I'll be providing.

[Suzi] Exactly. And you can even raffle off an hour of your consultation, or a copy of your book, or your top 10 list of whatever—something you create for the occasion.

Another thing is to use marketing gifts with your logo: I had a bunch of mugs printed up one year with my logo on them, cappuccino mugs, the giant ones. And every time I give a presentation, I'll fill one up with candy or hot cocoa packets, wrap it up in a box with a nice bow, and raffle that off. So they're getting a little something, it didn't cost me a whole lot, and I'm getting everyone's business cards to do with what I please afterward.

Proposal Formats

[Suzi] Well let's come full circle, back to the format for proposals. There are so many different ways to do proposals, and it really just depends on what your purpose is in doing the proposal and when in the sales cycle you want to use it. But there is a model I like for proposal writing that I call the Gilberg model, in honor of the colleague who introduced me to it: **situation, results, recommendation, rationale, implementation, and price.**

I'll start at the beginning. **Situation** is where you describe the client and the client organization, **results** would be the results they intend for you to produce in whatever services you're providing. The **recommendation** would be what you recommend they do in terms of first step, second step, etc. Then your **rationale** is why they should use your services, or why they should follow this approach, or why what you're recommending is going to get the results they want. **Implementation** is how you're going to do it: six training sessions over three months, or a training session followed by 14 coaching sessions, or whatever, for how many people. And then you **price** it out at the end.

There's another model that a colleague of mine used to use. She called it the PSR model, which is **problem, solution, results.** So the **problem** is the first part of the proposal where you define the problem. The **solution** is where you give the potential solution and what your services could do to help them solve that problem. And then the **results** are what the client can expect. And you follow that up with next steps, pricing, and recommendations, and that sort of thing.

Um, let's see, other models that I've collected over the years. . . . This one doesn't have a particular name, but the first part is a **project overview,** and that includes the context, the benefits, what services we'll provide, and what the deliverables will be. The next step in this one is the **project approach,** where you number the steps and do like a half a paragraph on each of the steps, and include a **proposed timeline**. And then the **program fees** and the **payment schedule.** I know in the case of training versus coaching, a lot of people will ask for money up front: either 50 percent to secure the date, or 25 percent on acceptance of the proposal and then 25 percent on some other milestone—they set up three or four different steps in delivering the money.

Qualifications and **references** are the last two in that model. And then there's something that, if I can, I like to include in a proposal: **success criteria.** Now obviously if it's early on in the sales process, and you don't really know enough about what they want or what they expect, you can't really do this, but if possible, I like to include success criteria in the proposal. In other words, I want to say how they'll know that they've gotten the value they're paying for, because then I can always go back to it at the end and use that as an evaluation tool as well.

[Len] Let me just ask about the references. . . . Are you referring to testimonials? Are you referring to other people you've recommended or you've worked with?

[Suzi] Well, it might be that. It might be, "We have provided coaching services to the following organizations, among many others," and then you know, you maybe list four or five organizations that are similar to the one that you're proposing to. Or it could be individuals for them to call, it depends. You don't have to offer references.

It all comes back to what you're trying to accomplish with the proposal. Just try different things until you find what works for you. I'm always changing my proposal format.

[Jeremy] The idea of gathering a bunch of sample proposals is a really helpful one; it allows you to think about different ways you can be with clients and different ways you can serve them and earn a living. I mean the thing that I'm continually struck with, and I will note this from the experience that I had last week, is that it's very hard for most folks to go in and sell coaching as the #1 service. Coaching seems to be something that we can sell based on a relationship that we already have with an organization or an individual. It's based on trust, and it's hard to sell that. It's a lot easier to sell your ability at delivering some sort of HR service, or doing some kind of assessment, or providing something else first—a training or lunch-and-learn. Then over the course of time, after seeing how you operate, people say, "Well, tell me about this coaching thing," and you are able to then roll that out.

[Suzi] I think that's right. And it does get to the point where if you can offer coaching about a specific skill development area that's in demand, that can be a way in the door as well.

[Jeremy] That's even another way of reducing their uncertainty about coaching, or it could be a skill demand. Say you're talking about emotional intelligence, you could use a specific topic or competence that people want to learn as an entry point to sell coaching.

[Suzi] An example of that is next week I'm going out to Chicago to work with a firm that I don't have a previous relationship with—they called me out of the blue.

[Len] That's based on a referral, right?

[Suzi] No. It's indirectly based on a talk that I gave in D.C. to the Legal Marketing Association on "Taking a Leadership Role in Your Law Firm." There were about 65 people there, one of whom was a woman who ended up writing an article for a website devoted to law—suddenly there was this article about my session on the web. And they had gone to my website and downloaded my picture, so my picture shows up on their website next to an article about the talk I gave in D.C., and then I get a call out of the blue from a law firm in Chicago that saw the article.

[Jeremy] That's a great example of working your niche.

[Suzi] And I didn't even work it myself! It was all pretty exciting, and what they've hired me to do is come out there and provide coaching for nine different attorneys who want some extra help in presentation skills. So I've got nine one-on-one sessions set up, and they didn't want to do it as a training because everyone wanted something slightly different. So I actually think, John, with the work that you do, that you could tailor something specifically to overcoming resistance; that's definitely a skill that people would want coaching for. So I think that you have a good "in" there to structure coaching right around that.

[John] Right. Some number I heard several years ago—that may or may not have been true then, but I've taken it as gospel since—was that when we give a public workshop or presentation, over the next five years, 11 percent of the people who attend the presentation will come back for consulting.

[Suzi] Wow.

[John] And this is before the internet. Your story might mean that it's gone up some.

[Suzi] Well, I have to tell you that story certainly isn't the norm for me. But I often have people approach me after I've given a talk, wanting to know more or wanting to hire me as their individual coach. But the Chicago work was completely out of the blue—to have a firm hire me that had not attended one of my talks.

[John] Another thing about people being skittish about coaching—I'm sort of new to the jargon—is that sometimes I get the impression that the coach wants to hear people validate them as doing coaching, and it seems like the client is more concerned about what's going to solve their problems. And the normal jargon for that is some kind of consultation—some kind of assistance—and in a very real sense, coaching is just one of several types of intervention. It's like a one-on-one training—a one-on-one consulting type of thing. One of the problems I have is deciding when to and when not to use coaching. And when I look at what's going on in me, it's more an exercise for them to validate me as a coach, as opposed to my wanting to solve their problems.

[Suzi] Well, there's a distinction there . . . you're pointing to a distinction that's been batted around the coaching community for quite some time: what is the distinction between *coaching* and *consulting*? And the distinction that I heard years ago—which is pretty much how I define it for my clients—is this: *Consulting* means that I am bringing an expertise to bear that will help you solve your problems, and that I will offer you recommendations and suggestions for how to solve particular problems based on my expertise. *Coaching* means I am a guide providing mastery in the process so that you can come up with solutions for your problems, you bring your own expertise to bear, and I am just helping you get out of your own way.

[John] Yes, I've heard that too, and that definition of consulting works when you're doing consulting for a group or an organization. But when you're working in an organization with *individuals*, one-on-one, any consulting that you do is very, very similar, if not identical to, what we do when we say that we're coaching. So to me, the big distinction is the size of the target group, because when it comes down to one-on-one, it's damn near identical.

[Jeremy] The important thing is that you get the work. You can call it what you want.

[Suzi] If you get paid for it, that's right. The important thing is to get *paid* work. In our call next week on networking, we're going to really get into networking activities as distinct from sales activities and marketing activities. So no homework on that—the ongoing homework for this course is to make calls, make calls, make calls. Get appointments, get appointments, get appointments. Get *paid* gigs!

Homework

Continue to make calls, set appointments, and move targets through your sales cycle.

The Purpose of Proposals

The truth of the matter is that I hate doing proposals, and try my best to avoid them or get around writing them. Sometimes that is not possible, so here are a few tips if you have to do a proposal.

First of all, find out the purpose of the proposal. Preferably, this should happen before you invest a week's worth of your time carefully crafting the ultimate marketing piece, because a proposal is either a marketing piece or it's an administrative piece. You need to know which it is so that you know how to write it. In many cases, if the proposal is required because the person to whom you have been selling needs to pitch your services internally, do your best to find out who these other decision makers are and attempt to set up a meeting with them directly. If that is not an option (perhaps you are already dealing with the key decision maker, but he has to get funding from the Board or a silent partner), then your role is to support your client in shaping the most effective communication to his audience. That involves having conversations and co-designing with your client what kind of proposal will best address the issues and concerns of those to whom he must pitch.

If, on the other hand, the client simply wants a proposal so that he will have something in writing, then you are not really writing a proposal; you are writing a letter of agreement, yet you might not have sealed the deal. Make sure you are not the one pushing a proposal as an extra unnecessary step in the sales process if the client is ready to get started. I see many of our colleagues do this: They offer a proposal instead of asking for business and writing a contract or letter of agreement. This only lengthens the sales process with an unnecessary step. If you are shy about asking for the business, will spending hours crafting a proposal help? I say not. My point here is that you must assess for yourself, in the context of your sales process, how relevant it is to write a proposal. Will it move your sales process forward? Are you using the proposal as an avoidance tactic instead of asking for the business? What is the purpose of the proposal and can that purpose be achieved another way?

Proposal Models

There are a great many models of proposals you can use; here are just a few to get you started. Ultimately, if you must write a proposal, and if you are completely clear about its purpose, the model doesn't really matter, so pick one you like and go for it! Of course, written communication is a reflection of your professionalism, so be sure to have someone proofread and edit your proposal for grammar, spelling, syntax, and clarity.

Gilberg Model

Situation
Results
Recommendation
Rationale
Implementation
Price

PSR Model

Problem
Solution
Results

Project Model

Project Overview:
Context
Benefits
Service
Deliverables

Project Approach:
Steps
Timeline

Program Fees:
Payment Schedule

Other outlines I've seen people use are variations on these themes:

Outline # 1

Program objectives

Our understanding of your
situation

Proposed solution

Program description

    Intake session

    Assessment

Development plan of action

    One-on-one coaching

    Team coaching

Costs

About your project leader

Why invest in coaching?

Outline # 2

Background

Assignment

Goals

Proposal

Recommended
timing/approach

Pricing

Outline # 3

Situation overview

Scope of work

Strategy/approach

Assumptions

Project timeline

Fees and payment schedule

Resources utilization

Outline # 4

Current situation

Goals and objectives

The solution (purpose,
approach, and deliverables
of each phase)

Confidentiality, coaching
ethics, and intellectual
property

Biographies

Client list and references

Schedule and budget

Project timeline

And the final two for your consideration:

VQC Model

Introduction:
    Who we are (firm overview, clients, capabilities matrix)
        Why choose our company (knowledge of your industry
        or company, extensive expertise and experience in similar
        situations—either listing similar companies served or similar
        industry—focus on performance and results, associates'
        qualifications and experience)
Statement of Work:
    Our understanding
    Our strategy and solution
    Expected benefits
    Deliverables
    Process
        Step 1: Needs assessment and results
        Step 2: Design and development
        Step 3: Ongoing support and consultation
    Bios of team members

Chiropractor Model

Answer four questions:
    1. What's wrong?
    2. Can you fix it?
    3. How long will it take to fix it?
    4. How much will it cost?

Pricing

Are you charging enough? At the risk of sounding flip or glib, my advice is to simply price your services as high as the market will bear. Do your homework, of course. Find out what others are charging for similar services. Be sure to include your cost of doing business, administrative costs, travel time, preparation time, and other incidentals. Also, be sure to state clearly that you will be billing the client for reimbursement for any out-of-pocket expenses associated with the fulfillment of the engagement.

You can price your services in a variety of ways: hourly, daily, annually, retainer agreements, by project, by results, or any alternative fee arrangement that works for your clients. But whether you price your services hourly, daily, on retainer, fixed fee, or some alternative fee arrangements, be sure you are clear about three things:

1. Is it worth it to you?
2. What is the value proposition for the client, and are they getting more than they are paying for?
3. Are you competitively priced in the market?

It is great fun to be priced at an hourly rate that feels ridiculous to you and yet you still have more clients than you have time to serve, so you keep raising your rates for each new client that comes along. Soon, however, you will find that there is a breaking point at which the market will no longer allow you to raise your rates. There is no need to box yourself into raising your rates only once a year. Raise your rates continually until the market yells, "Uncle!" or until you have a comfortable balance in terms of number of clients and income generated for your time spent. Of course, having products and multiple streams of income is always a good business idea.

Think about your current pricing. Is it hourly? Is it daily? Is it per product or service? Does it vary? Is it strategically designed to align with your overall vision or business strategy? The time and energy you have invested in your education, other professional training, and experience should factor into your pricing. What will the market bear? When creating your pricing, take into account the money you have spent to get where you are. Take into account your education, your degrees, your professional training, and any leadership or executive positions you have held. Take into account your coach training certification program (or whatever professional training you've had), any certificates earned, your coaching (or other) credentials, and all that you've learned from the fabulous mistakes you've made along the way. And please take into account your life learnings. When you consider all that, you can likely raise your current fees by 150 percent right now! Meaning, if you currently charge $100 an hour, you can raise your rates to $250 an hour.

Create some levels or scope steps to your top price. If you have different price points of entry to working with you, then there is always some way for clients to have the experience of what you have to offer. Have one or two free "tastes" you give away to people. No, I'm not talking about free coaching samples. I'm talking about marketing materials that you give away that add value. Perhaps you have a free e-course they can download, or a free guide or free report you wrote that you can send out by auto-responder from your website. Maybe you can create a free top 10 list of something that points to your expertise in a given industry or domain. Be creative!

Shifting the Money Conversation

"The world is awash in money! Do you hear what that means?
It is awash in money. It is flowing for everyone. It is like Niagara Falls.
And most of you are showing up with your teaspoons."

—Abraham-Hicks[1]

Are you under-valuing your experience and under-pricing your coaching, consulting, or other professional services? Our executive clients take us more seriously if we are priced in league with them . . . how credible are you if your hourly rate is more along the lines of what their administrative staff earns? There is a scarcity mentality prevalent in our professional community. This scarcity thinking or poverty outlook leads to coaches undervaluing themselves, their experience, and their education, which leads to under-pricing coaching services.

There are scarcity mindsets and coaching belief systems embedded in our professional community and propagated in our coach training schools that set up coaches to not make money. One such approach is the concept of giving away free coaching sessions to lure in clients. In reality, this method primarily allows the coach to under-value his services and to attract clients who are more committed to getting something for free than those who truly value the coach and the service. Once someone gets your services for free, it is very difficult to transition to paying high dollars for it. Do not diminish yourself or our profession by attaching a valuation of zero to our work. You can make a huge contribution to the world by providing pro bono services to those who cannot afford it, but giving it away for free as a sales ploy is inauthentic and gimmicky. Offer a reduced introductory rate, if you must, but stop giving away free samples.

I am continually amazed at the statistics I read about the coaching profession that estimate that fewer than 7 percent of coaches are making a living at it. Yet there is a small percentage of sufficiently abundance- and prosperity-minded coaches who are generating sustainable six-figure revenues through coaching, and even fewer who have successful business models such that they are sustaining multimillion-dollar coaching businesses. Financial literacy coupled with abundance thinking can help coaches shift the money conversation in our profession.[2]

Asking for What You Want

Closing the deal in a client meeting becomes very simple—almost a non-event if you've been fully present in the conversation. It is a matter of listening for the opportunity to ask for what you want. Yes, you have to actually *ask* for the "buy." You have to ask your client to contract with you. You have to ask for the money. However, if you have been selling through your natural style, using a coaching approach to sales, having an abundance mentality and a helping mindset, then closing is as effortless as falling off a log. If you find that you have blocks when it comes to closing deals, then I'd refer you back to "Shifting the Money Conversation" above and suggest that producing such a shift for yourself will allow you to generate a breakthrough in asking for and getting what you want.

Of course, first you must know what you want. It may sound simple, but this part often takes quite a while to sort through. You have to actually know what you want with extreme clarity before you can ask for it. It is useful to think through how you would ideally like to structure the engagement so that you'll have some ideas when going into your client meetings. Work with your clients to create a structure that will work for the organization, the end-user client, and you. Think of creative ways to encourage your clients to structure the deal in the way that you want. What do you want to encourage your clients to do? For example, I often work with lawyers and law firms. They prefer to structure coaching engagements on an hourly model, because that is how they bill their clients. However, I prefer to work on retainer. Knowing that ahead of time, I can offer a volume discount if a client is willing to pay on the retainer plan.

The Set Up: Structuring the Engagement

It is important to have a strategy going in to any deal. Think through your desired answers to the following questions:

How will you set it up to serve all parties involved?
What needs to happen? What are the steps to getting off the ground?
What initial conversations need to happen with the client?
What needs to be discussed initially with the organizational representative who is hiring you?

For example, when I get to this stage of the dialogue with clients, I typically lay out for them the process for how we will work together, how communication and reporting will work, what I am and am not willing to share in order to protect confidentiality and build trust with my client, how our work together will end, what results can be expected and the conditions for satisfaction therein, how progress will be measured, and what they might do to feel like they are in the loop and connected to the process.

Contracting and Setting Up an Engagement

When contracting an engagement with a client, there are several ethical points to consider.[3] Of course, in general, it is just plain good business sense to clarify at the outset of any engagement the roles, agendas, expectations, and results intended. But what about if you are in a situation where you have two tiers of clients inside the organization? You must contract with both the organizational representative and your end-user client. In both cases, you must make clear the boundaries of confidentiality and any reporting requirements that might impact your role.

Clarify the expectations and how they differ between the client and the organization so that you can manage the experience of both parties in terms of what your work will and will not do toward meeting their expectations. Encouraging your client to share his or her progress with others in the company will help you maintain confidentiality. Clarify the boundaries around what the company has a business need or right to know prior to the engagement. Determine and communicate up front your exit strategy and how clients will be cared for after you transition out.

Have your lawyer help you with specific clauses in your agreements. Have one agreement template that is the general agreement for the paying party, or the organization, and a secondary agreement template that is for the individual being coached. Then you can simply customize each engagement with a letter of agreement that details the specifics you've worked out with your client and attach the templates that are appropriate.

A word of caution: Be careful about promising complete and absolute confidentiality in your agreements. Because coach-client communications do not enjoy the same protections as other professions—we have no such thing as doctor-patient or attorney-client privilege—we can be subpoenaed to appear in court. I have heard of cases where an executive coach's notes were entered into evidence and the coach had to testify against her client.

Also, be super clear about the distinctions between coaching, consulting, and counseling. The precedent was set in a court case in Colorado where a coach was sued for practicing therapy without a license! Make sure you have mental-health practitioners in your network so that you can make referrals when you come upon clients with issues and needs that coaching and consulting cannot address.

Think through, prior to any client meeting, how you want to set up the engagement and what needs to happen and be discussed before going forward. What do you need to discuss initially with the client versus with the organizational representative?

One question that comes up a lot from clients is about reporting, particularly, for example, when a CEO and HR have hired me to work with a VP. In this case, the CEO and HR are the engagement sponsors, and my typical response is something like this:

[HR] Once you meet with James [the VP], how will you share feedback with us from his first session? Moving forward over the next few months, when and how should we expect you to share your findings?

[CEO] Yes, I want to know what's happening in his coaching as you proceed. Please keep me closely informed.

[Executive Coach] My initial priority will be to create a solid coaching relationship with James. Therefore, in order to build trust and confidentiality and earn his respect, I won't be sharing with you any *specific* things he shares with me.

I realize, however, the importance of keeping you (CEO and HR) informed. Usually how this works is that I can share with you overall observations about James's progress as we work together—how he's performing in the coaching conversations, my impressions of what the issues really are and if coaching is the right intervention, and whether he seems to be on track and engaged with the pursuit of the intended outcomes/goals of the relationship.

Typically, I encourage those I coach to give the more specific feedback to management directly. Thus, I will be urging James to share with you both how it's going for him and any specifics that come up in our conversations that are relevant. Part of my role will be to support James in sharing those things with you that he might not otherwise think to reveal.

It is important for the success of the coaching engagement that I create a safe space for James, where he knows I'm in his corner and feels comfortable with my role as his sounding board and trusted advisor. If he believes that I am reporting specifics back to you, it will diminish my effectiveness with him.

James and I will spend our first one or two sessions clarifying and formulating the goals for the coaching engagement. If you have specific input for those conversations, I'd love to incorporate it. Once we have clearly defined goals with observable and measurable results outlined, either James or I will share those with you, depending on his preference.

It is critical, from my perspective, to leave the lines of communication open between those of us who are stakeholders in this project. Thus, I am always available for questions or concerns or information you'd like to share with me, and I will be sharing with you what I can that doesn't violate or muddy up the confidentiality and trust with James. I will be encouraging him to share with you as well.

In addition to that informal communication, I would like to formally check in with you both at the mid-way point, if not sooner, to be sure that we are keeping each other informed of how it's going. I will be looking to you for your impressions of James's progress and any improvements you have noticed at that time. We typically call that mid-engagement meeting a lessons-learned meeting. We'll look at what's working, what's not working, and how we can improve for the remainder of the engagement if something's not working.

Coaching Agreement

Setting up the engagement has a lot to do with knowing what you want and communicating clear boundaries. It also, inevitably, requires paperwork. In the event that these might be helpful to you, below are my sample agreement templates. Feel free to steal shamelessly from them for your own use if any of it is relevant for your business; however, I strongly recommend that you have your own attorney approve the agreements and contracts you create before you use them.

Sample:
Coaching Agreement

This agreement is entered into on *insert date here* between Suzanne I. Pomerantz, MT, MCC, Executive Officer of Innovative Leadership International LLC (Coaching Consultant, hereinafter *Coach*) and *insert client name, title, company, and address here* (hereinafter *Client*).

1. Client shall pay to the Coach the non-refundable sum of $350 per hour for telephone coaching consultations and $3500 per eight-hour day for meetings, training, facilitation, preparation and travel time in consideration for the Coach's work with respect to the Client's chosen area(s) of performance and productivity. Payment is due in full within 30 days of receipt of the invoice for each scheduled phone session or personal meeting. Volume discount for retainer agreements is $1500 per month for four scheduled coaching calls and one hour preparation time to be paid in advance on the first of each month. *Alternate agreement should be noted here* _____.

2. The structure of coaching sessions in terms of frequency and duration will be determined and agreed upon by the Coach and the Client together. The Client agrees to compensate the Coach for all sessions based upon verbal agreement of structure.

3. The Coach reserves the right to bill the Client for a missed meeting if the meeting is not canceled or re-scheduled at least 48 hours prior to the scheduled time.

4. The Client agrees to pay for all of the Coach's travel, meal, and lodging expenses associated with the delivery of coaching consultation meetings, which will be reimbursed at cost.

5. The Client agrees to initiate all scheduled telephone conferences, or will pay for the Coach's associated phone expenses.

6. The minimum coaching agreement is six months unless otherwise approved by the Coach.

7. The Client understands that the Coach's processes and program materials are proprietary information and agrees NOT to disclose or use said information for purposes or business other than per the conditions of this agreement. Should the Client breach this paragraph, the Coach shall, in addition to all other remedies, retain the remedy of injunctive relief.

8. The Client agrees to communicate honestly, to be open to feedback and assistance, and to create the time and energy to participate fully in the coaching program. This includes full compliance with suggested practices, systems, tools, program terms, and completing all assignments. Client assumes full responsibility for results and outcomes produced from the coaching relationship, and Client agrees to save and hold harmless the Coach from any liability that may arise as a result of Client's negligent performance or any perceived act of omission or negligence on the part of the Coach in accordance with this agreement.

(continued)

Sample:
Coaching Agreement *(concluded)*

9. Coach makes no guarantee as to the results achieved nor is responsible for the results achieved from the coaching due to the subjective nature of the work. The Coach agrees to serve as guide, advisor, and consultant in the area(s) identified by the Client, however the Client is solely accountable for producing any and all results.

10. Coach agrees to maintain complete confidentiality of all verbal and written Client information disclosed or received unless permission is received from Client. Coach upholds ethical guidelines set forth by the International Coach Federation.

11. This agreement may be terminated with cause by either party with 7 days written notice to the other party, or without cause upon 30 days written notice to the other party. It is agreed that this agreement shall be reviewed to insure its workability. The term of this agreement is to be for six months and is automatically renewed for another six months unless otherwise specified. At a time of voluntary separation or termination of the agreement, both parties agree to make every effort to assure the welfare of both parties.

12. This agreement shall not be altered, changed, modified, or amended except by written consent of all parties to the agreement.

Should litigation arise out of this agreement, the losing party shall pay the prevailing party's attorney's fees and associated costs. This is the entire agreement of the parties, and any representations not contained herein shall have no force or effect. Except as may be otherwise provided in this agreement, all claims, counterclaims, disputes, and other matters in question between Client and Coach arising out of or relating to this agreement or breach thereof will be decided by arbitration if the parties hereto mutually agree, or in a court of competent jurisdiction within the State of Maryland. This agreement shall have been deemed to have been signed and performed in Maryland *if the client business is outside of MD, insert their state here* and the agreement shall be interpreted and any disputes resolved according to the laws of the State of Maryland.

Signatures:

For the Coach: For the Client:

_____   _____
Suzanne I. Pomerantz, MT, MCC   *insert their name here*
Innovative Leadership International, LLC

_____   _____
Suzi Pomerantz/Executive Officer
       print name/title   print name/title

Individual Coaching Agreement

The purpose of this document is to seal the intention for a powerful coaching relationship between the coach and the individual client. It details the expectations that will produce the specific outcomes the coach and client design together.

Sample:
Individual Coaching Agreement

Name: _____

Company: _____

Sponsors: _____

Address: _____

_____

_____

Direct Dial: _____

E-mail: _____

Fax: _____

Requirements:

1. Innovative Leadership International LLC receives from _____
   all coaching fees by the first of each month in advance except in a fixed-fee arrangement whereas payment is due upon receipt of invoice.

2. All payments are made payable to Innovative Leadership International LLC.

3. Client calls coach at the scheduled time, *on time* at 301-601-1525. If the client calls over 10 minutes late, the client misses the appointment.

4. Client agrees to abide by the following "Coaching Policies and Procedures."

(continued)

Sample:
Individual Coaching Agreement *(continued)*

Coaching Policies and Procedures

Sessions: Client receives five sessions over two month's time. The initial coaching meeting will take place in person, and the remaining four sessions will be by telephone and they are for approximately 45 minutes each. The client and the coach will schedule around holidays, vacations, and time off as requested by the client and coach. It is up to the client to make sure to get all the coaching sessions each month. For telephone coaching, the client calls the coach at a pre-arranged number, date, and time. If the client calls over 10 minutes late, the client misses the appointment.

Fees: Fixed-fee arrangement: $3000 will be billed to _____ through Human Resources. The fees are for the coaching service for two months including all scheduled coaching appointments, assignments, preparation time and post-coaching appointment work, administration time, reporting, and local travel. Client pays the full rate even when the client misses appointments.

Cancellations: To cancel an appointment, please call your coach as soon as you know. Cancellations must be made 48 hours in advance. If the client gives 48 hours notice and wants to reschedule an appointment, the client may do so during the same week of the original appointment, depending upon the coach's availability. If the coach is not available to reschedule the appointment, or if a rescheduling/cancellation occurs in less than 48 hours, the client loses the appointment.

E-coaching: The client may e-mail the coach at any time for brief "spot coaching" in between scheduled sessions. This may result in a brief telephone conversation, depending on the nature of the coaching request. If this exchange exceeds 15 minutes, the coach reserves the right to bill for the additional time at the hourly rate of $400. You can e-mail your coach at coach@innovativeleader.com anytime.

Time Duration: Coaching can last three months to multiple years, depending upon project requirements. Innovative Leadership International LLC typically has long-term, ongoing relationships with most clients. Our initial minimum

(continued)

Sample:
Individual Coaching Agreement *(continued)*

coaching agreement is for six months with a review at three months to assess the coaching progress and agreement terms. In some cases, we will arrange a different, mutually agreed-upon duration for a fixed-fee or retainer agreement. In those cases, the coaching will end at the pre-determined time unless the client requests a new agreement.

Completion: Client or coach gives at least a 30-day notice prior to ending the coaching relationship and agreement after the minimum six-month initial period.

This agreement, between _____ and Innovative Leadership International LLC will begin on May 01, 2006, and will end at the end of July 2006.

Service Provided: The service to be provided by Innovative Leadership International LLC to the client is executive coaching, both in-person and via telephone, as designed jointly with Human Resources, the client, her supervisor, and the coach. Coaching, which is not therapy or counseling, may address communication or leadership strategies, specific personal projects, business successes, performance and productivity, or general conditions in the client's life or profession.

Our Promises: Innovative Leadership International LLC promises that the information provided by the client will be kept confidential except when otherwise required by law. The only data shared with others is for learning purposes and will be non-identifiable. We may ask for specific business and personal information, and we respect the client's willingness to be truthful while we maintain confidentiality. Coach agrees to maintain complete verbal and written confidentiality of all client information disclosed or received unless permission is received from client. Coach upholds ethical guidelines set forth by the International Coach Federation.

Granting Permission and Power to the Coaching Relationship: Throughout the coaching relationship, the coach will engage the client in very direct and personal conversations. The client can count on the coach to be honest and straightforward, and to have integrity. The purpose of our interaction is to remind the client of his or her intentions and to coach the client to realize these intentions. The client firmly understands that only the client can grant power to the coaching relationship. Therefore, the client agrees to make the coaching relationship powerful. If the client thinks the coaching is not working at any given time, the client will communicate and take action to restore the power of the coaching relationship.

(continued)

Sample:
Individual Coaching Agreement *(concluded)*

The client understands that the coach's processes and program materials are proprietary information and agrees NOT to disclose or use said information for purposes or business other than per the conditions of this agreement and the coaching engagement.

The client agrees to communicate honestly, to be open to feedback and assistance, and to create the time and energy to participate fully in the coaching program. This includes full compliance with suggested practices, systems, tools, program terms, and completing all assignments.

Client assumes full responsibility for results and outcomes produced from the coaching relationship, and client agrees to save and hold harmless the coach from any liability that may arise as a result of client's negligent performance or any perceived act of omission or negligence on the part of the coach in accordance with this agreement.

Coach makes no guarantee as to the results achieved nor is responsible for the results achieved from the coaching due to the subjective nature of the work. The coach agrees to serve as guide, advisor, and consultant in the area(s) identified by the client, however the client is solely accountable for producing any and all results.

By signing below, you, the client, agree to keep your agreements, to regard our coaching appointment time frames with respect, and to keep the coach informed as to what you need in order to keep moving forward.

Your signature below indicates full compliance with and understanding of this agreement.

_____   _____
Client   Date
Approval:

_____   _____
Suzanne I. Pomerantz, MT, MCC   Date
Executive Coach
Innovative Leadership International, LLC

Coaching ROI Resources

It is always helpful in making the business case for your services to provide some data about the ROI of your services. In this case, if you are a coach, you can use some of the following resources when writing your proposals and agreements.

January 4, 2001, Manchester Inc. released a study that quantifies the business impact of executive coaching stating that "a company's investment in providing coaching to its executives realized an average return on investment of almost six times the cost of the coaching."

November 2, 2001, MetrixGlobal LLC determined the business benefits and return on investment for executive coaching programs. "Coaching produced a 529% return on investment and significant intangible benefits to the business. The study provided powerful new insights into how to maximize the business impact from executive coaching."

Anderson, D., & Anderson, M., (2004). *Coaching that counts: Harnessing the power of leadership coaching to deliver strategic value.* Boston: Butterworth-Heinemann.

O'Neill, M. B., (2005, February). An ROI method for executive coaching: Have the client convince the coach of the return on investment. *International Journal of Coaching in Organizations.*

Peterson, D. B., & Kraiger, K., (2004). A practical guide to evaluating coaching: Translating state-of-the-art techniques to the real world. In Edwards, J. E., Scott, J. C., & Raju, N. S. (Eds.), *The human resources program evaluation handbook* (pp. 262–282). Thousand Oaks, CA: Sage.

Phillips, J., Ph.D., & Phillips, P., (2004, Spring). Measuring ROI in executive coaching. *Executive Coach Magazine:* 18–21.

Phillips, P., (2002). *The bottomline on ROI.* Atlanta, GA: CEP Press.

Tobin, D., (1998). The fallacy of ROI calculations. *Corporate Learning Strategies.*

Corporate Executive Board and Corporate Leadership Council study on ROI on Executive Coaching, January 2002.
www.corporateleadershipcouncil.com

Endnotes

1. See www.abraham-hicks.com/for publications and quotations from inspirational speaker Esther Hicks and her Abraham group.

2. Financial Literacy is a booming coaching and training industry. Books by Robert Kiyosaki are a good resource, and you can learn more at www.Liveoutloud.com.

3. Pomerantz, S., & Eiting, J., (2004). Drawing lines in the sand: Ethics in coaching, contracting and confidentiality. *International Journal of Coaching in Organizations, (2)*3.

Step 8
Networking

> "And the day came when the risk to remain tight in a bud was more painful than the risk it took to blossom."
>
> —Anais Nin

This chapter starts out with a telecourse conversation about expanding the sale, and then moves into networking. The rest of the chapter explains what networking is, summarizes the Nine Mindsets of Networking, and outlines some networking actions you can consider trying out. Networking is not just for extroverts! Marianne Williamson, in *A Return to Love,* wrote these words of encouragement:

> Our deepest fear is not that we are inadequate. Our deepest fear is that we are powerful beyond measure. It is our light not our darkness that most frightens us. We ask ourselves, "Who am I to be brilliant, gorgeous, talented and fabulous?" Actually, who are you NOT to be? Your playing small doesn't serve the world. There is nothing enlightened about shrinking so that others won't feel insecure around you. We are born to manifest the glory that is within us. It is in everyone. And as we let our own light shine, we unconsciously give others permission to do the same. As we are liberated from our own fear, our presence automatically liberates others.[1]

Telecourse Session #8:
Expanding the Sale and Using Your Network

Ways to Expand the Sale

[Len] At one point in our last meeting, we touched briefly on expanding the sale, and I wanted to make sure I understood what that meant.

[Bill] You're referring to the sample proposal?

[Len] Well, actually I was referring to the goals in the sample proposal; there were about five of them, as I recall, and the fifth one related to the supervisors of the new-hire minority lawyers. What I thought Suzi was thinking was that a way to expand the coaching part of this contract would be to also provide the coaching to the supervisors.

[Suzi] Exactly.

[Len] Is that what you mean by expanding the sale?

[Suzi] That's one way of expanding the sale. Last week, I was specifically talking about situations where sometimes you can get into a corporation by closing with something smaller than all of the services you can help them with.

For example, there have been situations where I started with a company because they wanted one training session—a one-day thing, or a half-day investment on their part. That's all they wanted. The opportunity to expand the sale in that case is for follow-up work from the training (for example, to get into coaching after the training). Or if they sign up with you to coach one person, you can expand the sale by coaching more than one. There are lots of different ways to expand the sale. You could start out coaching one person, then expand to facilitating a strategic planning or leadership retreat for the whole firm.

What it basically means is just going for more. Sometimes you can't go for the whole enchilada; sometimes you just go for a small close, you get the close, you prove yourself, and then you can expand it from there. Seal a small deal, then once you're a known quantity, seal the big deal.

[Len] And I also thought it meant that if your original project didn't work out exactly as they had thought, you were telling them what else might be necessary—in the example of your proposal, providing direction to the supervisors who were providing direction to the employees.

[Suzi] Yeah. I always try to include the supervisors as much as possible, and if they don't want to get involved in coaching, I definitely want to create a relationship where I can provide feedback to them—not specifically about what happened in the coaching, but where they should go with it after I leave. I like to leave them with next steps, or predictions for the future that I see based on my coaching with the person—more of a diagnostic debriefing than anything else.

[Len] I see coaching as the kind of experience, for many people, that comes out of a trusted relationship or a relationship that involves experience with one another. It's one thing to be referred for a coaching engagement for an organization or an individual that's looking for coaching, and it's another thing to sell coaching to a new organization that knows nothing of you. It seems like it's a lot easier to have a training component, an assessment component, an OD component, or some kind of consulting component up front that you use as your lead-in, get-to-know-me, I-get-to-know-you relationship, which requires relatively small commitment from the firm in terms of time and money. And then you add on the coaching as you get to know one another over time. You can always tell them about it in your beginning sales pitch, but you don't necessarily lead with it.

[Suzi] That's right, Len! And you can also sell skill-based coaching right off the bat. For example, I'm leaving today for Chicago to go work with nine different attorneys at a law firm who all want different kinds of presentation skill coaching. So that's around a specific skill set.

[Len] Right. That's more like a training.

[Suzi] It's more personalized training, exactly. But that is a way that can open up the door to at least the concept of coaching in an organization, and then from that into the kind of coaching that we love to do most, which is the strategic, trusted advisor kind of coaching. So any other follow ups from previous calls or questions? I'd love to hear from everybody how you're doing on making your calls, and how that's going with setting up appointments.

[Len] I've gotten more involved in working with that outplacement company. After a lecture they sponsored at the Harvard Club the other night, I ended up coaching someone for one of the hours that my coaching partner had proposed to do. And I'm trying to expand that to an add-on to his coaching contracts. I'm trying to develop a model where my partner does one kind of coaching and I do another kind of coaching. So I seem to feel more comfortable expanding things than puncturing holes in and diving through.

[Suzi] Well, if you can design your whole strategy around expanding things, go for it—there's nothing wrong with that. Remember when we talked about cold calls versus warm calls or referrals? You can design your whole business-building strategy around warm calls and referrals, and never have to make another cold call again. So it's really about figuring out what works for you and having a strategy and structures to support that. If you have someone else—a partner—who can seal the deal for you, and you can just get in there and expand the sale, by all means: Let that be your strategy and go forth and prosper!

[Len] I have a question about what you see as that other entrée into coaching. What would you be selling if you're not selling coaching right up front; what is the easiest, fastest service to offer?

[Suzi] Well, I think Jeremy hit on it in our previous call when he talked about doing assessments and training or meeting facilitation. Those are great places to start.

[Len] Assessments, okay. Training, I don't know—that's kind of time consuming.

[Suzi] It doesn't have to be. A lot of organizations now don't want to devote full days to training, so you can do a training session over a brown-bag lunch, or a two-hour session, or a short seminar, or even a half-day. But you don't have to commit the time for a whole day, or two whole days. There are places where you can do one-on-one training, you know. But I usually call that coaching, just to get them used to the concept of coaching.

I can tell you from experience, though, it's so much easier to sell coaching into organizations now than it was when I started years ago, because now people have heard of it and it's accepted. There's a great article in the May 2001 issue of *Training Magazine* called "Proactive Coaching." It talks about coaching being a perk and a benefit for top producers, top executives, and top performers. It's really well done. And it talks about a couple different ways that organizations are measuring ROI on coaching. Their website is www.trainingmag.com. If you want to read the article, it's in the May 2001 issue and it's on page 58.

[Len] What do you think would be a hot presentational thing for an afternoon or a lunch?

[Suzi] It depends on what you want to focus on, and who you are and who they are. What's your strong suit?

[Len] My forte is interpersonal skills, but that sounds pretty generic.

[Suzi] So pick some particular element of interpersonal skills. I have a colleague whose entire business is built around dealing with difficult people. She has tapes, books, workshops, and keynotes about dealing with difficult people. Just pick one element of interpersonal communication that would be appealing to an organization or to a broad cross section of people in an organization. "Providing effective feedback to your colleagues in a team environment" is one idea. I actually had a request for that recently.

[Deb] That's a good one.

[Suzi] It was from a creative organization. . . . They're a marketing and communications firm with about 25 people in the company, all working together as teams and cross teams. And there are times when they have to give each other feedback about their work, or they have to say, "You know, I really don't think we should go in that direction, and here's why," only they don't do it very politely. Their interpersonal skills are such that they basically leave dead bodies all around and end up causing all kinds of friction. So that's a topic that's of high interest to them: How do you give feedback to a colleague when it's not positive? And do it in a way that protects the common desire to have a collaborative environment.

[Deb] I think that's a really popular one too, especially now that you have managers who don't know how to give feedback.

[Suzi] And especially because there was that huge movement a couple of years back to do everything in work teams, so now you've got all these teams. But you know, people don't know how to work in teams any more than they know how to work with difficult co-workers or bosses or subordinates. So you're going to have those interpersonal issues anywhere you have teams.

[Len] But the focus is teams?

[Suzi] Could be.

[Deb] Or could be individual.

[Suzi] You could get individuals.

[Jeremy] You could be providing effective feedback to your direct reports.

[Deb] We could make a whole list: teams, individuals, direct reports, coaching your employees to do that . . . you know, whatever.

[Suzi] That's another hot topic, too: how to be a coach. Do a seminar for managers or people who have to supervise others in coaching skills. Lots of organizations think, "Great, if we turn all these people into internal coaches, we don't need to hire external coaches."

[Len] Right, but it just turns out to be a great advertisement for you.

[Suzi] Of course it is, because they start to see how difficult and challenging it really is, and they realize, "I don't want to do that on top of my regular job. I'm getting paid to do X, Y, and Z; I don't want to add this whole other job on top of it," and then you end up getting the business.

So are we ready to move on to networking?

Ongoing Networking

[Suzi] On one of the early calls, we talked about the distinction between networking, marketing, and sales. So now we're going to focus on the networking piece of the triangle, which is really about seeking connections. It's not about closing the sale, or having the meetings, and it's not about the precursor to that, which is all the image-building stuff, the writing, and the presentations—that's marketing. What we're going to talk about now is the ongoing activity of networking and the networking mindsets.

What are the mindsets that are helpful in seeking as many network connections as you can, building your network to a place where it can work for you—where it can help support your marketing efforts and your sales efforts? To start out, I'd like to go and have each of you say what networking is for you. Then we'll get into the Nine Mindsets.

[Jeremy] For me, networking is the big schmooze . . . where in a very nice and friendly way, you're like Velcro with the people you run across in work and your seminars and elsewhere. You follow up with them and you keep some kind of a relationship going.

[Deb] I'm the conference queen, and networking I think is my strength. Being the eternal extrovert, I can talk to just about anybody, anywhere. I can do great at the initial meeting, and what I'd like to talk about is how you keep it going.

[Suzi] How to have it work for you?

[Deb] Right, because I've got tons of contacts, but I want to know where you put your energy and how do you make it work for you?

[Suzi] Yes, it does take a lot of energy and you can't keep up with everybody.

[Jeremy] So that's sort of the next question right?

[Deb] Yeah. And one other question would be how do you target who you network with?

[Suzi] So we'll deal with how you target them and how you keep up with it and how to be more strategic about it. Okay, who's next?

[John] It's your strength, Deb, but making the initial contacts and schmoozing are my weaknesses. I'm the most internal of internals, and so initiating a relationship, that type of stuff, is really tough for me.

[Bill] I'm in between introvert and extrovert. Networking for me is like putting on a suit, sort of talking the talk, and becoming that. I kind of discover who I am in that world when I do it. I gain confidence when I network. The closer I get to the thing, the more confident I am. So networking is a good thing for me. But I've got a lot of cards I collected at the end of the year when I did my first networking thing, and I tell you, you can waste an awful lot of time networking. I feel like I need to walk around with a billboard sign when I network: "Call me if and only if. . . ." I don't have time to follow up with all of them.

[Jeremy] And you're running into people who are also sellers, but you need to find buyers.

[Bill] Yeah, too many coaches who want to have lunch with me. It's like who needs this?

[Suzi] Well, you know what? That brings up an opportunity. Is there something you can sell to the coach?

[Bill] No, I don't want to do that. I don't think they have any money.

[Suzi] Oh, how funny. That's great. Observe your assumption. There are actually quite a few coaches who have multi-million dollar operations. Okay, did we get everybody?

[Len] Well, I pretty much think networking is like advertising myself to other people, and I would hope these people are the buyers. Also they tell me what their needs are, amongst the buyers, so that's part of networking.

[Suzi] I can see how if you equate networking with advertising yourself you'd only consider doing it with prospective buyers. I hope to expand your thinking here a bit.

Networking Mindsets

[Suzi] I'm going to share with you my Nine Mindsets of Networking. The idea with these Nine Mindsets is that they are to be used in conjunction with each other. I mean it's good to have one or more of them working for you, but using all nine of them *together* is the real secret to success in networking. Networking gives you access to so many other opportunities—not just for direct dollars and sales, but for all kinds of connections throughout life.

Nine Mindsets of Networking

1. It's a game. Have fun.
2. Connection-seeking
3. Partnering
4. Clear agendas, up front
5. Curiosity and genuine
   interest in others
6. Six degrees of separation
7. Climate of comfort
8. Giver's gain
9. Action

The first mindset of networking is to think of it as a game. Networking is fun if you stay open to it as a game. The trick is to start with the people you already know. As we went around the group, what I heard in common in what each of you said is that networking is "a thing that you go to"—that it has to do with meeting people for the first time, being an extrovert even if you are an introvert, and collecting business cards. Something else you said is that it requires a lot of follow up, and it's very time consuming. If you think of it as a game, and if you stay open to the fun of it as a game, and if you start with the people you already know, it's a lot more fun. It's not so much this task that you have to manage, with the time and the cards and making yourself an extrovert if you're not, and on and on. Networking is not about being outgoing if you aren't; it is about a sincere curiosity and interest in other people.

Start with who you know and systematically find out who they know. It's just like referrals for sales. You're going for the warm leads. Now you're not going for people who are specific to anything directed at your business; at this point networking is just everyone. So that's the first mindset: **Networking is fun if it involves people you already know—just start with who they know.**

The second mindset is: Become a connection-seeker. Now if you're not already doing this, make yourself driven to find connections. What that means is look to connect people with each other, connect people with information, and connect people into your life—include people and ask them to include you. Most of the time, you don't even have to ask, because if you're including people in your life, and if you're connecting them with information and what you're up to, they're going to start including you in things. And it snowballs from there. So the second mindset is: **Be a connection-seeker.**

The third mindset is about partnership, and that's just partnership in the general sense of the term. Look for mutual benefit—look for ways to serve the people you're networking with, whether you're meeting them for the first time, or whether they're warm leads, or whether they're people you already know. I've heard it called servant leadership. Ask questions like these: "What are things we can help each other do? What are you up to in your life? What are you interested in? What's important to you? What are you working on? What are your challenges?"

And when you're exploring and you're genuinely curious about that, you'll find all kinds of ways you can connect with them. The point here is that you **focus more on being *interested* instead of trying to be *interesting*.** You might be able to find leads for babysitters, I think I shared that example with you before. You know, you might say, "I just read an article that speaks exactly to your point, I'll fax it over to you." There's so many ways that you can connect with people and look for mutual benefit—look for ways to serve them.

[Jeremy] That's what I mean by the big schmooze. . . . You're just spreading out your influence. **There are layers upon layers of ways that you serve people in your network, and you just look to connect with them.** And it might not have anything to do with what your initial outcome will be or what you hope. It might just be on a very basic level.

[Suzi] Exactly, and that goes back to mindset number 2, being a connection-seeker, because if you're genuinely focused on that, and if your only agenda is to seek connections, then you're going to find usefulness in every person you interact with. And you're looking to find ways to be useful to them. So it's not just about sales. With sales, you are strategically targeting people in your network for the purpose of selling your services. And the purpose of those conversations is to get meetings, and the purpose of those meetings is to get more meetings, etc. There's a focus to it, there's a strategy to it, it's purposeful. You are focused on those who would be buyers of your services with sales, but not with networking.

Networking to me is very expansive. With networking, you're meeting people in your life, you're meeting the people in their life, you're finding out where the connections are, you're just exploring possibilities. There's no "should" or "have to" about it—it's just about a genuine curiosity about what's there. It's like going on a scavenger hunt, looking for something that might be out there. It's assuming there's something there, and looking for it, and continuing to look. Sometimes you keep looking and you find there's nothing there, and then you just go your separate ways. But most of the time, if you're looking hard enough, you'll find something to connect with people about.

The fourth mindset is about **keeping your agendas clear and communicated** up front. Networking gets hard when people go to networking events with the intention of selling something. Sometimes I find people are there to give out their card or collect cards, or because they want to talk about their particular service that they want you to buy. That's not networking, that's selling. Networking is when you're just there to make connections. You're in it to meet this person, and to explore who this person is and the ways you two can play together. And if you do have an ulterior agenda, you want to communicate it up front. You want to be honest, and you want to check your assumptions; that's part of keeping the agenda clear and communicated up front. If you have an assumption that the two of you are having a conversation simply to explore what's possible in having met each other or getting to know each other further, check that out—I wouldn't assume anything.

The fifth mindset is a **curiosity about what's possible and a genuine interest in others** all the time. And again, that ties back into being the connection-seeker: Be more interested than interesting.

The sixth mindset is based on the six-degrees-of-separation concept. Are you familiar with that one? The concept is that we are all, everybody in the world, separated by only six other people between us—six degrees of separation. So, for example, even though I met each of you for the first time over the phone when we began this class, if we sat down one at a time and explored everybody we know, chances are we are six people or less away from each other. In other words, I know somebody who knows somebody who knows somebody who knows you—five somebodies in between us, rendering us six people apart from each other.

The other way that this concept works is when there's somebody you'd like to get to know. Let's say you wanted to get to know Bill Clinton. The odds are, there are only six other people between you and Bill Clinton. There's a chain of people who know each other that's only six people deep, between you and anybody you want to get to know.

In that mindset, the application to networking is that everyone is on the squad—there are no benchwarmers or spectators in this sport, so nothing is a wasted interaction. **There is no wasted time in networking because everyone is connected, and if they're not connected to someone you want to know, they *are* someone you want to know.** Getting to know all the different people you could possibly want to know in your life is analogous to constantly strengthening the strands of your web, if you think of networking as a big spider web. Actually, it's more like a net: You are in a net of people all connected by different strands. And let's say there are people in your life you haven't talked to, or let's say you had great connections at conferences you went to with people whose business cards you kept, but with whom you never followed up. Those strands are very weak and thin right now, and the way to strengthen them is to get to know those people more by having the conversations and following up with them.

So with the mindset of six degrees of separation and everyone being on the squad, every moment is an opportunity for relatedness. And every opportunity for relatedness is a building block for your network. So every strand in your web, every strand in your net, adds strength to the fibers of your network. And if you're just focusing on strengthening all those strands, eventually you're going to find that it all starts working for you.

[Jeremy] Here's one way it works: When you're going for leads—whether it's a networking lead or a sales lead—you don't go away empty handed. You leave with another name.

[Suzi] Right. For me that's more specific to sales, because there's a "should do" implied in that, so it's more strategic. But the way I think about networking, it's an ongoing thing—it's all the time. It's not something that you do when you think about it. Sales activities are something I have to remember to do, and something I have to schedule to do, and something I have to keep track of in terms of where I am in the process. And networking is not. Networking is just ongoing, all the time. I'm not just strategically seeking connections or leads related to business, I'm just seeking connections in general with everyone, everywhere, all the time.

[John] Even if you don't exchange business cards?

[Suzi] Exactly. Networking is not about the business cards. Business cards are about marketing. Networking is about these Nine Mindsets working together.

Okay, mindset number 7 is wanting to create a comfortable atmosphere for the people you're talking with. It's about keeping in mind, as you're building relationships, that there are three things that people want: **People want to be loved. People want to be acknowledged. And people want to be taken care of.**[2] Being taken care of can mean being attended to physically, emotionally, spiritually, mentally, or simply being heard or being understood. Part of being taken care of is being well-served. In business, this translates into providing excellent customer service or exceeding expectations. But, in general, I have yet to find people who would argue with me that they don't want those three things. They want to be respected or loved, they want to be acknowledged, and they want to be taken care of. So in networking, as you're connecting with people, look for ways to do those things.

Mindset number 8 is the concept of giver's gain. The idea behind giver's gain is that if you focus on what you can provide for others, you're going to get some benefit out of that. **Rather than looking for what others can do for you, focus on what you have to offer them.** It's like President Kennedy's "Ask not what your country can do for you but what you can do for your country"—it's that concept. If you're the giver, you're going to gain, because generally people want to help you, so if you're focusing on helping them, it will come back to you.

The last mindset is the notion that networking is ongoing, all the time. It's not just at networking events, it's not just at conferences, it's not when you put on your suit, it's not just when you make sure you have all your business cards with you and go forth with the intention. **Networking requires constant action.**

Networking Vehicle: Informational Interviews

[Suzi] One of the things that I found really helpful in getting started in networking is the informational interview. It's a really powerful tool for meeting people and getting connected with who's in their life. For example, as you know, I was a schoolteacher before I became a coach and business owner. When I left teaching, I knew there was some other thing out there I wanted to do, I just didn't know what it was. So when I set forth, I didn't have a business network—I had been a teacher, and my network was my students and the other teachers in the school. So I set out to meet people in business. And I started with the people I knew through family and friends. I said, "Who do you know who's in business? I don't care what business, I want to go meet with them and do an informational interview and find out who they are and what they do and what skills it requires and whether or not it's something that a teacher could transfer skills into doing."

I spent six months conducting about 150 informational interviews. Now, I didn't start with 150 people, I started with 3. But what happened was, from each person I did the informational interview with, I asked for names of who else they knew whom I could talk to—who might be an interesting next step in my journey of exploring what's possible out there in terms of new careers. And that's how I met so many people and started my business as a coach; it was through people I found through the informational interviews. I ended up meeting a woman who connected me up with the president of her company, which happened to be a coaching and development company, and they were looking at the time to bring on new associates. They had a stringent selection process, then they provided intensive training and mentoring, and that's what got me started. So never underestimate the power of informational interviews.

Networking is the precursor to sales activities because in order to follow up and to keep strengthening the strands of your web, you've got to make phone calls, you've got to set up meetings, and you've got to follow up. And following up has to be ongoing. So it's not only getting out there and continually meeting new people and continually strengthening the strands of the web of people who are already in your network. It's also following up, following up, following up.

[Jeremy] And it's interesting because what we're looking to do here when we're networking is we're looking to be selfless, and giver's gain, and that's very real. On the other hand, there's a time when people are going to turn to us—after we've been very generous, connecting them to others, providing them information, giving them names, and faxing and e-mailing and all like that—and they're going to say, "Oh, and what do you do? Who are you?" And we have to be ready to not be self-effacing at that point. We have to be ready to turn on our little commercial and tell what we've been doing, and plugging it in to what they've been doing.

[Suzi] That's exactly right. And that is when networking transfers into the sales process: at that very moment, when they express that interest in what you're up to. You have to listen for it, because there comes a time when they're going to come to you and want to know what you do and where you do it. And this is why, in this telecourse, we didn't start with networking, which is somewhat the logical place to begin. We started with our 30-second commercial; networking is down here at class number 8.

The idea is that networking is a doorway into the sales process. It's a great place to continually keep your pipelines fresh and keep new things coming into the pipeline. And to answer Deb's earlier question about how you strategically target the people you want to be networking with, my answer to that is don't. Let that go. My answer to that is network with everybody, and then when you're in the sales process, be strategic about who you target in the sales process.

In networking, you want to throw open the doors and let everybody into the game. It's a big old party, it's a big game, everybody's in it. If you have that mindset about networking, you get to meet really interesting people on airplanes, walking the dog, getting your hair cut, waiting in lines—and you find out all kinds of interesting things about people. And it becomes like a game. And you know what else? If you keep it in your mindset as a game, you don't have to follow up on *everything*. So now, if you don't want to be strategic with who you've met in your networking, and put them into your sales process for follow up, then okay . . . yeah, I know we've said you've got to follow up, follow up, follow up with everyone. But to me, networking takes all of the "shoulds" out of it. There are no laws about who you should network with. Network with everybody—see what comes of it, see who they know. Any reactions, comments, questions?

[Bill] A few more words about the informational interview. What is that exactly?

[Suzi] An informational interview is where you set up a meeting with someone to gather information about them, either about what they do or what their company does. It's not a sales meeting at all, it's personal. You're looking for information that will help you figure out what's next for you. So these types of meetings are very nonthreatening for the other person, because you're clearly not coming to sell them anything; you are coming to pick their brains. It's flattering for people. It's kind of like you're asking for a small nugget of mentorship—mentoring in a small dose.

So you set up the informational interview for half an hour with somebody, or you set up lunch with somebody. I actually tried not to set them up around meals, because I didn't want to have any awkward moments. At the time, I was trying to live off my savings, so I didn't want to spend any unnecessary money, and I didn't want anyone else to feel pressure to pick up the tab. So I would set up these half-hour meetings. I would go to someone's office and I'd say, "Tell me about what you do, and how you got into what you do. What skills does someone have to have to be successful doing what you do? What do you like about it? What do you not like about it? What would you do differently if you had to do it over again?" And what I started learning were all the jobs that I didn't want to do after I left teaching. That's what was helpful for me, but you can design informational interviews around anything that you want to find out.

Also, there were two questions that I asked every single person in the informational interview: "Who else do you recommend that I conduct this interview with—who else would be good to talk to?" and "What do you recommend that I read?" And I followed up on just about all the people and some of the books that were suggested to me.

[Jeremy] So you *did* get another name. . . .

[Suzi] At that point it wasn't sales, it was survival. I had to ask the person in front of me where else to find people. It's amazing how people really want to help you. You call up and you ask for an informational interview, and they're happy to help.

[Jeremy] Well, people like other people who are vulnerable, which speaks to an interesting networking and sales and interpersonal dynamic. It's one thing to come across as authoritative and know your stuff, but it's also great if you can provide a balance by showing that there are areas that you'd like to get help in. People like that vulnerability.

[Suzi] I think that's right. So does this approach to networking sound far-fetched for you, or does this sound like something you could integrate into what you're already doing? If not, where are the obstacles for you?

[Deb] It's pretty much a lot of what I've been doing, and I think I need to take it to the next step, because I'm very much a connector and putting people together and networking and all that stuff. So now I need to go to the next stage and really keep in touch with some of these people, and follow through with some of the connections. I have a question, though. You mentioned a word, before the Nine Mindsets . . . you said *strategic*. Can you clarify what you meant?

[Suzi] That's more in the sales process. When you're in the sales process, you want to identify all the people in your network, and by *network* I mean all the people you know—everybody, even your three-year-old's best friend. There are people you know who know other people. So look in your network and find out who, of the universe of people in your network, are strategic choices for you to plug in to your sales process for business. In other words, if you had to focus your attention on just a handful of people in that network to pursue for a possible business development, who would those people be? That becomes your target list, and it isn't a list of everyone in the world; you strategically select it for the purposes of selling your services.

And then part of doing that is figuring out how you're going to access them. It may make sense to look at how you know those people. Let's say there's someone in your network who you know through your next-door neighbor. So maybe the way you're going to access that person is to have your next-door neighbor help you connect up with that person. It all depends on the relationship. . . .

And sometimes it's helpful to trace back how you know people to keep the connection—the strands of the web—clear in your mind. Who connected you to whom? How did you meet this or that person, and trace the connections to see how many degrees of separation back they go. When I started doing this, I could trace back my very first client through six people. I could trace back all the way to the person who started the ball rolling, the one person I already knew who said, "You should talk to this person." And then I met that person and they said, "Oh, you should talk to this person." It's fun sometimes to do that, to trace it back and see how it works—and to see how long and strong some of your connections really are.

[Jeremy] Also, something else I think that we can all identify in ourselves about networking is a continual availability—an openness—to be able to be open to new possibilities of connecting to other people, and thinking we don't have to judge them, and they don't have to judge us. In Myers-Briggs terms, I think networking is the ultimate key activity. You don't have closure. It's the opposite of project management. You're not managing any projects here; it's just keeping things open. Playfulness generates connections from others and an interest from others in playing. In the course of that expansiveness, you find out if there are possibilities for other forms of relating, ideally in terms of business.

[Suzi] There are so many things that we have to do that are "should do's." And for me, the sales process has a lot of "should do's" in it, but networking is just a place to sort of let your hair down and be fun and see what's possible. That's a lot of what attracts me to coaching; it is the exploration or commitment to what's possible, and for me, networking is just a natural place to express that.

[Jeremy] Suzi, do you have a specific networking strategy for being in conferences or trainings, aside from giving out your business card and taking business cards?

[Suzi] Yes, I would forget about the business card game and design for yourself a strategy or a goal for what you want to accomplish networking-wise during that time so that you're not just sitting there listening for the content. You also have a strategy: who you want to meet and what you want to find out about who you meet. What is your goal for the meeting or conference? What do you want to accomplish? Who are the kinds of people who are going to be there, and **how can you be useful to them,** and how can they be useful to you, and how many do you want to meet? It's different for me with each meeting I go to. Sometimes I'm at a conference and I'm looking to just meet as many new people as I can. And sometimes my strategy is more specific, and I know there's going to be one or two people who are going to be there who I want to meet, so I'm going to seek out those people. Or maybe there are people I've talked to or come in contact with whom I've never met in person. And so my strategy is to put faces with names and deepen my relationships with people I have at least a superficial contact with. So that's what I'd say in a nutshell: **Just have a goal or a strategy for every networking interaction.** The key at any networking event (i.e., any event where there are people) is to meet as many new people as you can through the people who are there who you already know. If you don't know anyone, introduce yourself to one person who seems to know everyone, and ask them to introduce you around.

[Deb] Okay. That's helpful because I'm still in the stage of "What can I bring to you?" So it's helpful in forcing me to think in that way.

[Suzi] Just identify for yourself what you want to learn at these conferences: not just from the speakers, but what do you want to find out from your colleagues who will be there with you?

[Jeremy] Now sometimes the people at those conferences who are often sought-after are very defensive—they're so used to being hit on by people who are trying to sell them that they're really weary of any kind of interaction with somebody new. So it's important to just try to get them outside the conference or to make an appointment to talk to them, or to be with them later on, where you're finding about what their needs are, because they're just burned out by sales pitches.

[Suzi] You know, there's nothing wrong with having your strategy be to seek out your colleagues, especially if you're in a transition phase. You could have your whole strategy be to meet other coaches who are going to be there to ask them some strategy questions about how they handle different things, or what their approach is, or what their strategies are. Because I find that folks in the coaching community are so open, it's a great time to gather information and get some good ideas for how you're doing things.

[Deb] Yeah, that's my goal. I think it's kind of turning it around and seeing what kind of value they actually bring, and how I differ and how I am the same.

[Suzi] Keep it distinct, too. This is a networking event, not a sales event. You're not there to sell: **The purpose is not to sell anything, the purpose is really to make contacts, make connections, and develop relationships.** And there's nothing wrong either with having your strategy be, "I'm just going to see who's drawn to me and see what comes of it."

[Jeremy] This is a good chance to work on your 30-second commercial.

[Deb] Exactly, that's what I was thinking about. And there are going to be some people from companies there. So it is an opportunity to maybe promote. But I think I can come in the side door on that.

[Suzi] See what your comfort level is, too. I always get burned out more quickly at a conference if I'm trying to promote than if I'm just creating relationships to explore later.

[Bill] This is good news to me, because too often I walk away from networking experiences and say, "Well, nothing's really come of that, I've collected a bunch of cards . . . and how many of these people are selling insurance?" But it's good to know that it's a much more open-ended thing, and that it's as much social and recreational as it is anything else—and you never know what comes of these things.

[Suzi] Exactly. You could meet your next best friend in a random networking incident. You just don't know. I would say take the focus off of the cards: Take the focus off of giving your card out and collecting their cards. If you get cards from people you know you're never going to want to keep in touch with, throw them out; there's no reason to keep them just because they gave them to you. I find people all the time who just have stacks and stacks and stacks of business cards with rubber bands around them, from every conference they've ever gone to.

[Bill] Also, I feel very guilty if someone's e-mailing me and they want to get together for lunch, and I don't want to get together with this person, or if there's someone who wants to show me space in his school business program in case I want to rent it out later and I'm not interested at this time. I feel guilty about not following up with these people. I respond with a polite e-mail, but I need to get away from that, too. The way we're talking about networking now it seems like a very loose, not necessarily responsive, thing.

[Suzi] Right. The trouble that I find a lot of people get into is that they confuse networking with sales activities. And if someone wants you to look at space for the possible future time when you might consider renting, then they have confused networking with sales. If that person were being strategic about contacting you for a specific sales purpose, they would have already figured out that you're not interested in pursuing that further. But because they've couched it in terms of networking, you're now left with all of this "should" feeling around following up with them. So it gets messy . . . which is why we want to keep networking distinct from sales, which goes back to the mindset about keeping agendas communicated and clear up front.

In networking, true networking, you don't owe the other person anything—you don't have to follow up, you don't have to go look at anything. If you're networking, you're exploring connections and possibilities. And for you, looking at that space to rent is not a possibility, so you don't have to explore that. I see this most often with attorney clients I coach, because they don't really have any concept of sales activities as being distinct from networking. They think that if they're networking, they're selling. And they don't see the distinction—they have it completely collapsed. So part of my challenge for them is to un-collapse that: to help them see that, in fact, networking is X, and sales is Y. And networking in and of itself does not get you clients, and it does not get you dollars. You get clients, develop business, and bring in dollars when you take your network that you've been building up continually, and you strategically target people in your network to bring them into your sales process—which is everything we have been talking about for the past eight classes.

[John] So, Bill, a way to get the folks off your e-mail tail is to just call it what it is, and tell them something like, "I enjoyed meeting you, but I'm not in the market."

[Suzi] Exactly. No harm in that. Another possibility is to go and meet with these people for lunch or to look at the space, and use that as an opportunity to explore other possible connections and see where it leads. If you want to do that you can, and then you're taking it back into the realm of networking, and you're keeping it there, which is fine. But you don't have to let anyone else take you out of networking and into their sales process unless you want to go with them.

[John] So what you could tell them is, "I'm not in the market, but if you'd like to have lunch anyway, I'd like to have lunch with you."

[Suzi] Right. I'd say something like, "We might still meet just to explore possibilities and see where we might be able to help each other."

[Bill] Right. That would be a good idea because I originally was interested in meeting with this person and starting a small business curriculum at SUNY—Purchase, which is about 10 miles from here, but then it sort of devolved into a discussion of space, and I think I fell into that too easily. This is a nice distinction.

[Suzi] Also, be assertive about how people can help you. When you go to explore this, it could be that the person who wants to rent you space picked up in conversation with you that that's something that could truly help you. You'll need to be assertive and say something like, "Well that's really not what I'm up to right now, but I'll tell you what I am up to: I'm interested in meeting clients in X industry, and if you know anyone in that industry, I'd love to meet them." Or whatever you're up to—tell them what you're up to.

[Jeremy] Then give them your commercial.

[Suzi] Exactly. But be conscious of where you are in the networking dance, or the networking experience, and the sales process.

[Jeremy] Now another important part of networking is to make other people your sales representatives—or maybe not sales representatives, more like information representatives, if you will. They become your affiliates who can pass along referrals to you. And the more you're able to do that, the more you're able to leverage your network.

[Suzi] That's right. People you meet ideally become your agents, and that's where you're going to start to see the return on the investment of time. That's where you're going to start to see your network working for you, when you've got such solid connections with people that all of a sudden, they're sending you people who are clients and prospects. Because they know who you are, they know what you're up to, and they know the exact profile of people you're interested in, and when they come across them, they'll send them to you.

[Jeremy] And when you have those kinds of people in your network, take good care of them!

[Suzi] So go out there and explore networking in a way that is about having fun, and see if you can transfer that attitude to your continued homework assignment of making calls and setting up meetings.

Homework

Apply the Nine Mindsets of Networking and start networking with everyone!

What is Networking?

In the beginning of this book, I said that networking is the relational aspect of your business. It is connecting with others for the purpose of sharing resources, information, leads, referrals, ideas, and so on. Cultivating a working network of relationships is crucial to your business development system. Networking is about connecting, meeting people, and collecting people. You are networking when you are:

- Building your pipeline
- Connection-seeking with genuine interest in others
- Meeting people
- Talking to people and getting to know them better
- Getting out there and creating relationships of all kinds
- Asking to meet other people—asking for introductions or at least requesting contact information and permission to use your contact as a reference

- Following up with someone you met in passing
- Applying or improving your manners, etiquette, and social graces
- Introducing people to each other with an eye to expanding others' networks
- Engaging in activities that yield human connection and interaction, not necessarily related to business
- Keeping in mind the Nine Mindsets of Networking
- Finding out what people do, where they do it, why they do it, and what they want to do
- Interacting with people in a way that generates relatedness

I particularly like the way Mary Foley describes it:

> Knowing how to network well can make or break your career. That's how powerful it is, because that's how powerful relationships are to your career. I'm not keen on the term "networking." The problem is the word "work." I mean how many times do you walk into a room full of people expecting to leave with actual work in hand such as a signed contract? It doesn't happen! Why? Because before someone signs their name or hands over a check, there's lots of getting to understand each other, lots of exchange, and making a connection. So, I say we rename "networking" to "netconnecting." Meeting and getting to know new people is about gathering—netting—several good connections. Once you've connected, sharing business cards is simply the convenience of not having to write down their contact information on a napkin.[3]

Networking is more than just netconnecting, though. It is netweaving, because you've got to weave together your connections—perhaps it is more like netknitting, because you are knitting together people and resources and ideas for everyone's mutual benefit. The more you can think in terms of weaving or knitting, the less working you'll have to do!

Networking is the backdrop of the sales process. It informs your strategic target choices, it lubricates the wheels of progress, it cultivates the garden of possible leads. And you'll make lots of new friends!

Nine Mindsets of Networking

1. It is a game, and it is fun if you stay open to it. Start with who you know, and find out who they know.

2. Become a connection-seeker, if you are not already. Make yourself driven to find connections. Connect people to each other, connect people to information, connect people into your life: Include them and they will include you.

3. It is about partnering: Look for mutual benefit and ways to serve. Keep yourself operating from and inside of a spirit of partnership, collaboration, and helpfulness.

4. Keep agendas clear and communicated up front. Include people in what you are up to—share and communicate. Be honest and check assumptions. Speak of that which is important to you.

5. Be curious about what's possible: Show genuine interest in others. Inquire as to what is important to others.

6. Understand the six degrees of separation: Everyone is on the squad— there are no benchwarmers or spectators. Strengthen the strands of your web constantly. Nothing is a wasted interaction. Every moment is an opportunity for relatedness, every relatedness moment is a building block for your network. Every strand in your web adds strength to the fibers of your network, and eventually you will find it working for you.

7. Set up a climate of safety/normalization/creating a comfortable atmosphere (there are three things all people want: to be respected, to be acknowledged, to be taken care of/well-served). Seek first to understand other people (like Stephen R. Covey says) and be trustworthy.

8. Operate from the perspective of giver's gain: People want to help you, so focus on helping them and it will come back to you.

9. Be in continuous action. Networking is ongoing, not at events only. Never underestimate the power of informational interviews. Make calls, set up meetings, and follow up with everyone.

Checklist:
Networking Actions

- List the categories in your life in which you know people—family, church, work, neighborhood, school, past employers, business associates, friends, associations or professional groups, those who provide services to you (e.g., your dentist).

- Make each category a separate page, and list all the people you know in each category.

- In each category, choose the top three people you know best as your networking starters.

- Set up time to talk to or be with your network starters and tell them your vision.

- Ask your network starters whom they know whom you could talk to about your vision.

- Seek out every person your network starters referred you to and tell them your vision.

- Ask each of these people whom they know whom you might talk to.

- Continue to work your way through your own network lists.

- Continue to follow up and meet people from your network starters' networks.

- Tell everyone you meet what you are up to in your business and in your life.

- Tell everyone a clear profile of your ideal clients.

- Remember the Nine Mindsets of Networking during all of these interactions.

- Explore collaborative, partnering, and alliance-building opportunities.

- Identify and list at least 10 people with whom you want to do a joint venture or other collaboration and have initial conversations with them about what that might look like.

Endnotes

1. Williamson, M., (1992). *A return to love: Reflections on the principles of a course in miracles.* New York: Harper Collins. Chapter 7, Section 3.

2. Alice Miller, who wrote *The Drama of the Gifted Child,* rev. ed. (New York: Basic Books, 1996), says that all people want to be respected, understood, and taken seriously.

3. Foley, M., (2005). *10 bodacious ways for a bodacious career.* Richmond, VA: Bodacious! Books.

Step 9

Lessons-Learned Meetings and Expanding the Sale While Serving the Client

"Take calculated risks. That is quite different from being rash."
—George S. Patton, Jr.

"People are always blaming their circumstances for what they are.
I don't believe in circumstances. The people who get on in this world
are the people who get up and look for the circumstances they
want, and if they can't find them, make them."
—George Bernard Shaw

The best part of the sales process is that once you've got new clients, and your schedule gets full, you can shortcut the cycle. An easy avenue for building business while you are billing time is to generate new business with the clients you are currently serving. This chapter covers tools for expanding business while you are working. The telecourse goes into the lessons-learned meeting concept and how to generate referrals while focused on client service and deliverables.

Telecourse Session #9: Expanding Business While Billing Time

A Glance Back: Networking, Marketing, and Prospecting

[Suzi] Since we spent the previous call talking about networking, let's just go around real quick and have everyone say how they applied the networking concepts this past week. And it's okay to say you didn't even think about it, but if you did have any thoughts or if you took any action around the Nine Mindsets of Networking, let's share those now.

[Len] I like the mindset that networking's fun. I've just been talking up a storm pretty much with everyone I meet, telling them what I do and asking what they do, and so I've just been very social.

[Suzi] And has it been fun?

[Len] Oh, yes—I've really enjoyed it. So that's the primary one that I'm focusing on.

[Suzi] Bill, how about you?

[Bill] I've been working on what's come from networking, revising my bio, and sending it off. And I really haven't had time to do anything else this week.

[Suzi] Okay. How do you feel about networking?

[Bill] I feel a lot better about networking now that I don't feel I have to walk away with a sale—that takes a lot of the pressure off.

[Suzi] Deb?

[Deb] I went to that Industrial Organization of Psychology conference, and one of the consulting companies was interested in talking to me further, so I told them I would go to work with them part time, just to get the experience. I'm not sure about that, though.

[Suzi] Couldn't you create a consulting relationship with them, where you are working with them, but remain an independent contractor?

[Deb] They don't do that, unfortunately. Maybe I should just do an adjunct-like thing.

[Suzi] See if you can get a contractor arrangement. That way your time is still your own, you don't owe them certain hours, and you can leverage both opportunities—being on your own as well as with the company.

[Deb] Yeah. That's a possibility. But whether I want to do that or not, whether that's going to work out, it certainly has forced me to start doing all my marketing materials. As far as networking goes, this past week, I talked to some people from the military, and they do some really cool stuff. But for me, it was more getting information about what other people are doing and how they're doing it.

[Suzi] Informational interviews.

[Deb] Well, maybe . . . because these were IO people and a lot of them were internal—they've done a lot of testing and research, that kind of stuff. So for me, it was more gathering information than networking. But I got a bunch of cards and I wrote on the back of them who each person I met was and what they looked like, and what the context of our conversation was. I don't know if there's any way to keep track of all that, and I still need to follow up with them. So in general, I think I just haven't done as much as I'd like to. Also, this morning, I went to the Technology Round Table, which is some of the executives for the telecommunications network up here in Sonoma County, and continued my connection with them. I was going to call one of the vice presidents from one of the wireless technology firms to see if I can have lunch with him. When I called his EVP, I learned he has left the company to start his own business. So I'm starting to track him down. That's what's going on. . . . I guess I'm all over the map.

[Suzi] And Jeremy, how about you, any new insights on networking since last week?

[Jeremy] I don't have anything new on networking, but to get back to an earlier previous topic: I've been going back and forth with somebody to see if I'm going to hire this person to sell for me—exploring the pluses and minuses. It would be great to have all these things opened up, but I'm still going to have to go in and pitch. So I have to see if this person's on the same page with me, and then train her to present what I want presented. And if we can make that thing go, we'll see if it's more efficient or not. I also have a meeting today with a guy who's an executive coach. He's putting together some kind of a coaching initiative and I'm not sure if it's a sales call, a networking call, or a nothing call.

[Suzi] Jeremy, what's your thinking about having someone sell for you?

[Jeremy] I think it's a good idea because it gets me off my butt, but it has to be the right person and I have to do the selling myself also. They'll qualify, and I'll close. I'll still have to be there to talk about my coaching.

[Suzi] That's right. So you're talking about a prospector, really.

[Jeremy] Yeah. You can't really sell coaching without being in there, too.

[Suzi] I like the distinction of having someone be your prospector as opposed to having someone sell for you, because no one's going to sell your effectiveness at coaching any better than you can.

[Jeremy] That's right. But they could sell some training initiatives that would get me in the door. They could sell some sort of preliminary training stuff or stuff that would be a way of getting to know me before the coaching, where I'd still be getting paid while they're getting to know me and I'm getting to know them.

[Suzi] The hard part, I would think (and you might want to work this out with the person you're talking to), is that so much of the initial sales conversations are about setting up the foundation for the relationship and learning about the issues facing the client or the client's company. If someone else is doing that, you're going to be getting it secondhand, and she might not know how to listen for the same opportunities that you know how to listen for, which is just part of the risk. Maybe in the beginning, you'd want to do things alongside her so that she starts to learn what you listen for.

[Jeremy] Yeah, whenever you begin something new like this, there's a labor-intensive part at the beginning, which is a pain in the butt, but worth it if it winds up taking off. What have you been up to, Suzi?

[Suzi] I've been traveling a lot—I've been billable since we last spoke. I've been off to Chicago and Delaware, and now I'm off to Oregon.

[Jeremy] When you go to a place, like you're going to Chicago, do you try to sell there also?

[Suzi] Generally I do. This trip I was in and out really fast, but generally I like to build in time for selling. I usually know people in the cities I'm flying to, so I bill time on either end to meet with those people, or to find new contacts, or to at least make phone calls when I'm there.

[Deb] What are you actually doing, Suzi?

[Suzi] On my trip now to Oregon? I'm actually doing executive leadership coaching with 13 different shareholders in a law firm. So they're all partner-level executives in a law firm, and they all have different leadership accountabilities—either management and leadership of the firm, or there's one guy who's in charge of operations, one in charge of different practice areas, that kind of a thing. So leadership coaching—one-on-one leadership coaching basically—13 meetings back to back. And then last week in Chicago, I had 9 back-to-back sessions with attorneys in a law firm about presentation skills.

[Deb] So you're focused on attorneys then?

[Suzi] It's looking that way these days, which works out well in this market.

[Deb] So you suggest that as a sales strategy?

[Suzi] Well, I definitely suggest when there's a downturn in the market, look for the people with the money, because a downturn in the market isn't a downturn for everybody. And while many companies are laying people off in giant chunks, that creates opportunities for the outplacement market and the legal market. Another way to think about it is when there's a downturn in the market, it means there are opportunities in certain niche segments. The strategy would be to seek those out.

Lessons-Learned Meetings

[Suzi] Okay, so lessons-learned meetings is the topic of the day. And lessons-learned meetings are not in the initial up-front piece of the sales process other than to mention to your client that they are part of your service process, but they happen either at the mid-way point of an engagement or at the end of an engagement. They are part of the sales process because they are a great opportunity to not only find effective client feedback, but to ask for referrals and to build new business with existing clients—to expand the sale or to expand existing business into new business.

The point of a lessons-learned meeting is very simple: If you're in a long-term coaching relationship with a company or with an individual, you want to check in at the three-month point. You want to tell them in the very beginning of your sales process while you're doing the contracting with them, "Part of our process is that at the three-month mark and the six-month mark, we will have lessons-learned meetings. The lessons-learned meeting will be a one-hour meeting where you and I will get together with whoever else our organization has been serving in your organization, and we will have a conversation about how it's going."

The lessons-learned meeting allows not only the opportunity to see what might have gone wrong and how we can fix it for the rest of the engagement, but what's going right. And when clients talk about what's going right, it generally ends up being a big love fest, because they start telling you all of the things that are working, at which point you've got all sorts of opportunities to expand a sale. It's like you've got your foot in the door and you can crack it open to new business.

It's also an opportunity for you to say, "Great, I'm glad you had that experience with us. Can you put that in writing for us to use in our marketing materials?" or "Fabulous! I'm so glad that that worked out for you. Can I quote you on that?" So the lessons-learned meeting is a great opportunity to build up your marketing file with testimonials, when you're finding out what went well with your client. It's also an opportunity to explore issues of communication—how well is the communication going between our two organizations? You want to look at how the working relationship is working, and if there's anything that hasn't been working, look at it now and see what you can do differently in the future, before the engagement ends.

And all this is true, too, for the meeting that you have at the end of the engagement, because the meeting at the end of the engagement still gives you the opportunity to say, "You know, if we were to continue working together in the future, what might that look like? What should we be doing differently? What could you be doing differently?"

That last point is an important one: In these lessons-learned meetings, please take the opportunity to tell your clients what they could be doing differently, too, to better support the process. There will be times when your client could inadvertently sabotage things, and this is an opportunity to communicate that to them. But what the lessons-learned meeting mainly does is build the formal structure for feedback to one another, and you can then take the opportunity to find out what worked and turn that into a referral, turn that into more business with your clients, and so on. Is anyone doing that already?

[Jeremy] I'm not calling it a lessons-learned meeting—I don't give it a formal name. But I do talk with the client and the manager about what we've been doing, and what people are getting or not getting out of coaching, and places that people can apply what we're doing.

[Suzi] And at what point in the engagement do you do that, Jeremy?

[Jeremy] I do it from the beginning.

[Suzi] You're doing it continually? How frequently?

[Jeremy] Well, if there's a third-party contact, I'm involved with them as a resource person. So that's initially it, and then at some stage early on also.

[Suzi] And do you build that in as an expectation from the beginning?

[Jeremy] What do you mean "expectation"?

[Suzi] An expectation with the client that they will be required to be at these meetings with you, because they have a role in participating.

[Jeremy] I try to do that, yeah.

[Suzi] Because one of the things that I've found is if you don't build that expectation in from the beginning, it's hard to manage your client expectations down the road. It's really hard to all of a sudden come out and say, "We've been doing this now for three months, so let's get together and talk about how it's going." Sometimes they will and sometimes they won't, depending on how much time they've got. I find with my executives they say, "Yeah, yeah, yeah, that's great," but they never have enough time for it.

[Deb] So you're saying set it up within your contract?

[Suzi] Set it up within your contract so that you can manage the expectations around it—so that you can say, "This is a part of our process, it's part of the coaching process, it's how we do business." You want to make sure, not only from a customer service perspective, that you get that feedback, that you're asking questions, and that you're giving feedback, too. And you also want to use that opportunity to get new business—either from them or from other people to whom they can refer you in the organization, or from other people outside the organization to whom they could refer you.

[Jeremy] Sometimes it can get tricky: I've had a situation recently where they're trying to make a substitution to put somebody else in to take their place.

[Suzi] What do you mean?

[Jeremy] Well, I had somebody who was finding it tough to sustain the coaching relationship—there are a lot of control issues. So she told me she'd met with some big HR person at an insurance company, and said she thought I'd be a great coach for that person. And what I really sensed there was that she was going to substitute this HR person for herself.

[Len] That happens with therapy, too. They send you their best friend and they're gone in a month.

[Jeremy] Exactly. So my response was, "Um, gee, it's so nice of you to think of me, but you're my client and I want to continue working with you. We have all these issues to work on here. But if you have a referral for me, I'd love to be able to talk to her if that works for you to give it to me." But I kept the focus on my client.

[Suzi] And how did that work?

[Jeremy] Very well, actually. She liked that. I mean she was definitely testing.

[Suzi] See, it sounds like that was a perfect opportunity for a lessons-learned meeting. The hard part in managing the lessons-learned process is that it's outside the context of the executive coaching conversation. So you have to be very distinct about the boundaries there—this is not a coaching conversation, this is a "how are we doing" meeting. We're taking a periodic step to the side—one giant step outside the coaching process—to look at it from a different angle. And that's why it's useful to build in that expectation from the beginning, because then you can manage it.

[Len] Do you call it a lessons-learned meeting?

[Suzi] I do. I know a lot of people have trouble with that. So I've had clients decide that they're going to call it an engagement review meeting, because they didn't like the term *lessons-learned meeting*.

[Len] Well, I don't like that either.

[Suzi] You can call it whatever you want. Name it whatever works for you, just so long as you're using the same concept, which is the opportunity to **celebrate the successes, explore what new business is coming down the pike, and capture whatever you can capture that's going to be useful in testimonial letters or referrals or endorsements from them.**

[Len] If the business is coming from a sponsoring client there—say it's coming from HR or a vice president—how do you manage talking that business with your coaching client sitting there?

[Suzi] You have everybody in the meeting. You include everybody. You include the client as well as the HR person or the executive who hooked you up. Because what happens is it builds credibility for you back with the original hierarchy in the hiring organization. So if HR hired you and then HR sits in on this meeting, they then get to hear all the fabulous accolades from your coaching client.

Likewise, if it's the CEO who brought you in to work with another senior-level exec, he or she (the CEO) will be listening to someone they value at a high level in their organization singing your praises. And what's going to happen is it creates a brainstorming situation where the two of them start thinking where else you could be useful, especially when you ask that question with the two of them together. Because the person you're coaching will be saying, "Here's what I got out of it, here's everything that's been great about it," while the CEO is listening to that and thinking, "If you got this much out of it, then I know six other people who would really benefit if they got the same thing."

[Len] And they don't have to name that person?

[Suzi] No, they don't have to name names then, but they can say to you, "I really see other places where we can use this," and you can say, "Great, let's set up a meeting to talk about it. How's next Tuesday at 3:00?" See, then we come back to that.

[Jeremy] It's great when they start thinking about you as their special resource that they can apply to other people and places and situations. They take sort of an ownership interest in your career. That's the best!

[Suzi] Absolutely.

[Jeremy] It's like they start seeing you as a way to handle all kinds of situations—"I'll just send you my coach."

[Suzi] I just had that happen yesterday with an executive I work with who's in the Legal department in a giant corporation. At the end of our conversation, she said, "You know what, I'm wondering if you've worked with anyone outside of Legal in our corporation? Have you worked with any of the folks in Corporate?" And I said, "Well, I haven't yet. I've been having too much fun with the folks in Legal." She said, "Well, you're so good, I'm going to connect you up with them." You know, it's great when they do that for you because then *you* are no longer doing the selling.

[Jeremy] That's my favorite kind of sale.

[Suzi] So the lessons-learned meeting—or engagement review meeting, or whatever you want to call it—is an opportunity to expand your sales. Again, you have to design the questions for this, just like you designed the questions for the initial sales meeting, because it is part of the sales process even though it's got more of a customer service focus. Questions to ask include: "What have I done that's been of value to you? How can I better serve you in the future? Have I met your expectations in terms of communication throughout this engagement, or what could I have done better? Where do you think you could have better supported the process?" Give them a chance to evaluate their role in the process before you give them feedback about how well they did in the process.

[Deb] Suzi, could you write down some of those questions for a follow-up e-mail to us? Or should we just copy them as you tell them? [See page 286 for sample Lessons-Learned Meeting Discussion Points.]

[Suzi] Well, actually your homework assignment is to generate those questions for yourself. And we're going to start next session talking about them. Each of us will have different questions because there are different things that we're looking to learn from our clients in these meetings. So your homework assignment is to think about what you want to learn from your clients in a lessons-learned meeting, or to design a template for the questions you would ask in the meeting. And remember, the whole purpose of it is to build a service relationship, create a partnership, and make possible future sales.

And really think through it. Think through, "Okay if I'm meeting with my client and all the other relevant people in the organization, and it's the end of the engagement, or it's the middle of the engagement, what do I want to learn from them? What do I want to find out?"

Any questions about the homework assignment or the lessons-learned meetings in general?

[Len] How do the lessons-learned meetings go when you're coaching various individuals in an organization?

[Suzi] When I'm coaching several people at once, I usually have them all present for the lessons-learned meeting. And it's really neat to see what happens when one of them says something like, "Well what I really value is I had that great conversation with you on strategy on getting ready to present to the Board on X, Y, and Z subjects," and all of a sudden you'll see the light bulbs going off in other people you've been coaching, who haven't thought to use you for that application yet. So then they start saying, "Oh my gosh, I didn't even think about that! I could do that with you, too." You start to see ways to deepen your influence, not only with individuals you're already working with, but other ways the organization can use you.

[Jeremy] Well I think I have a caveat instead of a question: I like to control for positive outcomes as much as possible. In terms of timing, a good time to have a lessons-learned meeting is when you're in a positive phase. If, however, you've just done something that has had a not-so-good impact on the client, or something's happened where people are just flipping out, that's a not-so-good time to have a lessons-learned meeting.

[Suzi] Actually, it is a good time as well. There is no bad time to have a lessons-learned meeting. When you're conducting it during a difficult situation, it's great because it builds up your points in the client's eyes, because you're handling it right at the moment. It's almost a damage control, customer service move.

[Jeremy] Maybe we're talking about different things here. It seems to me you could risk exposure issues with some of your clients.

[Deb] Maybe both of you could give some specific examples.

[Jeremy] For example, if your client had some thoughts about quitting the organization, this would be a bad time to have a lessons-learned meeting.

[Suzi] I don't know about that. You could really learn a lot about why.

[Jeremy] I know, but you've got to work out the issue with your client first, I think.

[Len] You're talking about the confidentiality aspects when there's something you don't want the rest of the organization to know?

[Suzi] Oh, I see. Well, in that situation you can do a mini, lessons-learned meeting with your actual client before you include other folks in that conversation.

[Bill] Well how often would that happen? Would that happen across the board? I mean would you have that as a routine feature?

[Suzi] I wouldn't make it a routine practice at all. I would just do it once in the middle and once at the end.

[Bill] No, I'm talking about would you have a lessons-learned meeting with your client beforehand, then offer a group meeting?

[Suzi] Oh, no. I wouldn't do that routinely, only in a case like Jeremy's— in a negative situation. Because what happens is the client will say great things to you in private, and then they won't articulate it in the same way in front of the people you want them to say it to. You want it to be genuine in the moment. You don't want to have to prompt them or say, "Remember what you told me when we did this in private?" Then it looks like you've crafted their responses and coached them into the right responses, and you don't want it to appear that way.

[Deb] So do you say up front, "We'll have a review of the work we're doing together, and these are the people involved, and these are the confidentiality issues, or whatever?" Do you set up the expectation up front?

[Suzi] Yes.

[Len] But also it sounds like you'd have to be sort of reserved when speaking with your coaching client in front of other people, because you don't want to be disclosing too much.

[Suzi] Right. And you definitely set that up in the beginning. You set up the ground rules and the context. You tell them, "This is not about revealing the stuff we've talked about; it's really about the process."

[Len] So both you and the client have to have some generic vocabulary for the process. Also, as I understand this meeting, it's not only an opportunity for you as the coach to get the feedback from the people you're working with, but also an opportunity for getting repeat business.

[Suzi] And there's yet another side to it: There's also an opportunity for you to provide feedback to the client and the client organization about where they have made things difficult for you, and how they could make it easier. There are lots of things that happen on the organization's side that impede the coaching process. For example, you frequently have situations where there are communication loopholes, where you can't get the information as quickly as is necessary. That's an opportunity for you to say, "You know what? This isn't working so well, and in order for me to achieve the results that you've commissioned me to achieve with this person, here's how you can better support that process."

[Len] So you're also focusing on system issues in the company.

[Suzi] Yes. And it's not so much about the content of what you've been discussing. It's more about the process and how everybody's feeling at that moment. Most of the time, these meetings are just a big love fest— they really are. Most of the time your client is saying, "Oh my gosh. I can't live without this person as my coach. How did I ever survive?" They're talking about all the different successes they've achieved, and how they're seeing things more strategically or more clearly, and they're accomplishing all these things. They're really glowing about how great it's been to be working with you. And they understand that it's an opportunity for them to tell their boss, or whoever hired you, to make sure that they get to keep working with you.

Damage Control and Handling Critical Feedback

[Deb] Suzi, can you give a quick example how to do damage control if something negative comes up in those meetings?

[Suzi] Okay. The one that's most frequent for me is a billing issue, and it's usually not from the client—it's usually from whoever in the organization handles payment. They say, for example, "I got your bill, and I was surprised that you billed for travel time. I didn't think that was going to happen." At which point it's uncomfortable for everybody, but it's a great opportunity to sit down, show the signed documents you've brought with you from when you created the relationship, and say, "Well, our original letter of agreement says I'm going to bill for travel time." And then you have the conversation about whether you want to reduce that or waive it, or whatever you want to do about it for customer service purposes, right? But for me, negative remarks have only been about billable stuff.

[Jeremy] So you do that in public? You don't say, "Let's meet on the side about that?"

[Suzi] Oh, right, that's all part of it, because it impacts the value that your client ascribes to you, too.

[Deb] Is there ever a time when your client is unhappy and expresses that out in public?

[Suzi] You mean expresses it in a lessons-learned meeting and it's a surprise to me? No. Most of the time I can either read dissatisfaction or whatever in them and ask about it well ahead of time, or they've brought it up already and we've worked through it prior to the lessons-learned meeting.

[Deb] I was thinking if they bring up something negative, that's great, because you can use that as an opportunity to problem solve with them and show that you're open to doing that, making them feel that they can come to you with even negative stuff. They can trust you basically.

[Jeremy] I think what Suzi's also implying is—and I don't know if you actually set it up this way—that you can say to a client, when you're meeting with them one on one, "This is going to be a good opportunity for you to make a pitch to extend the engagement. If you want to do that here you can do it."

[Suzi] I've never actually said that overtly—they sort of get it. You know, they see that opportunity. But most of the people I'm dealing with are pretty high-level executives. And most of the time I find that they've already had this conversation without me in the room. Most of the time they've already gone to the CEO and said, "Thank you so much for making this coach available to me, I'm getting all this great stuff out of it," so there are usually not very many surprises in these meetings.

But, again, it comes back to how you design the questions, which brings us back to your homework assignment. Think of a client you're already working with and think about whom you would invite to the lessons-learned meeting and what you would ask. We'll talk about all that at the beginning of our call next week, which is also going to delve into the subject of referrals.

Any other questions or concerns before we wrap up?

[Deb] Would you put this business about the lessons-learned meetings into the written contract also?

[Suzi] Yes, that's useful. I don't always do that, but I definitely talk about it up front. It might be in a letter of agreement. I basically have a contract and a letter of agreement. The contract is a pretty standard coaching contract, and the letter is where I put all the specific coaching stuff for their particular situation.

[Jeremy] Speaking of billable time, is the lessons-learned meeting a billable thing?

[Suzi] Oh sure, this is billable time . . . unless they balk at that, in which case you might choose to figure it's part of your sales and marketing time. But it's really a review of how it's going and how you're serving them. I bill for lessons-learned meetings and it is a standard part of our process, because it is time entirely devoted to the client situation— that's billable time in my book.

[Jeremy] Do you have any thoughts of offering this gratis, or do you think that's unnecessary?

[Suzi] I think you should always bill for it, because it's your time focusing on this client, therefore it's billable. If you find that you're in a situation where you would like to create a greater sense of good will, or you feel like you've really been billable for so many hours for this client that you're starting to feel that you're taking advantage of them, then that's a great place to show them that you're watching out for their bottom line.

[Jeremy] I think I would prefer to do that because the way I contract with people is I'm requiring minimum days and such, so I'm going to get paid anyway. So I could say, okay, this is going to be gratis, and I could give everybody a little extra incentive.

[Suzi] Sure. But definitely make sure that you point that out to them. That's just my thing: Anything that you do gratis, you make it actually show up on the bill and then zero it out so that they see it.

[Jeremy] That's a good idea.

[**Suzi**] Because there's no point in giving them a gift if they don't know you're giving it to them.

Homework

Your homework assignment is to generate some questions to use in a lessons-learned meeting. Remember, the underlying purpose of the lessons-learned meeting is to build a service relationship, create a partnership, and launch future sales. Each of us will have different questions because there are different things that we're looking to learn from our clients at different points in our work with them.

Think about the things you want to learn from a particular client and form them into questions, or design a template for the questions you would ask generally. And really think through it: "If I'm meeting with my client and all the other relevant people in the organization, and whether it's the end of the engagement or it's the middle of the engagement, what do I want to learn from them? What do I want to find out?"

Building Business While Billing Time

We are all familiar with the frustration of the cycle that has us generate a full pipeline of leads that suddenly start to pop like popcorn, generating business that we then devote our time to delivering. While we are focused on client service and deliverables, we often lose our focus and momentum on marketing and sales, finding ourselves in the uncomfortable position of wrapping up projects or client engagements with no further gigs on the horizon—we must start all over again to build up our business development bench strength.

"But I'm too busy to do any marketing or sales now. I need to focus on being billable, and the time I spend selling is not billable time." Does this sound like anyone you know? In a systematic business development process, you can use two strategies that will allow you to continue to build business while billing time, thus cutting your overall sales cycle in half and expediting your acquisition of additional billable time while reducing the amount of time you spend in between gigs.

One strategy is to use the lessons-learned meeting as a business development tool, and the other is actively and consistently building your business through referrals. The lessons-learned meeting is a structured interview with your clients and key decision makers in the organization that takes place in the middle of the engagement as well as at the end. It is a time to check in with your clients and learn from them what is working and what can be improved. It's also a time to share with them what they can do better or differently to help you do your job better. Typically, these sessions turn into a mutual admiration and acknowledgment fest, which is a fabulous time to (a) ask for testimonials, (b) ask for referrals, and (c) ask what other challenges, issues, projects, or needs are coming up for your client so that you can shift the lessons-learned conversation into a sales conversation. Whenever you are interacting with your clients and they express gratitude or appreciation for your skill and contribution, ask for referrals. (There are three keys to getting referrals that we'll cover in the next chapter.) Of course, once the referral becomes business, you close the loop with a handwritten note or small gift to the referral source.

Lessons-Learned Meetings

When holding these informative sessions, do not take things personally, should something less than positive come up. Consider it an opportunity for genuine apology and rekindling of the relationship. You can use these meetings for damage control before things get ugly. Do not be defensive. Listen and accept the feedback as fact. It is the client's reality, and they need your empathy, not your reasons why they are incorrect. Do not invalidate their experience, but gather all the information you can for your own growth and development. Handle the confrontation with grace and you will turn around a potential upset into a fruitful relationship. Even if you do not continue to do business with the client, you still would like them to be a referral stream for you.

The sample below shows typical questions and topics for discussion in lessons-learned meetings.

Sample:
Lessons-Learned Meeting Discussion Points

What went wrong?

What went right?

Success stories

Are there any new cases, new issues, new products, new programs, new business coming down the pike?

Get permission to use work product

What changes are anticipated in the future?

How client can use your services more effectively in the future

What client did well

Referral (internal and external)

Letter of testimonial

Testimonial quotes

Status of your business agreement/working relationship

Expanding business/new business

Depth in organization

What have we done that's been of value to you?

How can we better serve you in the future?

What are your expectations of us in terms of communication, work product, timing?

What benefits did you see in the consulting aspects of what we did?

(continued)

Sample:
Lessons-Learned Meeting Discussion Points *(concluded)*

How did our process work for you?

How did you find your overall communication with our organization to be?

Were you satisfied with the team that served you?

Was there anyone on the team you were not satisfied with?

Were there other issues that your team shared with you about us?

How can we help your firm expand its successes in the future?

Is there anyone else you feel can benefit from the services we provide?

So what's next?

What's next for you?

Will there be other cases/issues/situations related to this one? Will you be working on them? Will we?

Who else should we be talking to?

Are you familiar with our X services?

Can we videotape you talking about our services for use with other prospects?

Could you write a letter for us to use in our marketing materials?

Can I quote you?

Will you write a letter of reference?

Was *your* client satisfied (in the case of a different end user or internal client)?

Initiating New Sales Conversations

The lessons-learned meeting is also a tool for you to initiate a new sales conversation. One of the keys to building business while billing time is to strategize how you can manage both current and past relationships and bring those individuals or companies into your sales process. You've heard the common sales fact that in order to really keep in touch and keep yourself top of mind, you need to be in contact (called a touch) with every client seven times per year. If you think about seven touches per client per year, that means you will need to be calling everybody approximately every two months. When you are fully billable, you do not have time to do this, so you will need to brainstorm ways to "touch" clients multiple times per year when you are too busy to call. You can fax articles, e-mail relevant information, invite them to join you at events or social gatherings, or keep a mental list of who you know in each city you happen to travel to and reach out when you're in town. With the increase in popularity of Blackberry technology, it is easy to send a quick hello note whenever you are thinking of someone on your list. You can now add lessons-learned meetings to your repertoire for rekindling or reviving client relationships. It is a tool that gives you access to adding some old, past relationships to your target list because now you have a tool for revisiting contacts with whom you may have lost touch.

Of course, keep in mind that the primary purpose of the lessons-learned meeting is to ascertain whether or not you are delighting your clients and exceeding their expectations. The sales aspect of the meeting is secondary, and you want to keep clear for yourself that a new sale is your agenda, not the client's. Keep the client's agenda your primary focus, while listening in the background for the opportunities to gather information that would serve your agenda.

Step 10
Building Business
and the
Art of Referrals

"What I know for sure is that what you give comes back to you."
—Oprah Winfrey

You can build your entire business without ever making a cold call. Learning how referrals happen so that you can intentionally cause them is crucial. It is wonderful when someone out of the blue refers a client to you, but you can't bank on that as a predictable stream of income unless you know how to cultivate referral relationships and can design strategies and systems to encourage and track referrals. There's an art to it, and it is not magic. The telecourse delves into these issues, and it is followed by a summary of referral guidelines to adapt to your business.

Telecourse Session #10:
Referral Relationships

Great Lessons-Learned Meeting Questions

[Suzi] Let's start with reviewing the homework, which was to generate questions that you might ask in a lessons-learned meeting, were you to consider having one.

[Len] I'll start. I understand that you named it a lessons-learned meeting, but when we were talking last time, it seemed to me like it was an opportunity for clients to express various viewpoints and outlooks. You would want to get an idea of what you're going to be doing from the name, right? So I changed the name of the meeting to viewpoints and outlook meeting. And this is designed to evoke responses such as, "We want more."

[Suzi] I love it.

[Len] So I was thinking that if I were Suzi and I were in that kind of meeting, the kinds of questions I would ask to evoke more responses from people would be more open-ended questions—they wouldn't be yes/no types.

[Suzi] Correct.

[Len] So I would ask questions such as, "How does what we are doing look to you? And how does what we do relate to your purposes? Are we on target?" And I was also thinking that they could write down various thoughts that they had about our service, and then share them with the person next to them, and see if they have similar ideas. Then I'd ask people to share that in the larger group. And the reason I would do that is to get them all involved.

[Suzi] Now, in the event that you were in a meeting with one person, how would you tailor that exercise?

[Jeremy] Ask him to talk to his imaginary friend.

[Len] Exactly—the empty seat technique. Well, that's one way. Also I was thinking of using a flip chart. I saw that Post It offers a flip chart, and it's like their Post It notes—you can take them off and stick them anywhere.

[Suzi] There's another really cool product that I just discovered. It's individual sheets of white plastic film. They stick to the wall with static electricity, and you write on them with a white board marker. So it's like a white board but it's flimsy like a piece of paper, and you can just roll it up and carry it around with you—and they're completely reusable.

[Len] And I've also been thinking about the idea of using the client's positive comments for marketing material. I would say, "Some of these ideas are so good, could we use them for our marketing material?" And I would let them know that I'm really interested in having them pass the word around about our service.

Here's another question I would ask: "In the bigger scheme of things, how important are our consulting services to you?"

[Suzi] That's a great question! I like that question because that gets right to the value.

[Deb] It also lets them think out of the box a little bit.

[[Len] Or it could be something like, "Can you give a sample of how coaching has helped you move up to a higher level—to something better than before?"

[Suzi] Or you could ask, "Can you give me an example of how our coaching has helped you?" And let them say the ways in which it has helped them, because you might be limiting it too much by saying, "How has it helped you move to something better than before?" That may be one of many things, so you want to expand it even further.

[Len] Exactly. So it's even more open-ended—like "Could you say what we have done and what we haven't done so far to improve our services?" And then, "What would you like to do in the future?"

[Suzi] That's nice and open-ended because they can either talk about what they want to do in a coaching context, or they can talk about what they'd like to do in their business, in their career, in their life . . . they can answer that however they want, and however they answer it, there's a nugget for you as a coach.

[Len] Exactly, it opens another door.

[Suzi] That's great.

[Len] Here's another idea: "If we could restart our contractual relationship from the beginning, what would you like to add or take out of it?"

[Jeremy] Good question.

[Len] "What would move you closer to your vision of success?"

[Suzi] Oh, I like that.

[Len] "If you surpassed the results in one area in six months, what would you expect it would be like if we started to focus on another area?" Now maybe that's too closed again, like the one before in helping you.

[Jeremy] It's a great question, but it's a little hard to follow.

[Suzi] I would break that into two questions, actually. The first question is, "What have you accomplished in the past six months?" So rather than, "If you have accomplished results in the past six months, what new direction would you like to go in?" break it down into two: "What results have you accomplished in the past six months?" And then the follow-up question is, "What new results would you like to accomplish, or would you hope to accomplish, in a coaching relationship moving forward?"

[Len] Good. Here are some more: "What other areas would you like to focus on? Do you know of others inside or outside the company who could benefit from our consultative services? How many more people in your company might benefit from beefing up your performance in coaching?"

[Suzi] Great.

[Deb] Can we write these on our hands when we . . .

[Suzi] Well, you probably want to go in with a prepared list of questions for any of your lessons-learned meetings. Because while you may generate the conversation off the cuff, it's just like any coaching meeting or any sales meeting—if you have your list of questions ready, then you can focus your attention on listening for the nuggets in the responses rather than thinking of the next question.

[Bill] Can you provide a list of questions to the participant in advance so that they can prepare?

[Suzi] You can, although I've had really mixed results with that. I've found when they have time to think about it, their responses are often more stilted or toned down. Or if they've taken time to think through the responses, they've maybe even talked to other people, sort of lobbied for a common reaction. You don't really get the candor that you get when you're hearing it for the first time.

Also, with more time to think, ponder, and interpret the questions, they might not give the initial knee jerk response that you want from them—they've thought through it too much. On the other side, it also depends on knowing your client, because some clients really value thinking things out. I worked with one woman executive who more than anything hated being put on the spot. I had to feed everything to her ahead of time, because if she was going to be in front of anyone but me, she was going to feel put on the spot if she hadn't thought about it ahead of time. So, again, you have to know your clients. . . .

[Len] Okay, here's another question for our clients: "What do you expect the overall benefit to the company is as we achieve our goals?"

[Suzi] So that's along the lines of "What's the organization getting out of your being in coaching with me?"

[Len] It is, along with: "In what other ways can we help focus you on your most important goals? How can we encourage learning and growth opportunities throughout the company? If our consulting services haven't helped yet, what can we improve?" These kind of overlap, I think. . . . Oh, and there's an interesting image I got from public-speaking expert Dottie Walters, but I use the image for coaching: "If you think of success as a stairway and coaching as a way to turn those steps into an escalator, where do you want this coaching escalator to bring the company now, and in six months from now?"

[Suzi] Oh, I like that.

[Len] It was just a quote to start with: "Success is not a doorway, it's a staircase." Something like that, but I got the staircase part from her. And then the coaching I added, and made it an escalator.

And another question I came up with was: "If you want to expand the scope of our agreement, what other important goals would you like to reach?" And here, if they couldn't offer an idea, if they just couldn't fashion words, I would just write out things like "Fashion actionable strategies" or "Help more employees shape up their areas."

I was thinking along a number of options. If I stump them with a question like that, they might not know exactly what to say, I thought.

[Suzi] Well, I think the only stumping point in that question is the opening phrase where you say, "If you want to expand your coaching agreement," because that could be perceived by the client as presumptuous. So you don't want to assume that they want to expand anything. For example, you could ask the next part of the question without assuming an expanded contract.

[Len] Okay. Just ask, "What other important goals would you like to reach?"

[Suzi] Yes.

[Len] "What has to change so that we can move up to a higher level?" And then I wrote options: "Attain higher standards, help more of you, or more important business expansion goals." Or maybe something like that; maybe that's not such a good question. There's another one that you said earlier—leave it open.

[Suzi] You may find that they've already answered that in previous questions that you've asked.

[Len] Exactly. I was just thinking of questions, one after another, and rephrasing things, so some are essentially duplicates: "What know-how and strength have not been fully tapped that we could expand upon?" That's a question. And, "What in your estimation is the real value of our services, personally, professionally, and corporately?"

[Suzi] And when you ask *real value*, are you asking for a number?

[Len] I'm really not asking that . . . I wanted to ask what they felt—how valuable they felt the assessments, feedback, coaching, and group training were.

[Deb] You mean sort of assessing each piece?

[Len] Exactly. Well, I mean that's a question . . . I don't know, what do you think about that question?

[Suzi] I think it's good because it gets at value again from a different angle.

[Len] And then I had questions for them to ask themselves. They don't have to respond out loud, but just think about them—for example, "What personal meaning do you find in what we are doing?"

[Suzi] Oh, I would love to have them answer that out loud if they felt comfortable with that.

[Len] Well, I'll give them an option, how about that?

[Suzi] Yeah, because that could be very rich.

[Len] This one is for older baby boomers: "What do you want to leave for the next generation?"

[Suzi] It's a legacy question.

[Len] And, "What do you think would happen if we did nothing?"

[Suzi] Oh good, I like that one.

[Deb] Wow, you've really done your homework.

[Len] Yeah, I worked on it. I really thought about it. It was interesting thinking, if I were Suzi, how would I write these things? Yeah, so that's what I did.

[Suzi] Excellent. The trick now is to think about how you would do it if you were Len.

[Len] That's great. But I can use you as a model.

[Suzi] Oh, definitely—keep me on your shoulder during these meetings, if it helps. But make sure the words and concepts are something that you can follow up on, because it's like playing chess, where you can think two or three moves ahead. You want to have the seeds somewhere in your mind to point to where you would go depending on how they answer it. How do you then take their response and leverage that into new business or a referral or whatever you want to leverage it into?

[Len] Well, that example you gave last time, when someone in the group says, "I know about five or six other people who could definitely benefit from this." And you say, "Great, let's get together on Friday at 8:00 and talk about it." That's one type of response in following up to get more business.

[Deb] Well, I did the homework, but I don't have the kind of questions that some of you have. I'm more of a process-oriented person. So I would go in with just a few questions.

[Len] Well, give us examples.

[Deb] Well, my process questions include whether they viewed the work as useful or not useful—it's kind of a therapy technique too. If you ask a direct question, sometimes people are afraid to answer it, or if it's something that might be kind of touchy, it doesn't give them very much room to respond. But if we take both at the same time, such as, "What's been useful for you and what hasn't been useful for you?" it's often easier to respond. And then I start to look at the things they bring up and then go through each one on the list.

[Suzi] So, would you do this on a flip chart?

[Deb] I think I would do it on a flip chart. I love the questions you have, Len. But sometimes you go in with these questions and then they start talking and you lose it all. They just want to talk about what they want to talk about. And I can guide the conversation, but it's hard to come back to the question you have in mind—"Well, I've got to ask this question now."

So I guess I just kind of go with the process and try to guide it and facilitate it. And then I also liked some of Len's organization questions, but I think I would save those for the end. So I have more general questions and more of a process than a structure thing. But I don't know: Suzi you've done this more than I have—I don't know what works, what doesn't work. Are there any . . .

[Suzi] You have to try it out with your clients and your personality style. It sounds like Len might take more of an interview approach, and you're going to take more of a group facilitation approach, where you're going to get up with the flip chart and ask what everyone says and delve into that more deeply. So there's no right or wrong way to do these, and you've got to figure out what works for you, and a lot of that comes from trial and error.

[Deb] Right. I'm thinking in lessons-learned meetings, though. Does it work better to have those types of structured questions?

[Suzi] I think it's always useful to have them, and you can make the call in the moment about whether or not you use them. However, if you don't have them, and you've got a room full of really silent people, then you're floundering. If you've got your prepared questions in your back pocket, you can pull them out at any time.

[Deb] It's true when you're working with engineers; they're introverts, and they love the structure. That's a good point.

[Suzi] And for some people, the structure of knowing that you have designed questions that you're going to ask them gives them a sense of safety. They feel that they are being taken care of in the process—that you've designed the process and they just have to go along for the ride. Although some more creative types or extroverted types would really love to generate the questions with you.

[Deb] More brainstorming. Okay, you're right. I think it depends upon the group and individual and what works best for them.

[Suzi] Yes, and what works for you, too.

Now, give us a sense of some of the other kinds of process questions you might ask.

[Deb] I think when I asked what's useful, I would also ask *how* it is useful. As we're identifying what's useful, I would also want some questions to get at how they see that that's useful.

[Suzi] And what would you do with that? Where are you looking to guide the conversation? In other words, finding out what's useful may be limiting in terms of how helpful it is for you.

[Deb] The way I see it is that you can ask questions and I can ask questions, but sometimes it doesn't really get to the meat of what you want. Or I can ask the question, "What's useful or not useful?" and then sometimes you're not quite getting to the core of it. So to guide the conversation, I think I would just be delving more and saying, "How is it useful to you? In other words, how is that particularly useful to you?" So it becomes more a personal ownership thing.

[Jeremy] You want to go over the process and talk about the processes that helped, and build on them in discussion.

[Suzi] I understand, Deb, but what I'm trying to get a sense of is the trajectory of the conversation. If you think about it as being in a car and driving, I hear that you're really paying close attention to a whole lot of things, almost at the same time: "You know what? We just passed this beautiful park, let's pull off and go visit the beautiful park, and let's explore what riches are in the park, and oh, look! There's a tree back there. Oh look, under the tree there are all these wonderful little flowers and mushrooms, let's get even closer and explore those." And this is great, but now you've gotten off the road and I still don't have a sense of what your intended final destination on that road was.

[Deb] Right. Well . . . I don't think I would go right off into visiting every little tree; I think I would tag a couple of things and explore them. You mean, what's the road?

[Suzi] Where's the road going? Do you see what I'm asking?

[Deb] Kind of . . . because I'm doing this off the top of my head and I'm not thinking it through clearly. But to get an overall picture of what that experience is like for that person, and the different pieces that have been important, I don't know if I'm always asking a question to get that.

[Suzi] That's all very valuable information.

[Deb] It's a given, you're saying.

[Suzi] Well, it's not that it's a given. It's very valuable information to find out. However, I think that before you get in the car and turn it on, you want to know where you're heading the car. You want to know where your ultimate destination is. Whether it's a brand new city or whether it's the grocery store, you have an ultimate destination in mind. And if you get distracted along the way, that's fine . . . but in this case, at least in my thinking, the ultimate destination of the lessons-learned meeting is some kind of new business, some kind of referral, some kind of deeper understanding of how you can best serve them in the future.

[Deb] Okay, then to answer your question, I'm thinking when people start to focus on this kind of stuff and start to look at their experience, at the benefits and usefulness of this piece and that piece and this piece, then I can take that at the end and do a recap. I'd talk about the things that have been a good experience, and then start bringing in some of those organizational questions and some of those "who else might benefit from this" questions. You've mentioned that kind of question: "Is there anybody else you're working with who might benefit from some of the things that you've benefited from?"

[Suzi] Okay, good, as long as you get there.

[Deb] Yeah, to me it takes a dual focus. It's having them look at it and what their own process is, what they're gaining from it, and how we could continue to work or change or whatever. Then the other goal is to ask all those other questions that Len came up with—"Who could benefit in the organization?" or "You've mentioned this . . . do you think they might be interested in it?" And when you have a sense of what the organization is like and what the needs are like, you could bring in some of that knowledge too—"Well, do you think so-and-so might benefit from that?" Those are the kinds of things I would try to do.

[Jeremy] I had some very brief questions that I came up with, which Len has pretty much covered. For example: "What has this experience been like for you thus far? How could this turn out to be more of a win here? What would you change? What would you add?"

[Suzi] I would also ask some specific referral questions. Len touched on it by asking, "Who do you know internally or externally who would benefit from this kind of a service?" But I might also fine-tune it a little bit. I might seek it out in the context of referrals: "What would either allow you to or prevent you from referring us to the CEO of your company?" I like to give them some specifics and let them say, "Well, I couldn't refer you to that person because of, whatever." You might find some feedback in there; you might find some nuggets about whatever it is that might prevent them from providing a referral to you. And then you come back and figure out how to earn back their trust in that area.

The point is, you want to really delve into questions like this, not only for what's been great, what's helped, what we can do differently in the future to improve, but also to uncover whether there's some little nugget of distrust in some arena. You want to get that out too so that you have a chance to know it and solve it, and thereby move on.

So, be looking for all those things, or be listening for all those things.

[Bill] You know after this tour de force, the only thing I would add is there were words that were missing for me. I wanted to hear thoughts like, "I want to know what we've done together that really matters to you. I want to know what expectations I have succeeded in meeting, or how I've failed."

I can imagine having a meeting where I didn't understand what anybody's talking about because they're not speaking with enough emotion, or going right to their personal issue, or speaking to the heart of the subject. Some of our examples sounded a little too detached to me—I think maybe I want a little bit of a revival-meeting flavor . . . I want something to happen. I want to remind people that something will really occur. That's the clinical psychologist talking. Some shaking has to happen there, too.

[Suzi] Absolutely. And I think that's why, rather than just giving you a list of questions to ask in a lessons-learned meeting, I wanted to give you a shot at generating them. Because as you can see here, we all have a different style and different concerns. There are the value questions, the future of the individual in the organization questions, some questions about referrals, and—Bill, you're raising a good point—some questions about meaningfulness.

Leveraging Referrals

[Suzi] So, on to referrals. There's a reason that our last class is dedicated to referrals, and that is because success in all of the other sales activities—any of the cold calling, networking, marketing, all of that—is heightened by your ability to leverage referrals. In fact, I would encourage you to develop a referral mindset, where you are building your entire business by referrals. Because then you don't have to make the painful cold calls. Referrals allow you to build on not only successful experiences you've had with clients, but also on trusted relationships you have in your network. And they allow you to use your sales and marketing and networking time more fruitfully so that you can spend more of your time doing what you really love, which is the actual coaching, and not spend so much time in the sales activities.

Some of the secrets with referrals involve relationships with people you already know—people in your network, people you have ongoing contact with. And that's the best way to develop business through referrals. This is going to sound a little bit like one of the networking mindsets, but the point here is to focus on who you know, focus on who you already have contacts with, focus on who you already have relationships with. As you're building your network, be in a referral mindset—what I mean by a "referral mindset" stems from a foundation of helpfulness and service, and things like partnership and trust. So if you're building relationships that are trusting relationships, you are coming from a place of genuinely wanting to help people and provide service to people; from that state of mind, referrals are a natural outcome of networking.

We've talked in the past about achieving depth in your client organizations, meaning getting to know more people than the one person you are coaching so that you have more leverage. That's also valuable in the context of referrals: the more people you know in an organization, the more potential referral sources you have.

Again, it comes back to thinking long term and exploring long-term possibilities. If you're seeking to grow your business through referrals, you're going to be thinking long term about the relationships that you're building now and how those relationships can support your referral base in the future. **The real secret to referrals is that referrals breed referrals, so continually look for ways you can give referrals.** One way to do that would be to think of a client or a contact who could benefit from a referral to somebody else in your network; it comes back to that mindset in networking about being a connection-seeker.

[Jeremy] It's about service, also.

[Suzi] Yes. So if you're in a referral mindset, you're thinking about referrals all the time—you're looking to give referrals, and you're going to be building your network and continuing to seek connections in the form of referrals. You're looking for where you can give referrals to people and request referrals from people already in your network and as you build your network. The trick is to make requests about the kinds of referrals you desire. You know, they're a nice thing when they just happen, right? But you can't count on that—it's wonderful when they just happen, but you can also be proactive about it. You can go out and seek the kinds of referrals you want, you can target them specifically, you can be strategic about it, and you can make specific requests of the people you know. You can tell everybody, for example, "I'm building my business through referrals, I could really use your help."

The one pitfall in the referral game is not really understanding, or not having almost a reverence for, the potential risk faced by people who give you a referral. What I mean by that is, think about someone who's in your family or in your circle of close friends. If they refer you into an organization, they have put their relationship with that organization on the line for you. And if they're a family member or a close friend, they may or may not have seen you in action professionally. They may or may not have a personal experience of your competence in the professional arena. So they're taking a risk in referring you. When they're doing that, it's completely out of their relationship with you, but it's scary for them—they want to help you, and they know that you're a good person because they love you, but if they don't know firsthand how good you are professionally, then they're putting their relationship with whoever they refer you to at risk. Does that make sense?

[Jeremy] Yes, absolutely.

[Suzi] So understanding that, and not expecting or feeling entitled to referrals from people within your closest circle of influence, is key. We must respect the vulnerable place it puts them in.

[Jeremy] I thought you were going to say something about the dilemma an executive would face when she refers you to someone else within the organization. Say someone's referring you on to the CEO, and you deliver or don't deliver—what does that mean for them? It's obviously a big risk factor one way or another, or a big reward factor one way or another.

[Suzi] Exactly. And that's a risk on a different level. The risk with your closest family and friends is a deeply personal one—these are people who love you and want you to succeed. If they refer you to a place where they think you can help, whether or not they have firsthand experience of your actual competence, they put themselves at risk with whoever they refer you to. And even if you do well, it doesn't necessarily translate into a payoff for them; it's more of a relief. But if you don't do well, then it's kind of the thing they're going to be holding their breath about all along.

[Bill] How about a concrete example? A friend of mine is corporate counsel for the corporation that her father originally developed, and he passed away recently. I haven't approached her because I don't want to put her in the position of feeling like I'm using our friendship. There have been political battles in this company having to do with control of the corporation that she's been a participant in. And I wouldn't want to put her in any trouble. But how could I present my services to her in such a way that she feels comfortable saying no—and it's important that a friend be able to say no—and the issue just goes away? How can she feel comfortable saying no? Who can she send me to? How would you handle something like that?

[Suzi] In a case like that, I would seek to provide service to her and friendship to her by offering her someone else as a coach, rather than yourself. Because what you're doing in that situation—if you're approaching it as networking—is making a referral that will help her and possibly someone else you know. You're being respectful and reverent of the dynamic there by not assuming what she should do. And that allows her to talk to you in a very safe way about what coaching could or could not provide, and why you're referring or recommending some other coach. And then she can, and most likely will, come back and say, "Well . . . why don't you do it? I don't want this new person, why don't you do it?"

[Bill] That's a great idea.

[Jeremy] And the other thing would be, which comes from a therapy model, is to learn to be abstemious. When I do this with people, sometimes we can talk about the pluses and minuses of referring us to somebody else, and what that would be for them and the potential client. And maybe it's not a good idea for them, for me to be coaching this other person. Maybe it is, but maybe it's not. When I'm able to take my self-interest out of the equation, people like that a lot.

[Bill] Well, I've been abstemious, but it hasn't resulted in anything.

[Jeremy] In your situation, Bill, you might want to just give her choices, as Suzi is suggesting. You give people choices, and then they can be aware of what they could be choosing.

[Suzi] And it protects you from being perceived as swooping in at her time of sorrow and taking advantage.

[Bill] That would be the wrong road. . . . I can imagine many cases where it could be important to talk around the subject. We all run into this: We know a lot of people it turns out who work at places we'd like to do work for, and it would sure be nice to do that without putting people on the spot.

[Suzi] Well, part of this, again, is knowing your client profile. Who are the ideal clients for you? Who can you help? And when you ask people to help you, let them know you're building your business through referrals and really need their help—chances are they know somebody who fits your client profile. "Who do you know that's an executive dealing with change?" "Who do you know that owns a business of $50 million or more in annual revenues?" "Who do you know that is an attorney in a leadership position?" Ask those kinds of questions, zeroing in on your client profile. That's a way you can start to focus people's referrals to you so that you're not just saying, "By the way, who else do you know that I could talk to?" because then they'll say, "Well, nobody comes to mind right now," and that's the end of the conversation. You want to help them narrow that focus.

The other option for referrals is to create referral streams not just with your contacts and prospects and clients, but also by creating alliances with colleagues who are not your clients, people you couldn't get business from. This is a great way to use the relationships you develop with other coaches. For example, "What's your specialty? Here's what my specialty is. Who are the kinds of clients that you're looking for? Great, if I run into someone who fits your description, I can refer you to them, rather than me. And we can do that back and forth." So creating those types of alliances is another option for referral streams.

Organize your networking, your marketing, and your sales strategies and activities around the ultimate goal of referrals. Tell people how they can help you, tell them you're building your business through referrals, and ask for referrals. Asking for referrals isn't as painful as asking for business. Consider specializing in a niche market or in a community where you can focus your relationship energy in a way that's going to more quickly generate referrals for you because it's all in the same community. Part of what I'm finding in the last few years of my business is once I've started focusing on the legal community, the referrals are incredibly fast. It's a much faster time frame from the request for referrals to referrals turning into business compared to taking on the world at large—the whole business world.

[Jeremy] You've narrowed your universe into a niche.

[Deb] And they often talk to each other.

[Suzi] Of course they talk to each other. So you start to get known in a community; it snowballs. A woman I met recently at a meeting said, "You know, I've heard your name a lot." I've never met her before in my life: She's an attorney in Oregon for gosh sakes. I'm just outside of D.C., but I do a lot of work in the legal community around the country. So it was that kind of a thing. Somehow you get known, and that helps with the relationship building, too.

What about other opportunities for referrals? We talked about lessons-learned meetings, but consider that if there's ever a breakdown in a relationship, a breakdown in service—handling that effectively is a really powerful opportunity for referrals, too.

[Jeremy] Say more about that.

[Suzi] Well, when you resolve a problem in a very powerful way for people, it repairs the relationship and makes it stronger than it was before.

[Jeremy] It's like when you have an argument with your partner and make up, you love each other more.

[Suzi] Yeah, you get closer after conflict. In that warm, fuzzy, happy place in the closeness after conflict, in a professional relationship as well as a personal relationship, that's a great time to talk about referrals.

Some other mindsets for you to have when asking for referrals include thinking of it as fun, or thinking of it as a scavenger hunt or playing detective or looking for lost treasure.

[Deb] Or you could do it as a game.

[Suzi] Yes, there's no end to it. There's no end to the referral trees that are out there. And I often like to chart them in my mind or on paper, as in I met Jackie through Rachel through Shawn, which I can trace back 17 people, and isn't that cool?

And always assume that people want to give you referrals, because if you don't assume that, it's hard to ask for them. Assume they want to give you referrals. Don't you want to give referrals when you can help others? Assume other people want to do the same.

Referrals 1-2-3

[Suzi] Okay, now, when do you ask for referrals? One time to ask is, of course, when someone compliments you on your services or on your skill in a certain area. That's a great time to say not only, "Great, can I quote you on that?" but also, "Who else do you think would benefit from that sort of thing?"

Another time to ask is when you have provided some type of value or service to someone, whether or not they paid for it. For example, there are times when I have gotten referrals after an initial meeting with a prospect who didn't end up signing on with me. But after that initial meeting, they got so much value that they referred someone else to me. So if you're constantly planting the seeds that you're building your business through referrals, whether or not people actually sign on with you, they're going to remember that and think about where they can refer you.

But also don't wait for them to express satisfaction. Periodically check in and ask for referrals, so that way you can be more in control of the referral process, rather than wait for someone to say something nice and then jump on that opportunity.

[Bill] Ask how you're doing . . .

[Suzi] Yes. Okay, so here's the 1-2-3 of referrals:

> 1. Give excellent service.
> 2. Express the importance of referrals to your business.
> 3. Ask for referrals.

Number 1 is provide excellent service or value to a prospect or client. Number 2 is plant the seed that you're building your business through referrals, or plant the seed that referrals are critical to you. The third one is, at a moment when rapport is good, directly ask for referrals.

So how do you plant seeds? One of the ways to plant seeds is just to say it up front: "I'm building my business through referrals." Or you can weave stories into your initial dialogue about how you've received referrals. You can add it into your written materials: "97 percent of our clients came from happy customers who trusted us enough to refer us into their network," putting it in language that fits with your community or niche market. There are a lot of ways you can build referrals; just get the concept of referrals in and be prepared to describe your ideal client profile to potential referral sources.

On the back end of getting a referral, you want to keep your referrer posted about how it's going and what happens. This means that when someone gives you a referral, you can't just take it and run. You've got to keep them in the loop, to some degree: "I called the person you referred me to, I left a message, we haven't connected up yet, I'll keep you posted," or, "We had a great conversation last week, I'll keep you posted." So you want to check back in. That helps you continue to build the relationship, but it also keeps them aware that you value referrals, and also allows them to remember that next time they think of someone they'd like to refer you to.

And then once the referral becomes business, definitely close the loop by sending a handwritten note and maybe even a small gift back to the referral source—again, reinforcing how much you value referrals, how you depend on referrals to grow your business, and what they mean to you.

[Bill] What kind of note, what kind of gift?

[Suzi] A brief, handwritten note on your personal stationery. Or a small gift—I send mugs with my logo printed on them. I know some folks who send a little letter opener with their logo on it. Some people don't do anything at all with their name or logo or insignia on it; they might send a book. I have a colleague who is a sales trainer—that's her whole world, that's what she does. And she sends out a book called *Selling the Invisible* when she gets a referral. It doesn't have to be much, but it should be something that makes a meaningful link to what you do.

> **Homework**
>
> Begin systematically seeking referrals, using the basic technology of referrals.

Referral Guidelines

"The best way **not** to get referrals is to ask for them as soon as you make a sale. BIG MISTAKE. What have you earned? Why would someone risk a referral on an unproven person or product?"
—Jeffrey Gitomer

There are several guidelines to keep in mind when playing the referrals game. You can build your entire business through referrals, and never have to make a cold call. Referrals require active relationship management so that you are continually planting the seeds by sharing with everyone that you are building your business through referrals, and all referrals are greatly appreciated. It is important to also continually ask for referrals. Beyond planting those seeds, you must water them by reminding folks in all your circles that you love referrals. Sprinkling these references to referrals into conversation wherever you see the opening to do so will result in a garden of referrals in full bloom. Give referrals freely and to everyone. Don't expect immediate return referrals. Ask for referrals in an ongoing, continual loop. Be specific about the kind of referrals you want. Follow up on all referrals and follow through by getting back to the person who gave you the referral. Identify fruitful referral streams and nurture those relationships. Acknowledge and appreciate your referral sources, and use the checklist on the following page.

Checklist:
Four Keys to Referrals

1. Give excellent service.

2. Express the importance of referrals to your business.

3. Ask for referrals.

4. Acknowledge referral sources.

Remember the giver's gain concept from the chapter on networking? That applies here, too. Sales expert Jeffrey Gitomer tells us "The best way to get referrals is to give them first. The second best way is to earn them." This is where networking and referrals work together. Go back to your networking list from which you made your strategic target list. Of that list, pick the top five you think would be powerful referral sources for you. Now, think about what you know about their work, about their ideal clients, about their needs and challenges. Using that information, you can most likely come up with a couple of prospective clients you could refer to them. Giver's gain: If you can come up with a few referrals to give your top five chosen referral sources, then you'll be leading by example. It is much easier to ask folks to give you referrals if you have already given them something of value.

Want to know more about referrals? Bill Cates wrote a great book called *Unlimited Referrals: Secrets That Turn Business Relationships into Gold* (Thunder Hill Press, 1996).

Integrating it All

Getting in Action

Action follows thought. Action precedes motivation. What will it take to keep you in action?

Worksheet:
Personal Action Plan

1. What new ideas will you implement immediately? _____

   _____

2. Which tools from this book will you incorporate and use in your ongoing work life? _____

   _____

3. What structures for accountability will you put in place for yourself?

   _____

   _____

4. How often will you communicate with your colleagues for support and to eliminate isolation, share resources, and discuss best practices?

   _____

   _____

5. How often will you meet with your coach or another consultant to identify targets? _____

   _____

6. How many calls will you make each week?_____

   _____

7. How many qualified appointments will you set up each week?

   _____

   _____

8. Who are your top 20 targets right now, and by when will you contact them?

   _____

   _____

Template:
Personal Strategic Business Development Action Plan

Are you making as much money as you want or need?
Is your business where you want it to be?
Is your life where you want it to be with regard to your business?

You've chosen to build a business or start a practice doing work that is meaningful to you. Perhaps you call yourself a sole proprietor, perhaps you are set up as another entity. You might be a coach, a consultant, a therapist, or a trainer. Whether you are just thinking about starting your business, have just begun, or are several months or years into your business ownership life, there are questions that inevitably arise.

As human beings, we are caught in a strange dilemma. We know we want something, yet we don't always know what it is we really want. Once we figure out what we really want, it becomes the world's biggest secret. We don't make a practice of telling people what we want. Why is that? What do we fear? Why don't we believe that we can have anything we want?

Design your business to fit your life, rather than living your life around your business. The formula is simple:

- Know what you want. Clarify the specifics of what you want by when. You don't have to know the *how,* just the *what specifically by when.*
- Hold clear the vision of what you want. Be willing to hold the vision for as long as it takes.
- Tell the universe exactly what you want. Write it down. Tell everyone.
- Trust that you deserve what you want. If you didn't deserve it, you wouldn't be capable of wanting it in the first place.

(continued)

Template:
Personal Strategic Business
Development Action Plan *(concluded)*

Consider this:

If you are not telling those around you (and the universe) what it is you really want, you are causing your own deprivation.

Surrender struggle.
Surrender deprivation.
Surrender attachment to any particular outcome.

Create your Strategic Business Development Action Plan (see worksheet page 317).

One way to write down what you want for your business is in a Personal Strategic Business Development Action Plan in three distinct domains: networking, marketing, and sales. Use the template in the four boxes on the following pages to:

- Select the clients and work that you want

- Work from your strengths while reducing your limitations

- Determine how you will cope when your commitment is tested

- Boost your revenues

- Expand your work opportunities

- Leverage your time

Use each box on the following pages for ideas when determining which actions you want to take in each area. Consider these lists as a way to kick start your brainstorming. After the four trigger boxes, there is a blank template to fill in with your own actions for each cell.

Remember, **action precedes motivation,** so just get going!

8 Visioning Ideas

1. Clarify your vision: What do you want (ideal state)?

2. Identify where you are now: What is the current state of your business situation or activity level in each area?

3. Identify what you need to do to build a bridge from where you are now to where you want to be.

4. Identify your core values and the core values of your company.

5. List the core competencies for you and your company.

6. Determine your product and service offerings.

7. Ideal client profiling: Determine with whom you want to work and map out a profile of the ideal.

8. Revisit your business plan or write one.

13 Networking Ideas

1. List the categories in your life in which you know people: family, church, work, neighborhood, school, past employers, business associates, friends, associations or professional groups, and those who provide services to you (e.g., your dentist).

2. Make each category a separate page and list all the people you know in each category.

3. In each category, choose the top three people you know best to be your networking starters.

4. Set up time to talk to or be with your network starters and tell them your vision.

5. Ask your network starters whom they know that you could talk to about your vision.

6. Seek out every person your network starters referred you to and tell them your vision.

7. Ask each of these people whom they know that you might talk to.

8. Continue to work your way through your own network lists.

9. Continue to follow up and meet people from your network starters' networks.

10. Tell everyone you meet what you are up to in your business.

11. Remember the Nine Mindsets of Networking during all of these interactions.

12. Explore partnering and alliance-building opportunities.

13. Identify and list at least 10 people with whom you want to do a joint venture.

12 Marketing Ideas

1. Determine if your priority is retention, acquisition, or reacquisition. **Retention** is growth, maintenance, and reassessment of new and existing buyers. **Acquisition** is seeking and contracting with prospective buyers. **Reacquisition** is rekindling lost, discouraged, or past-successful buyers.

2. Create or update collateral materials (logo, business identity, cards, letterhead, etc.).

3. Website development: Create or update your website.

4. Create or update brochures.

5. Write a column, articles, or books, or create products.

6. Explore direct means of outreach to your target market:
   - Direct mail
   - Promotional offers
   - Survey/Research
   - Advertising
   - Public relations
   - Invitational seminars/events

7. Explore indirect means of getting your message out through intermediaries:
   - Speaking engagements
   - Teaching opportunities
   - Writing and publishing
   - Association involvement
   - Survey/Research activity
   - Media engagements
   - Pro bono work
   - Sponsoring programs/events

8. Have 15 to 20 ways of generating leads.

9. Consider e-mail and web campaigns.

10. Offer free bonuses and free downloads.

11. Link your products and events.

12. Vary your offering so that you have entry-level price points and premium products.

12 Sales Ideas

1. Determine your target market and make a target list.

2. Determine who you would like to approach with which offering and list them.

3. Determine potential referral stream sources and begin requesting referrals and leads.

4. Determine your call list to set up first appointments/meetings.

5. Start making calls, keeping the numbers game in mind.

6. Track your progress and move people through your sales process systematically.

7. Continually keep your pipeline filled so that you will not be attached to any one particular lead or prospect.

8. Explore direct and indirect means of keeping in contact with every-one in your process.

9. Keep making calls and keep setting up meetings.

10. Follow up, follow up, follow up.

11. Ask for the business!

12. Provide excellent customer service.

Worksheet:
My Personal Strategic Business Development Action Plan for Networking, Marketing, and Sales

Action Plan	Actions I will take	Resources required	By when	How I will know
I. Vision				
II. Networking				
III. Marketing				
IV. Sales				

Worksheet:
My Individual Selling System

General notes of things I remember most clearly from this book that I will apply to my own selling system: _____

_____

Ideas for customizing my selling system that are different from what I read in this book: _____

_____

My integrated selling system has this core strategy: _____

_____

I will track my selling system using: _____

_____

My first goal for applying my selling system is: _____

_____

My stretch goal for the application of my selling system is: _____

_____

My structure for accountability is: _____

_____

Mental Positioning Checklist:
Critical Mindsets for Success in Sales

- Partnership

- Be a connection-seeker.

- *Sales* is not a dirty word: Reframe sales as an extension of your service cycle—it is about helping your clients.

- Approach sales from a service context: Use your coaching skills in a coach-approach to selling.

- Ask "How can I help?" Focus on service, taking care of others, and being helpful.

- Do what you do—and think referrals.

- Giver's gain

- Six degrees of separation

- Integrity and business ethics

- Keep a broad view of who the client is (strive for depth in organizations).

- Think long term.

- Develop and sustain long-term, meaningful relationships.

- Your sales style and approach must be natural and authentic to you: No tips, gimmicks, or techniques will seal the deal for you.

- Ask for specific help, referrals, leads, business deals.

- Referrals breed referrals.

- Expect to grow your business by referrals.

- Listen more than you speak.

- Provide exceptional service by making bold promises and overdelivering.

(continued)

Mental Positioning Checklist:
Critical Mindsets for Success in Sales *(concluded)*

- Learn what clients need, want, expect, and give them more.

- Value is defined by the client, not you.

- Operate from a foundation of commitment. Articulate what you are committed to and find out what is important to the client.

- Act as if the client is already a client and treat them with that level of care through the sales process.

- Follow through is critical.

- Link individual goals with organizational goals and generate measurable results.

- Every interaction is an opportunity for a relationship.

- Challenge assumptions: yours and theirs.

- You are always in a sales conversation: Either you're selling or you're being sold to.

- You always have a choice.

- Adopt an abundance mentality. You can make a difference *and* make oodles of money. There are dynamic laws of prosperity. You can read all about them in Catherine Ponder's book, *The Dynamic Laws of Prosperity.*

- Never give away free coaching samples! If you believe people need to have an experience of your service before buying, offer an introductory rate or a discounted sample rate rather than giving it away for free. If you give it away for free, you interfere with your own value proposition.

Final Thoughts
and
Next Steps

Checkpoints on the Road to Success

Authenticity yields enrollment. Enrollment happens when a person or group sees a possibility large enough that they can see themselves in a future that inspires or motivates them so much that they become compelled to take action toward making it happen. Sales is all about enrollment. Authenticity is your access to that.

If you aren't already a natural trust-builder, do whatever it takes to get really great at getting people to **trust** you. As far as I can tell, there's only one way to do that: ICE, which stands for **I**ntegrity, **C**haracter, and **E**xcellence. **Integrity** means simply that you say what you'll do and you do what you said. **Character** is your unique configuration of qualities that build your reputation as a person of substance and honor. **Excellence** is about consistent, outstanding performance and a commitment to the highest result possible.

Of course, you must have a clear **vision.** Know where you want to go with your business and take steps in that direction. Yogi Berra said, "You've got to be very careful if you don't know where you're going, because you might not get there," so make sure you know where you are going before you begin to apply the concepts in this book. Determine where you want to go and take steps in that direction—have an end goal even if you don't have a strategy, and keep your eye on that end goal. The universe is yours: The 10 steps outlined in this book will help you open its floodgates, so it is important to know which ones you want to open so that you can control the deluges and manage the flow of the process.

The importance of vision: All things being equal, you can't get "there" if you don't have a clear idea of where "there" is. If you don't know where you are going, you could end up someplace else. So if you were to apply all 10 of the Seal the Deal steps, and start producing record sales, what will that get you? Why bother? What are you reaching for? What is the ultimate vision that will inform your work inside of a larger purpose? This is important to articulate for yourself. Write it down and keep it visible wherever you usually make your sales calls. Keep your focus on your daily practices, and keep your mind's eye on your vision. The results will happen.

Then there's the **money** consciousness thing. Coaches in general need some help with financial literacy. Just look at the language in the industry for an example. One pet peeve is when coaches call their business a "practice." You are not building a practice—that is for therapists and dentists. Nor are you practicing coaching like you would practice yoga or a sport. You are running a business or you are self-employed—either way, profit is not a four-letter word! This links back to the abundance mentality. Who are you not to have everything you dare to dream about in terms of wealth creation?

Consciously design your **attitude.** What is your current belief about what you need to do next to grow your client base? What new attitudes, beliefs, or mindsets will help you get there? Which actions will cause an attitude shift? Remember Eleanor Roosevelt's statement: "No one can make you feel inferior without your consent."

I would be remiss if I didn't tell you about the **Daily Chafes.** A chafe is something that rubs you raw—it is uncomfortable and painful, like a rug burn. Expect three things to chafe you every day. That way, when things go wrong, you won't be surprised. This is similar to preparing responses for the objections you hear in the sales process, only it is applicable to all of life. You can't always prepare your response to the little surprises in business or in life, so one way to cope is with the concept of the Daily Chafes. Your personal agency—your personal effectiveness and power—as well as your ability to persist in the face of adversity come from your internal capacity to source your energy and stay grounded. When one of the Daily Chafes interrupts your otherwise peaceful existence, you can laugh it off and say to yourself, "Well, that's one! Two more to go today!" It is your choice how you respond to the chafes in the sales process (and in life). Here's my warning: Even if you follow the 10 Seal the Deal steps as a focused, conscious practice, you will still run into about three chafes a day. Expecting Daily Chafes may just help to keep you on track, staving off such maladies as road rage and going postal.

And don't forget the notion of **fake it 'til you make it.** The route to confidence is often to act as if you are confident until you start to believe it yourself, thus demonstrating confidence. While at first some of the steps in the sales process may seem foreign to you or feel uncomfortable, with practice, you will gain facility and ease with the system, and then you will be able to personalize it, own it, and make it yours. It is okay if it all feels a bit contrived or forced at first. Just keep at it and you will learn to tweak the elements to make them work best for you. You've got to master the rules before you can break them.

Persistence and resilience are valuable skills to study. There is a fine line between persistence and being a pest; likewise there is a fine line between resiliency and resistance. Sales requires persistence and an unstoppable spirit. You have to be resilient and have ways to manage and grow your resilience. Sandy Davis of Changewise has tremendous resources about resilience that you can take advantage of. He even has a Resilience Game! He defines the term as "Resilience is a state of being that allows humans to recover quickly and reliably when they are stressed or thrown off balance by change or adversity." Go to www.changewise.biz for more. Mike Jay links resilience to the power to persist: "Resilience is the differentiated power to persist when things do not work out at first, the capability to navigate ambiguity and uncertainty, the motivation to transcend common problems and barriers and to collaboratively anticipate the future in sustainable ways." Check out his book on coaching personal resilience, *CPR for the Soul: Creating Resilience by Design* at www.cprforthesoul.com.

If you want to get to the top of any mountain, you simply take one step, then another step, and then keep going up. You will have to be prepared, you will have to be capable of handling surprises along the way that you couldn't have prepared for, and you will have to have a certain amount of faith; it takes real grit to stay the course and reach your goal of the mountaintop. The sales process is the same way. To reach the zenith, the summit, the peak, you must persist along the path, which in this case is the ten-step process we've been talking about. I once had a mentor named Kathy Griffin who taught me, "Others can stop you temporarily, only you can do it permanently." The flip side of that, of course, is that you can be unstoppable, which is entirely in your control.

Sales is a numbers game. Persistence and resilience are part of the numbers game. I've heard that 80 percent of people stop trying to connect with a prospective client after their third attempt, but 80 percent of all sales are made after the fifth attempt to connect! Recognizing that it is a numbers game will allow you to keep your pipelines fully loaded and to create the bench strength you need to continually generate sales.

The gift in this numbers game is that it removes any of those pesky attachment issues many of our colleagues face. It is nearly impossible to be attached to the outcome of your sales activity if you have more leads than you can track! Sales is only frustrating and emotional if we do not have enough possibilities in the pipeline and therefore get attached to needing each lead to become business. If you are actively pursuing five strong leads, you have time to think about each one and to pine for it to work out in your favor. If you are pursuing 150 leads, it becomes very difficult to have high hopes pinned on any one of them—you are freed up to focus on the sales process rather than specific potential opportunities.

You're Only as Good as Your Weakest Link

You've heard this phrase in reference to teams before. We know a team is only as effective as its weakest person. If we apply this concept to the individual, it becomes an inquiry into what Peter Senge calls *personal mastery:* Know your limits and learn to leverage and exploit your strengths. Have a strategy to counter your known areas of weakness such that they manifest as a strength. For example, I tend to act as a know-it-all, which can get me into trouble when I operate from that stance during a sales conversation. I have learned to interrupt that pattern by recognizing when it starts and by shifting to asking questions, seeking input, and becoming interested in the views or reality of others. What is your weak spot, and how can you reframe it into something that works for you?

Play Big

Once you've removed your blocks and left scarcity thinking behind, it is time to invent. Without the shackles of thinking small, what's possible? Can you double your rates? Can you re-think your sales strategy? Can you transition to a new business model? If the restraints are off, what do you really want? Do you have a coaching practice or are you building a coaching business? Are you doing coaching as a hobby or are you building a business? How big is a big enough business? Do you have the right team around you to build something that will continue to support you, sustain your continual learning and development, allow you to focus on continual improvement in the areas of customer service and product development? Are you working as much or as little as you wish? Do you love all your clients? If you could have anything in your business, what would it be? What will it take to get there from here? What might it look like if your business surpassed even your own wildest dreams?

Mailbox Money

Eventually, we get tired of selling our time for money. You can grow your business only so big that way, because time is limited to 24 hours in a day and you are limited in how many of those hours of each of your days you can sell. The answer is to find multiple streams of income, and multiple revenue sources outside your professional service area as well. Perhaps you create products that leverage core content in a specific niche market, or perhaps you catch the wave of the current trend to harness the internet to reach prospective clients and sell products. Perhaps you have secured an in-house position to use your coaching or consulting mastery, or you have branched into real estate or other investment strategies to put your money to work for you.

If you are not thinking about or doing anything to generate passive income—money that you earn that is not directly linked to an exchange for your time—then you might consider one or more of these avenues to take your business to the next level. How can you leverage those teleclasses you lead? Can you videotape yourself next time you are in front of the room leading a meeting or training session? Can you find a colleague to interview you on video or by telephone line that is then recorded and put into an MP3 file that folks can download from your website? Have you written a book or been meaning to? Can you take the materials that you have created for various client engagements and link them together somehow into a workbook or monograph that you can sell? Do all your products and services support a common vision, purpose, or set of values that you stand for? Where are you not accountable to yourself for what you and your business stand for and how can diversifying your revenue streams support that?

How Big is Big Enough?

To expand or not to expand? That is the question. If so, how? Stop to think about if your business is big enough. That means you have strategically created an entity separate from your profession that has the capacity to hold the systems, people, strategies, financial goals, streams of income, and outreach methodologies that will attract and create the business that matches your values, vision, purpose, goals, intentions, and dreams. Does your business serve you while you serve your clients? Are you leading your business, or is your business running you? If you trade your time for money without additional streams of revenue, then you are self-employed, which is distinct from being a business owner. Did you intentionally choose that? If so, and it has been working for you, is it time to explore what it would take to go from a self-employed practitioner to a business owner?

Business owners focus their strategies on systems and people. There are two ways to make money: Either people work for you or your money works for you. To build a million-dollar coaching business, we need to leverage other people. Do you want to manage people and create systems, or do you find that by remaining more of a freelance self-employed coach you have more flexibility to create joint ventures and alliances and partner with colleagues to expand your market offering without having to build a business to do so? Do you define yourself as a practitioner, manager, entrepreneur, or all three? There are some great resources to guide this inquiry further: *The E-Myth* books by Michael Gerber,[1] the *Rich Dad, Poor Dad* series by Robert Kiyosaki,[2] and the www.liveoutloud.com website, which has free downloads and free teleseminars that support financial literacy and strategic business building. If you want to multiply your income, you will likely need to change what you are doing. The business strategy you choose will determine the size of the business you can build, providing you have done the pre-work to clarify for yourself how big is big enough for you.

Having said all that, I hereby give you permission to not grow your business at all. It is okay to accept that running your own business may not be the highest and best use of your personal strengths, and you might be better served to take an internal position in an organization in which you can use your skills with your peers and employees.

Harness the Sales Process

Knowing that sales is a process, respecting the numbers involved, and increasing your awareness of your own sales cycle will allow you to leverage the information in this book to take your business to the next level.

In order to truly harness the sales process, there are three things required:

1. Give up attachment to any specific outcomes.
2. Trust the process.
3. Have fun with it.

In order to work the system, we must be in continual action. It is also critical to understand the distinctions between networking, marketing, and sales so that you can track your progress in all three areas. It takes activity in all three domains to produce dollars, clients, and business. Networking involves all the steps you take to meet people and begin to develop relationships. Marketing is all the stuff you do communicate about your credibility and service offering to the world. Making calls, scheduling meetings with those in your target list, and asking for the "buy" are sales activities.

Try the Self-Assessment Quiz at the beginning of this book again and note your improvement!

Onward . . .

As you gain sophistication and ease of use of the steps outlined in this book, you might find that it is helpful to keep in mind the core process navigation points to help you keep your course:

- **Credentials.** There's an assumed baseline of credibility: You have the training, experience, education, and credentials to deliver the service and get results.

- **Value.** You have a track record of proven value (results/worth).

- **Interview.** You understand and can facilitate a sophisticated interview.

- **Mindsets.** You are aware of and can manage your mindsets and attitudes during the process, and you have integrated the key mindsets from this book in ways that work with your natural style and personality.

- **Sales cycle.** You understand and can keep all your activities clear and consistent within a specific sales cycle.

- **Pipeline.** You constantly fill and track your pipeline of leads.

- **Numbers.** You know your numbers and what it takes to play the numbers game (both quantity and time) to move people through your sales process.

- **Technology of referrals.** You build your business routinely using the technology of referrals.

- **Networking.** You are always networking.

Reminder: You are always in the creation seat in your life and in your business. What shows up around you is always consistent with what you are putting out there. Rather than spending energy on the ultimate result that you want that isn't coming fast enough, place your energy on the practices and steps to getting what you want. Do the actions and trust that the results will follow.

Endnotes

1. See, for example, Gerber, M. E., (2001). *The E-myth revisited: Why most small businesses don't work and what to do about it.* New York: Harper Collins.

2. See, for example, Kiyosaki, R., (2000). *Rich dad, poor dad: What the rich teach their kids about money—That the poor and middle class do not!* New York: Warner Business Books.

More Homework

For your convenience, the homework suggestions from the telecourse content are re-captured here by each corresponding step of the sales process.

Step 1: Practice your 30-second introduction commercial 15 times. Find 15 different ways to practice it—with 15 different people, and include yourself as one of those people, meaning practice it in front of a mirror. Try to do it face-to-face. If you can't, do it over the phone. Find different ways of practicing it, and allow it to evolve and be fine-tuned, but keep in mind the key points (credibility, say what you would do, who you help, and what you help them do). Make sure it's within **30 seconds.** The shorter and more succinct you can get it, the better. Practice it until it starts to feel natural, and see what happens. Observe as you practice it 15 times over the next week. Observe how it evolves, and observe how you feel about it, and observe how natural or fluid it starts to feel.

Step 1, part 2: Assess your mindsets about sales. Use the worksheets in the book to capture a baseline of where your mindsets currently are so that you can clearly see how the shifts in your attitudes and beliefs directly generate a shift in your sales results and enjoyment!

Step 2: Start thinking about the entire universe of users of your services, and strategically think about whom the most likely targets are for you in that group. In generating your target list, you can look at current clients, referral sources, previous clients, your network, databases that you might have, books of lists, newspapers, or trade or business publications. In addition, you can search the internet, and look through associations. Start generating your target list using the Targeting Worksheet.

Step 3: Begin making calls to those on your target list to set up appointments.

Step 4: Write down your set of objections, and what you hear or what you expect to hear, or what you think the finite set of objections is, and also write down your responses for each one of those. Use the Overcoming Objections Worksheet.

Step 5: Create strategic questions for the client meeting. Use the Elements of Successful Client Meetings as a guide. Think about your success stories for your business and how you might work those into a sales meeting.

Step 6: Create your tracking system and review your proposals and contracts.

Step 7: Continue to make calls, set appointments, and move targets through your sales cycle.

Step 8: Apply the Nine Mindsets of Networking and start networking with everyone.

Step 9: Design a template for the questions you would ask in a lessons-learned meeting. Remember, the whole purpose of it is building a service relationship, creating a partnership, and generating future sales.

Step 10: Begin systematically seeking referrals, using the basic technology of referrals.

Chapter on Integrating it All: Complete the Personal Strategic Business Development Action Plan Worksheet and the My Individual Selling System Worksheet.

Recommended Reading

The following is a list of books that every salesperson should read. Some are focused on specific sales skills while others address the more theoretical aspects of selling.

Albrecht, K., & Zemke, R., (1990). *Service America!* New York: Warner Books, Inc.

Beckwith, H., (1997). *Selling the invisible: A field guide to modern marketing.* New York: Warner Books.

Childre, D., & Martin, H., (1999). *The HeartMath solution.* New York: HarperCollins Publishers.

Gitomer, J., (2006). *Little red book of sales answers.* Englewood Cliffs, NJ: Prentice Hall.

Heiman, S. E., & Sanchez, D., (1998). *The new strategic selling.* New York: Warner Books.

Khalsa, M., (1999). *Let's get real or let's not play.* Salt Lake City, UT: Franklin Covey.

Loehr, J., & Schwartz, T., (2003). *The power of full engagement.* New York: The Free Press.

Mackay, H., (1988). *Swim with the sharks without being eaten alive.* New York: Ballantine Books.

Miller, R. B., & Heiman, S. E., (1987). *Conceptual selling.* New York: Warner Books.

Parinello, A., (1999). *Selling to VITO (the very important top officer),* 2nd Ed. Cincinati, OH: Adams Media Corporation.

Ponder, C., (1962). *The dynamic laws of prosperity.* Marina del Rey, CA: DeVorss & Company.

Schiffman, S., (1997). *High efficiency selling: How superior salespeople get that way.* New York: John Wiley & Sons.

About the Author

Suzi Pomerantz, MT, MCC, has been described as "an exciting kinetic force" and is an executive coach, facilitative consultant, corporate trainer, and mom who serves on two international boards and writes articles and books when she's not busy serving Fortune 100 clients or chasing her two year old and four year old. She is the CEO of Innovative Leadership International LLC and specializes in leadership coaching in organizations and business development coaching for solopreneurs. She lives with her husband and children in Maryland. (Find out more at www.innovativeleader.com.)

About
Innovative Leadership International
LLC

Innovative Leadership International LLC (ILI) is a woman-owned executive coaching firm specializing in organizational coaching, leadership development, and business development. The master coaches and consultants of ILI provide executive coaching, team coaching, and emerging leader coaching in organizations to assist executives and their teams with setting strategic direction for their organizations, managing talent, and developing leadership bench strength. We help organizations develop and retain leadership capacity by coaching leaders in executive presence, presentation skills, personal power, communication, and vision work. We specialize in business development coaching for attorneys, coaches, trainers, consultants, and other professional service providers in the areas of sales, marketing, and networking. Since 1993, we have coached and trained thousands of leaders and teams in over 110 organizations internationally, including 7 Fortune 100 companies, 11 law firms, and 6 corporate law departments. We help leaders clarify their vision and exceed prior performance. We help attorneys and coaches demystify the sales process and implement a systematic process for business development. We help organizations improve communication and leadership, transforming cultures one individual at a time. We provide coaching, training, facilitation, and leadership development services. http://www.innovativeleader.com

Dear Reader,

In order for you to be able to better use the templates in this book, I'd like to send you the worksheets from the chapter titled Integrating it All. Just send me your e-mail address with the words REQUEST TEMPLATES in the subject line and I will send you (for free) a PDF file of the Personal Action Plan (page 310), Personal Strategic Business Development Action Plan (page 311), and My Individual Selling System (page 318). Send your request to templates@sealthedealbook.com.

Also, we update the website frequently, so please be sure to visit www.sealthedealbook.com often for free reports and other resources.

Thanks for reading and recommending the book!

Suzi